W9-BMD-742

BASIC TYPES OF PASTORAL COUNSELING

BASIC TYPES OF PASTORAL COUNSELING

HOWARD J. CLINEBELL, JR.

Abingdon Press

Nashville
New York

BASIC TYPES OF PASTORAL COUNSELING

ISBN 0-687-02491-9
Library of Congress Catalog Card Number: 66-21187

MANUFACTURED BY THE PARTHENON PRESS AT NASHVILLE, TENNESSEE, UNITED STATES OF AMERICA

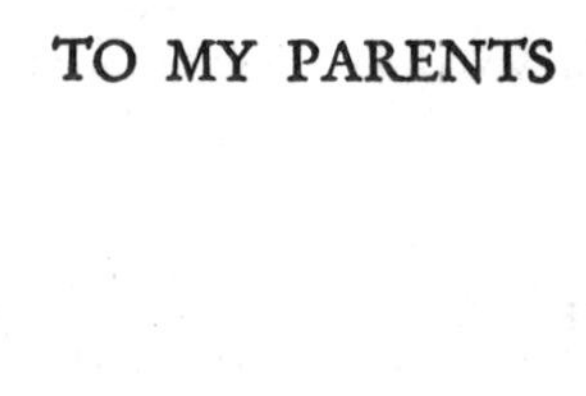

TO MY PARENTS

And his name will be called Wonderful Counselor.
(Isaiah 9:6)

Where there is no guidance, a people falls; but in an abundance of counselors there is safety.
(Proverbs 11:14)

Be transformed by the renewal of your mind.
(Romans 12:2)

TO THE READER

Let me introduce this book by mentioning briefly the experiences out of which it grew. For some twenty years I have been doing pastoral counseling in a variety of settings—thirteen years as a parish minister, two as a "minister of counseling" in a downtown church, and five in a pastoral counseling center. During these years, my thinking about counseling and my practice of this pastoral art have gradually changed. In these pages I have tried to set forth the ideas that now "make sense" and the methods that "work best" for me.

The conviction that pastoral counseling needs to revise its basic model, if it is to flourish fully, grew over the years as I found myself forced to modify my Rogerian-psychoanalytic assumptions and methods in order to meet the obvious needs of parishioner-counselees. The tentative "revised model" described herein has a broader theoretical base and a more varied methodology. It reflects both the changes that have occurred in my own practice and the impact of certain new thrusts in psychotherapy which have challenged my earlier understanding of counseling.

This book is beamed at the parish minister and the seminary student preparing for a general parish ministry. Its approach is based, I believe, on an awareness of the potentialities and limitations of counseling in that setting. One of the things that encouraged me to put the revised model on paper was the response of several groups of parish ministers, with whom I had an opportunity to discuss the approach during its formative stages. A number of them said of the revised model, "It provides a way of understanding and improving on methods I have been using intuitively for a long time." I present it, then, as a means of clarifying and strengthening what many pastors are already doing, rather than as a radical innovation.

At certain points the book overlaps my earlier book on the church and mental health, *Mental Health Through Christian Community*. I have attempted to keep duplication at a minimum and to treat such overlapping as was unavoidable, because of the related nature of the topics, from a somewhat different perspective.

The case material from my counseling used herein is disguised so as to protect the anonymity of the persons concerned. All identifying data have been carefully deleted or altered to this end.

Many people have guided, challenged, and stimulated my thinking in the area of counseling. I stand in their debt. In some cases, this is acknowledged in footnotes or references to their ideas. In other cases, the influence has been general, indirect, or, I suspect, unconscious, so that specific acknowledgment is not possible. I am grateful for the impact on my life of my teachers, students, and faculty colleagues, all of whom have helped to mold my thinking about counseling. The most powerful source of influence over the years has been the persons with whom I have entered counseling relationships. From their suffering and courage and growth struggles they have taught me much of what I know about counseling. The frustration of my failures and the quiet lift of those moments when counseling became an instrument of healing and hope provided continuing motivation for wrestling with the issues discussed in this book.

A special word of gratitude is due Frank W. Kimper and Robert L. Brizee, who read the manuscript and made cogent suggestions for changes, and Robert G. Hagelbarger and Doman Lum for their research assistance. I wish particularly to express appreciation to my wife, Charlotte, for her invaluable help with the various revisions of the manuscript.

I look forward to receiving feedback from both practitioners and theoreticians of pastoral counseling regarding the ideas and methods presented here. If counseling in the parish context is to realize its full potential, we must have many efforts to develop more effective methods. Equally important is vigorous interaction among persons who are experimenting with varied methods.

I trust that this book communicates something of the renaissance excitement that is currently rising in the field of pastoral care and counseling. My own enthusiasm has increased as I have moved in the directions of the revised model, and discovered how effective pastoral counseling can be when it uses a differential methodology and strives to be truly pastoral.

There is no doubt in my mind that counseling is one of the areas "where the action is" in every local church that is doing its job. My hope, as this book is launched, is that it will be a useful instrument to both ordained and lay ministers in this crucial area of service to suffering persons.

Howard J. Clinebell, Jr.
Claremont, California

CONTENTS

1

The Present Challenge of Pastoral Counseling

On a dangerous seacoast where shipwrecks often occur there was once a crude little lifesaving station. The building was just a hut, and there was only one boat, but the few devoted members kept a constant watch over the sea, and with no thought for themselves went out day and night tirelessly searching for the lost. Many lives were saved by this wonderful little station, so that it became famous. Some of those who were saved, and various others in the surrounding area, wanted to become associated with the station and give of their time and money and effort for the support of its work. New boats were bought and new crews trained. The little lifesaving station grew.

Some of the members of the lifesaving station were unhappy that the building was so crude and poorly equipped. They felt that a more comfortable place should be provided as the first refuge of those saved from the sea. So they replaced the emergency cots with beds and put better furniture in the enlarged building. Now the lifesaving station became a popular gathering place for its members, and they decorated it beautifully and furnished it exquisitely, because they used it as a sort of club. Fewer members were now interested in going to sea on lifesaving missions, so they hired lifeboat crews to do this work. The lifesaving motif still prevailed in this club's decoration, and there was a liturgical lifeboat in the room where the club initiations were held. About this time a large ship was wrecked off the coast, and the hired crews brought in boatloads of cold, wet, and half-drowned people. They were dirty and sick, and some of them had black skin and some had yellow skin. The beautiful new club was in chaos. So the property committee immediately had a shower house built outside the club where victims of shipwreck could be cleaned up before coming inside.

At the next meeting, there was a split in the club membership. Most of the members wanted to stop the club's lifesaving activities as being unpleasant and a hindrance to the normal social life of the club. Some members insisted upon lifesaving as their primary purpose and pointed out that they were still called a lifesaving station. But they were finally voted down and told that if they wanted to save the lives of all the various kinds of people who were shipwrecked in those waters, they could begin their own lifesaving station down the coast. They did.

As the years went by, the new station experienced the same changes that had occurred in the old. It evolved into a club, and yet another lifesaving station was founded. History continued to repeat itself, and if you visit that sea coast today, you will find a number of exclusive clubs along that shore. Shipwrecks are frequent in those waters, but most of the people drown! [1]

In this striking parable Theodore Wedel depicts the perennial danger confronting the church—irrelevance. The peril is acute in periods when the church is outwardly "successful." The parable highlights the fact that the only relevance that really matters is relevance to the *deep needs of persons*—relevance to the places in their lives where they hurt and hope, curse and pray, hunger for meaning and for significant relationships. Pastoral counseling is a valuable instrument by which the church stays relevant to human need. It is a way of translating the good news into the "language of relationships," as Reuel Howe expresses it—a language which allows the minister to communicate a healing message to persons struggling in alienation and despair. Pastoral counseling is an essential means by which a local church is helped to remain a lifesaving station and not a club; a hospital and a garden of the spiritual life and not a museum. Counseling can help save those areas of our lives which are shipwrecked on the hidden reefs of anxiety, guilt, and lack of integrity. An effective counseling program, in which both minister and trained laymen serve as *shepherd-counselors*, can help transform the interpersonal climate of a congregation. It can make that church a place of reconciliation, healing, and growth.

Pastoral counseling contributes to the renewal of a church's vitality by providing an instrument for the renewal of persons, relationships, and groups. By reducing the crippledness of our ability to give and receive love, counseling can help us to *be* the church—the community in which God's love becomes an experienced reality in relation-

[1] This parable originally appeared in an article by Theodore O. Wedel, "Evangelism—the Mission of the Church to Those Outside Her Life," *The Ecumenical Review*, October, 1953, p. 24. The above is a paraphrase of the original, by Richard Wheatcroft. It appeared in *Letter to Laymen*, May-June, 1962, p. 1.

ships. Thus, counseling is an instrument of *renewal through reconciliation,* helping to heal our estrangement from ourselves, our families, our fellow church members, from those outside the church, and from a growing relationship with God. It can create windows of new awareness, restoring sight to eyes previously blinded to the beauty, tragedy, wonder, and pain which is all about us, by our anxious, guilt-ridden self-concern. Counseling can allow us to discover fresh dimensions of our humanity. It can release our trapped potentialities for authenticity and aliveness. By helping us achieve more genuine intimacy in relationships, it can help to release our trammeled creativity—the creativity that is potentially present in every person. By renewing us as *persons,* counseling helps prepare us to become renewal agents in a church and in a society which desperately need renewing.

Pastoral counseling can be an instrument of renewal by helping us develop what is most difficult to achieve in our period of history—depth relationships. Most of us can identify with the pain of the minister who said to his psychotherapist, "My life is characterized by a plethora of contacts and a poverty of relationships." This is the common blight which threatens the creativity of each of us in our "touch-and-run" culture—a culture oriented toward interpersonal superficiality. *This* is the blight which militates against the renewal of a church as a redemptive social organism, preventing it from becoming a renewer of persons. This is what prevents a church from being a lifesaving station engaged in rescuing persons from our society's many forms of lostness.

It is far from easy to relate to the depths of another person. To do so is to come alive to his personhood—to his pain and potential, his emptiness or fullness, his own unique blend of hope and despair. It is painful to relate to the depths of another because it inevitably exposes us to the dark rooms of our own inner world. His emptiness reminds us of our own. His anger and guilt cause ours to resonate. Yet only as we relate to others in depth can we become growth-facilitators in their lives. Only those who have discovered new life in their own depths can become spiritual obstetricians, aiding the birth of new life in individuals and in the church. Pastoral counseling can help prepare such obstetricians of the spiritual life.

When people touched Jesus' life, they undoubtedly sensed in him the power which comes from openness to oneself, others, and the universe.

When people touch our lives, what do they sense? The noisy static of our harried times, perhaps? As an instrument for deepening relationships, counseling can help to bring that renewal to a church, which comes as a refreshing rain to a parched land.

THE CONTEMPORARY RENAISSANCE IN PASTORAL COUNSELING

In each period of history and every new environment, the church must find fresh ways of meeting the needs of troubled persons—new channels for its century-spanning ministry of reconciliation, healing, and growth. Only thus can it remain relevant to the deep needs of people. The various methods of pastoral counseling offer widening channels of healing and growth in our period of church history.

One of the signs of hope on the contemporary religious scene is the rising wave of activity in the field of pastoral care and counseling. Since World War II a surge of lively interest has been evident in the field. The ministry of counseling has been flowering with steadily increasing vigor. The growing impact of clinical pastoral training, the strengthening of seminary education in counseling, the remarkable proliferation of church-related counseling programs, the emergence of pastoral counseling as a specialty within the ministry, the strengthening of seminary doctoral programs in counseling, the rise of the American Association of Pastoral Counselors, the burgeoning literature in the field, denominational counseling programs, and the current experimentation in the pastoral care ministry of the laity—these are some of the signs of the surging vitality. It is thrilling to realize that we are in a renaissance period in the church's age-old ministry to the burdened. The challenge to each of us is to be a *participant* and *contributor,* and not a mere observer, in this dynamic movement—a movement which provides fresh responses to the needs of those beside our modern Jericho roads, robbed of their self-esteem and beaten by the crises and tragedies of life.

PASTORAL COUNSELING AT THE CROSSROADS

If the pastoral counseling renaissance is to become the powerful force for renewal which it can become, certain decisive changes must occur. Pastoral counseling must come of age in both theory and practice. It must find a new level of self-identity and maturity, by deepening its theological roots, broadening its methodology, and discovering its unique contribution to the helping of troubled humanity, with reference to both its own heritage and the other helping disciplines. The minister as counselor needs a unique self-understanding of his image, role, functions, and goals. As a clergyman, his self-understanding obviously must have a theological base derived from his awareness of the grounding of what he does in the ongoing life, message, and tradition of the church. Major contributions have been made to this theological self-understanding in recent literature.[2] The particular thrust of this book is toward broadening the methodology and enriching the model of pastoral counseling.

It is my conviction that pastoral counseling theory and practice are at a crossroads and must turn a corner if they are to respond to the opportunity for a renewal ministy of enlarged dimensions. If the corner can be turned, a new chapter will begin in the church's ministry to the heavy-laden.

This new chapter can be without equal in the history of our faith. Never before have we had such rich resources as are provided by the contemporary renaissance in pastoral care and counseling, the renewal movement in the churches, the sparkling new insights from the sciences of man, and the new techniques from the psychotherapeutic disciplines. As these converge in the pastoral counseling ministry, a broad stream of healing will be released through the churches. A dramatic breakthrough in this area is now possible. Whatever any of us can do to contribute to it should command our most disciplined self-investment. It is my hope that the ideas and approaches described in this book will make a contribution toward this objective.

Actually, pastoral counseling *practice* has already begun to turn the necessary corner. Older methods are being challenged, their effectiveness questioned by many practitioners of this pastoral art. Basic modifications have taken place in the way many of us practice pastoral counseling. It is important that our conceptual understanding keep abreast of these changes. Otherwise a foundation of understanding for making future changes will be lacking.

[2] Seward Hiltner, *Preface to Pastoral Theology* (Nashville: Abingdon Press, 1958); Wayne E. Oates, *Protestant Pastoral Counseling* (Philadelphia: Westminster Press, 1962); Edward E. Thornton, *Theology and Pastoral Counseling* (Englewood Cliffs, N.J.: Prentice-Hall, 1964); Carroll A. Wise, *The Meaning of Pastoral Care* (New York: Harper & Row, 1966).

THE MASTER GOAL OF PASTORAL COUNSELING

To understand the role of counseling in the work of a renewal-oriented church, a sharply focused picture of the *master goal* of this pastoral activity is needed. Is there a single, underlying difficulty from which all who come for counseling suffer, to some degree, regardless of their particular problems in living? An illuminating approach to answering this question has been given by psychiatrist William Glasser.[3] He holds that every person requiring psychiatric help suffers from one basic inadequacy—*the inability to fulfill his essential personality needs.* It is this inability which causes personality problems and interpersonal conflict. A person's behavior, however distorted, represents his attempt to satisfy his basic needs. To the extent that his efforts are unsuccessful, he will be a problem to himself and/or to others. This is an insightful way of viewing the basic problems of those who seek pastoral help.

Glasser maintains that persons have only two essential personality needs—to love and be loved, and to feel that one is worthwhile to oneself and others. I would reduce these to a single, indispensable need—*to experience authentic love in a dependable relationship.* An individual's personality hungers are *all* met to the degree that he participates in a relationship characterized by mutual "sensitivity and responsiveness to the needs of others." [4] This is what I mean by "authentic love." Having received a dependable supply of such love in his early life, one becomes a loving person who naturally responds to the needs of others and thus fulfills his own need to *give as well as receive love.*

Man's other personality needs[5] are derived, from his basic need for this quality of love in at least one relationship. He needs a *sense of his own worth,* which will make it possible for him to feel that others have inherent worth. Such basic self- and other-esteem is an essential ingredi-

[3] *Reality Therapy* (New York: Harper & Row, 1965), p. 5. Glasser's approach to therapy is highly significant for the minister-counselor.

[4] This succinct definition of mature love is from Regina Wescott. It should be emphasized that a mature relationship is never strictly a *quid pro quo* relationship. As Donald H. Rhoades puts the matter: "There are . . . two 'reasons' for mature love. One is that the other person needs it, no matter who he is and all the more the less he deserves it. The other reason is that love is natural to maturity" (*Faith for Fellowship* [Philadelphia: Westminster Press, 1965], p. 115). A person must have at least a minimal satisfaction of his basic needs in order to continue satisfying the needs of others. But, one who has achieved an appreciable degree of maturity has the inner security and resources to give in relationships in which he does not receive. This is the meaning of grace in relationships.

[5] For a more comprehensive discussion of these needs, see Howard J. Clinebell, Jr., *Mental Health Through Christian Community* (Nashville: Abingdon Press, 1965), pp. 147-48.

ent in authentic love. What often passes for "love"—a disguised form of manipulating or using others—diminishes self-esteem in both the one giving and the one receiving it. But to the degree that love is genuine, it enhances the esteem *of* and *for* the persons in the relationship.

Man also needs *to live responsibly*—i.e., in ways that do not diminish the personhood of others or block the fulfillment of their needs.[6] Responsibility, structure, limits—these are integral to a genuinely loving relationship. Something essential is missing from a parent's love for a child if he cannot set limits or discipline the child. Mature love always involves the dimension of responsibility and respect for the needs of others.

Another personality need of man is for *inner freedom*. As the wife of an alcoholic put it, a person needs to "own himself." Such freedom is also the freedom to *be* oneself. This freedom is the result of a warm, accepting relationship during one's early life with a person who possessed inner freedom and could therefore respect one's need for growing, autonomous selfhood. Inner freedom is created and nurtured in such a relationship. Respect for the inner freedom of the other is an integral part of authentic love.

The need for a *sense of meaning* is also a basic personality hunger. It is not for some abstract, philosophical meaningfulness that persons long. Rather it is a deep "gut-level" conviction that life is trustworthy and worth the struggle in spite of its cruelty, agony, and contradictions. This inner conviction is the product of loving, trustful relationships in early life and later. Psychoanalyst Erik Erikson used the term "basic trust" to describe the foundational feeling that life is trustworthy.[7] It is derived from the infant-mother relationship which develops during the first year of life when the mother is a warm, dependable, loving person.

Closely linked with the need for a sense of meaning is the need for a loving, *trustful relationship with God*. This is the vertical dimension of man's needs. This need is the reason why man is "incurably religious." Augustine's familiar line states it: "Thou hast made us for Thyself and our souls are restless until they rest in Thee." When translated into psychological (and much less beautiful) language, this simply means that by nature man requires a meaningful relationship with God to be whole.

[6] The emphasis on responsibility is at the heart of Glasser's therapy.

[7] *Identity and the Life Cycle* (New York: International Universities Press, 1959).

Pastoral counseling is the utilization, by a minister, of a one-to-one or small group relationship to help people handle their problems of living more adequately and grow toward fulfilling their potentialities. This is achieved by helping them reduce the inner blocks which prevent them from relating in need-satisfying ways. This is the master goal. Persons who need counseling help are those who are blocked, to a painful degree, temporarily or chronically, in their ability to maintain need-satisfying relationships. Many factors may be involved in such blockages—the lack of an adequate supply of mature love in early life, a traumatic crisis (e.g., bereavement, illness, unemployment), the paralysis of inner conflicts, debilitating anxiety, the accumulated results of irresponsible living, or the vicious self-perpetuating cycle of dysfunctional (nonneed-satisfying) relationships. Whatever the particular causes, such persons are unable to relate in ways that satisfy their need for the fundamental foods of the spirit. They seek bread but are able to find only a stone. The painful hunger-for-love produces an endless variety of inner distress, psychological symptoms, and interpersonal conflicts. It is this pain, and the hope of alleviating it, that brings them to counseling or gives them whatever openness to help they may have when the minister goes to them.

Pastoral counseling is effective to the extent that it helps a person increase his ability to relate in ways that satisfy his basic personality needs. To the degree that an individual is able to satisfy these needs, the following things become possible: *He will be able to handle his load of problems and responsibilities. He will continue to grow toward the fulfillment of his unique personhood. He will develop constructive relationships. His relationship with God will become increasingly meaningful. He will become a renewal agent in his family, community, and church.*

THE PURPOSE OF THIS BOOK

The overall purpose of this book is to help the parish minister (and the seminary student preparing for a general parish ministry) develop maximum skill in the various counseling methods which are required in that setting. Subsumed under this generic objective are more specific purposes:

(1) *It is the purpose of this book to review the procedures which are fundamental to all pastoral counseling* (see Chapter 4). These general

procedures provide a foundation for the differential use of particular counseling methodologies, as described in Chapters 5 through 15.

(2) A further purpose is *to develop a differential typology of pastoral counseling*. This represents a fresh approach to the task of conceptualizing and thereby understanding the full range of the minister's counseling activities. "Pastoral counseling" is not a species but a genus of pastoral activities. It is not one entity with one methodology. Instead, it is a helping function which requires a variety of methods to be fully effective. To minister to the varied needs of those who seek his help, a pastor must be able to shift gears in his counseling—to utilize approaches which are appropriate to the needs, resources, problems, and limitations of each person. *He must be able to utilize different facets of his personality* freely and flexibly. With a person floundering in catastrophic crises, he needs to use his supportive, nurturing "Parent" [8] side to give him stability in coping with his situation. To help a person who has never achieved dependable inner standards or controls, the minister must be a firm and accepting, but *not a permissive*, parent figure. In contrast, the counselee with a punitive, hairshirted conscience needs desperately to experience the minister's more permissive side. It is not that the minister puts on a varied "act." To do so would destroy the interpersonal integrity which is the *sine qua non* of an effective counseling relationship. Rather, he employs different dimensions of his many-faceted personality in responding to varying counselee needs.

The counseling methods described will be grouped under the following types of counseling: Methods of—Informal, Marriage and Family, Supportive, Crisis, Referral, Educative, Group, Confrontational, Religious-Existential, and Depth Counseling. More than one method will be presented within several of these types.

A minister's functional self-image is derived from his picture of the types and goals of the counseling which he must do in order to fulfill his ministry. With the exception of depth counseling, opportunities to do the above types are unavoidable in a person-centered ministry. Furthermore, *the minister is in a strategic position to do them well,* provided he is adequately trained. Proficiency in all these types (excluding depth counseling) is necessary for a fully effective ministry. For these reasons they may be regarded as *normative* for *pastoral* counseling.

[8] This usage from Eric Berne will be discussed in Chapter 7.

It should be made crystal clear that several counseling methods are almost always employed at various stages of a counseling relationship, often during the same session. The methods are *tools* to be used selectively by the pastor. Just as a carpenter needs a variety of tools to build a fine piece of furniture, a counselor requires a variety of methods to help rebuild a marriage or a person's value structure. As any experienced pastor knows, the varied counseling opportunities which confront him require both flexibility and ingenuity in applying what he knows about counseling methods. What he has learned from his own inner struggles may be more useful to him than his knowledge of the "techniques" of counseling. But the more he knows about the various counseling approaches, the better use he can make of his unique experience, personality resources, and creativity. It is the intent of this book to encourage the reader to increase his versatility and effectiveness *by developing his own differential approach to counseling methodology.*

(3) Another purpose of this book is *to introduce the reader to some of the creative new methods in psychotherapy which are relevant to pastoral counseling.* These new approaches are presented as adapted through their use in pastoral counseling. Ours is a period of amazing fecundity in the field of psychotherapy. New theories of the nature of therapy as well as new therapeutic techniques are springing up like flowers in a spring meadow. We in the church must be open to experimenting with these fresh approaches as we search for more effective ways of shepherding in depth.

The new thrusts which have the most direct relevance to the theory and practice of pastoral counseling are these: *Role-relationship marriage counseling, family group therapy* (John E. Bell and Virginia M. Satir), *transactional analysis* (Eric Berne), *crisis intervention theory* (Gerald Caplan), *reality therapy* (William Glasser), *existential psychotherapy* (Rollo May, Viktor Frankl, J. F. T. Bugental), and the broad thrust of *ego psychology.* All these are rich sources of insights and tools for the counseling pastor. The aim of this book is to make some of these readily accessible to the parish minister and directly applicable to his work.

In *Pastoral Care in Historical Perspective,* church historian William A. Clebsch and pastoral care specialist Charles R. Jaekle describe the present as a "transitional period in pastoral care." Speaking to the issue of whether it is proper for the church to draw on secular psychotherapies for its pastoral tools, they declare:

The lesson to be learned in this connection from the history of pastoral care is simply that openness to new psychological theories and notions in fact represents and continues a powerful trend found in every epoch of pastoring. The great tradition of pastoral care stands constantly ready to receive its ideas and its vocabulary both from psychological theoreticians and from popular language about the soul. The normative feature of pastoral care in historical perspective is neither a uniquely Christian psychology nor a particular language in which human trouble must be described, but it is the constancy of the pastoral posture and of the four pastoral functions of healing, sustaining, guiding, and reconciling.[9]

The authors go on to glean this maxim from the pastoral care heritage for the present period of transition: "Remain open to the insights of various and even conflicting psychological theories, for man's capacity for trouble is complex, intricate and inventive." [10]

This heritage-informed guidance is sound. Openness to new understandings of personality and therapy on the part of contemporary pastoral counseling practitioners will help us turn the corner discussed earlier. Alert openness will facilitate the creative breakthroughs which will release the renewal potentialities of counseling as a pastoral art. Time undoubtedly will prove that some of the new methods are of limited usefulness for pastors. The road to better pastoral skill may have dead ends and detours, but the only alternative is not to travel at all!

It is my belief that direct encounter with the ferment of new developments in current psychotherapies will broaden a minister's counseling horizons, deepen his general approach to pastoral care, and stimulate his interest in further reading, study, and training.

(4) It is the purpose of this book *to offer a revised model for pastoral counseling based not on insight-oriented, uncovering psychotherapy, but on relational, supportive, ego-adaptive, reality-oriented approaches to therapy.* I call this model "relationship-centered counseling." Many of the windows which have opened in my thinking through contact with new psychotherapies have revealed the same or adjacent

[9] (Englewood Cliffs, N. J.: Prentice-Hall, 1964), p. 79.
[10] *Ibid.*

aspects of the ideological landscape. The model of pastoral counseling which has emerged in my thinking and practice gradually developed coherence and unity. This model links the diverse methodologies described in this book into an integrated thrust. I offer the model to guide the counseling pastor and to encourage him to experiment with various methods, to the end that he will discover his own unique style of counseling utilizing the many sides of his personality. What I offer is not a finished system or a recipe book of counseling methods, but a tentative model linking a variety of methods. It is my hope that this will prove to be something of a catalyst for research in parish counseling, leading to further revisions in theory and innovations in practice.

(5) The final purpose of this book is *to encourage the widespread use of the reality-practice or role-taking method* which has proved to be useful in increasing both the self-awareness and the counseling skills of pastors. The reality-practice or role-taking approach is utterly simple to use. Its value has been demonstrated repeatedly in seminary counseling courses and in a variety of counseling workshops, clinical seminars, and pastoral case conferences for parish ministers.

HOW TO DERIVE THE MAXIMUM BENEFIT FROM THIS BOOK

Here is an approach to using the book which will maximize its practical value.

Step 1: Skim the entire book. Get an overview of the various approaches.

Step 2: Go back to the beginning. Read carefully, reflecting on each chapter. Write your responses, criticisms, agreements, rebuttals, and unanswered questions in the margin. Underline key ideas. Challenge the theories and approaches. Talk back. Keep asking, "How does this apply to my counseling?" Carry on a dialogue with the ideas which hit you. If possible, discuss the major ideas and methods with another minister or theological student who is reading the book. A small group of such persons will stimulate learning through interaction.

Step 3: Find one, two, or three reality-practice partners—fellow ministers or theological students who are interested in experimenting with new methods designed to increase their counseling skills. Reality-practice sessions with one's wife are also valuable (providing one has a sturdy marriage). The reality-practice team should participate in regular (preferably weekly) sessions, using the case material from one's counseling and/or the cases described at the end of the chapters on counseling methods. These practice sessions should become a kind of counseling laboratory. Their use will allow the seminary student to develop basic counseling skills and the seasoned minister to experiment with new methods, both without the danger of mishandling disturbed persons.

Here is the *modus operandi* of reality-practice. If only two persons are available, they alternate as "pastoral counselor" and "parishioner." If three are involved, the role of "observer-evaluator" is added. One person begins by taking the role of a person with whom he has counseled unsuccessfully or someone else whose problems he knows well. He attempts to get within that person's "internal frame of reference" (Rogers) as he takes his role. This provides valuable practice in empathic understanding. Unlike the conventional role-playing approach, the person who is "pastoral counselor" ordinarily is encouraged to function as he normally would. He plays *himself* as counselor, as he experiments with various methods. After a practice session has gone on for ten to twenty-five minutes, the participants come "out of role" and discuss what has happened. The "parishioner" begins by telling the "pastor" how he felt during the interview. The "pastor" then shares his feelings and observations. Both evaluate what has occurred, shift roles, and try another "counseling" session.

An observer-evaluator increases the learning value of reality practice sessions. If he is sensitive to interpersonal dynamics, he will observe things in the counseling of which the active participants are unaware. For example, he may say, "I got the feeling that you were involved in a verbal power struggle. I wonder if this was the case and, if so, why?" Tape recording and playback of reality-practice sessions is highly useful. This is crucial if there is no observer-evaluator. Counselors who hear themselves in action are usually as astonished as a person hearing his own voice for the first time. A typical reaction is, "I had no idea I talked so much in my counseling!" Since there are different learning values in each of the three reality-practice roles, it is important to rotate frequently enough to give each participant practice in at least two roles during a session. If the counselor is experienced, it is often productive for the counselee who desires to do so to use his own problems as the counseling "case." If all the participants are inexperienced, an experienced counselor should be invited to meet with the group as a consultant, as often as possible.

The value of reality-practice increases as a group gains experience with the method.[11] It is important that the participants become secure enough with each other to be utterly candid in their comments about the counseling. I recall one session in which the "parishioner" said during the evaluation period: "I felt as though you were overwhelming me with words. Somehow you weren't hearing my feelings." This was the first time that the "pastor" (who had done considerable counseling) had had any awareness of how he was affecting his counselees. This confrontation opened a door to self-awareness. Most serious participants discover that there are many aspects of their personalities which they are failing to utilize in counseling and others which they are misusing.

Step 4: Use your new counseling tools as opportunities arise in the parish, while continuing reality-practice sessions. Current counseling situations, particularly those which are going badly, should be used as material for reality-practice.

Step 5: If you encounter major blocks to effectiveness, not reduced by reality-practice, *by all means obtain supervision* from a clinically trained chaplain, a psychiatrist, psychologist, social worker, or a clergyman with graduate training in pastoral counseling. Don't give up in discouragement. Acquiring counseling skills and sensitivities usually takes time and struggle. Unless you have unusual natural aptitudes in this area, it will require disciplined practice and repeated self-encounter. As is the case with all artistic skills, the way to one's maximum effectiveness as a counselor is straight, and the gate narrow. There does not seem to be any other route to this important objective.

[11] Early sessions may seem to have little or no value. The uneasiness of the participants may elicit an excessive amount of nervous humor, or competitiveness may cause them to engage in "one-upmanship" by making the counselee unrealistically difficult or uncooperative. When such symptoms of anxiety are observed, they should be discussed openly in the reality-practice group. For further information on role playing see: Alan F. Klein, *Role Playing in Leadership Training and Group Problem Solving* (New York: Association Press, 1956).

2

A Revised Model for Pastoral Counseling

Pastoral counseling is in peril of becoming repetitious, the next step beyond which is sterility. This can be avoided by asking new questions.

—Wayne E. Oates[1]

This book grew out of the process of asking some new questions concerning the aims, methods, and basic model of pastoral counseling in the parish setting. Here is the general shape of the model which emerged. It emphasizes:

(1) *using supportive* rather than uncovering *methods;*

(2) *improving relationships* (through couple, family, and group methods) rather than aiming at intrapsychic changes;

(3) *maximizing and utilizing one's positive personality resources* in addition to reducing negative factors;

(4) *coping successfully with one's current situation and planning for the future* rather than exploring the past extensively;

(5) *confronting the realities of one's situation* including the need to become more responsible, in addition to understanding feelings and attitudes;

(6) *making direct efforts to increase the constructiveness and creativity of behavior* as well as feelings and attitudes;

(7) *dealing directly with the crucially important vertical dimension* (the dimension of values and ultimate meanings) in relationships as well

[1] *Protestant Pastoral Counseling* (Philadelphia: Westminster Press, 1962), p. 13.

as the horizontal dimension of physical and psychological interaction.

With these emphases, short-term pastoral counseling frequently can produce significant improvement in a person's ability to establish and maintain mutually need-satisfying relationships—the goal of this approach to counseling. The revised model appears to "fit" the parish minister's situation and to allow him to use the advantages of his *pastoral* orientation more than did the older model based on "Rogers with a dash of Freud." In proposing a revised model, my intention is to broaden and modify rather than to reject the methods and goals of the older model. Without sacrificing the important values of the Rogerian thrust in pastoral counseling, it seeks to recover the strengths of the pre-Rogerian period.

OLDER MODEL COMPARED WITH REVISED MODEL

During the formative period of contemporary pastoral counseling (the nineteen forties and fifties), five seminal ideas played decisive roles in shaping the literature and the approach to seminary teaching of counseling:

(1) The formal, *structured counseling interview* as the operational model;

(2) the *client-centered method* as the normative and often exclusive methodology;

(3) *insight* as *the central goal* of counseling;

(4) the concepts of *unconscious motivation* and

(5) the *childhood roots of adult behavior.*

Each of these has a degree of continuing validity and usefulness for the counseling pastor. But they pose serious problems if they dominate either his understanding of his counseling function or his practice thereof. Taken together, these influential ideas do not provide a solid conceptual foundation for his self-understanding or an operational base for maximizing his unique effectiveness as *pastoral* counselor. If these ideas alone form his working model, his ability to help many who come to him is drastically limited. Much of the widespread frustration felt by clergymen in their counseling activities is a direct consequence of such an inadequate model.

The setting and structure of counseling: The formal structured counseling interview, the major operational model of the older approach, was derived directly from the counseling clinic and psychotherapeutic interview. Parish experience shows that much of a minister's most productive counseling occurs in informal settings—in a parishioner's living room, in a committee room following a meeting, or standing in a hospital corridor outside the operating room. The "structures" of formal counseling—appointments, definite time limits, a private meeting place, and the label "counseling"—are often missing. It is important that a pastor discover that these features of the "fifty-minute hour" are not essential to helping people with their inner problems in significant ways. The minister who makes the structured interview his primary operational model will miss many of his finest counseling opportunities.

The revised model regards the formal, structured interview as *one of several* useful approaches. In general, the minister's image of the setting, structure, and process of counseling needs to be much more flexible than the psychotherapist's. To render significant help to the maximum number of people, the clergyman must be able to apply his counseling skills to the host of informal and often chance opportunities which he has to relate to those struggling with complex decisions, staggering loads, and agonizing problems. He should work hard at increasing his effectiveness in informal counseling so that these contacts can become bridges for transmitting help. (See Chapter 5.)

Methods of counseling: The profound influence which the client-centered method has had on the development of contemporary pastoral counseling has been generally salutary, helping to rescue it from a legacy of overdirectiveness. It was (and is) particularly needed by *clergymen* to alert us to the twin professional hazards of facile verbalizing and playing god in the lives of counselees. It has demonstrated convincingly the crucial importance in all counseling of disciplined listening and responding to feelings. For ministers in authority-centered traditions and for theological students learning counseling, a time exposure to Roger's approach is highly beneficial.[2] A grounding in this

[2] Many theological students need the Rogerian influence to "discipline their mouths" and to teach them to listen. Ministers from traditions which have taught them to be "answer men" need it for the same reasons. Rogers' later emphasis on the personality of the counselor and the general quality of the relationship can help one avoid the trap of "technique-itis"—an overevaluation on technique as an end in itself. (See Chapter 17.)

philosophy and method is an excellent *starting* point for increasing one's counseling skills. It is not an adequate *stopping* point. It gives one the fundamentals of establishing a therapeutic relationship, but it does not provide guidance in the *varied* methods of utilizing this relationship to help troubled persons. The Rogerian method provides a firm foundation but not the entire edifice of an adequate approach to counseling. The pastor must stay *person-centered* in his counseling, but this is not synonymous with remaining "client-centered" in methodology.

With some counselees the client-centered method is sufficient by itself. This is true of those whose main need is for emotional catharsis —the opportunity to pour out their burdened feelings and have them shared by an accepting listener. It may also be true of those whose need is to think through a situational problem. As a method of longer-term psychotherapy, this approach is useful with reasonably intelligent, verbal, young or middle-aged neurotics who are strongly motivated to get help.

But the pastor sees many troubled people who lack the ability to respond to the relatively passive Rogerian approach. It must be modified in a more active direction if they are to receive help. My experience has been that a *majority* of those who come for pastoral counseling cannot be given maximum help by an unmodified Rogerian approach.[3] Their defenses are too ingenious or their personalities too rigid, limited or ossified. Gordon Hamilton describes casework's "adventure in passivity." [4] Rogerian-trained pastors will resonate to this phrase, recalling counseling experiences characterized by long-term, fruitless reflecting and rambling—exercises in mutual frustration. Many of those who cannot respond to a Rogerian approach *can* be helped to greater adequacy in living by the use of other counseling methods.

The Rogerian model has tended to make the minister feel that he should strenuously avoid the use of his authority—i.e., he should not advise, direct, inspire, or teach in his counseling relationships. In

[3] For a succinct discussion of the limitations of client-centered therapy, see psychiatrist Lewis R. Wolberg's *The Technique of Psychotherapy* (New York: Grune and Stratton, 1954), pp. 42-44.

[4] See *Ego Psychology and Dynamic Casework*, Howard J. Parad, ed. (New York: Family Service Association of America, 1958), p. 26. John W. Drakeford refers to the "filibustering counselee" and the inadequacy of client-centered methods in dealing with this problem. The same is true of the counselee who indulges in fruitless orgies of self-pity. (*Integrity Therapy, A New Direction in Psychotherapy* [Fort Worth, Tex.: mimeographed manuscript, 1965], p. 92).

contrast, the revised model is based on the conviction that it is often constructive, even essential, for the pastor to use his authority selectively in sustaining, guiding, feeding (emotionally), inspiring, confronting, teaching, and encouraging persons to function responsibly. The authority derived from the minister's knowledge, skill, and role is an invaluable asset in counseling, provided he knows how to use it appropriately.

Instead of regarding teaching as alien to sound counseling, the revised model regards creative teaching methods as indispensable to much pastoral counseling. Helping a person learn certain facts and skills may change his entire perspective on his problems. In one sense, counseling in general is a sharply focused form of depth teaching.

The overall impact of Rogerian training has been to make ministers feel that they should assume a special, relatively passive stance when counseling. Often this does not fit their personalities and contradicts their general approach to people. In contrast, the revised model picks up the later Rogerian[5] and existentialist (in psychotherapy) emphasis on the counselor bringing *himself* to the person rather than some image of a "counselor." The minister's essential humanity is one of the precious things he has to share in all his relationships. If he puts on a "counseling approach," of whatever kind, he confuses his counselees by the mask which obscures his personhood.

Pastoral counseling methodology has tended to center on one-to-one relationships. The "relationship-centered" thrust emphasizes counseling with married couples, entire family units, and other small groups. Individual problems are rooted in relationships which are not satisfying personality needs. Couple, family, and group counseling approaches are especially efficient because they deal directly with troubled relationships.

The goals of counseling: Typical of the mainstream of pastoral counseling theory as it has developed is Seward Hiltner's statement: "The generic aim of counseling is new insight, with proof in action."[6] The emphasis on insight represents a giant advance over the advice-giving or mere problem-solving approach to counseling. For some who seek help from a pastor, insight is an appropriate goal. These are persons who

[5] I refer to Rogers' emphasis on "congruence"—the counselor's inner consistency, awareness, and genuineness (see Chapter 17).

[6] *Pastoral Counseling* (Nashville: Abingdon Press, 1949), p. 95.

possess considerable ego strength, inner resources, capacity for introspection, and the motivation to do more than solve immediate problems. Anyone who has profited from psychotherapy can attest with gratitude to the positive changes in feelings and relationships which accrue from enhanced self-awareness.

Several problems loom large if insight is regarded as the "generic aim" of pastoral counseling. For one thing, many people are apparently incapable of achieving insight[7] because of lack of ego strength, the absence of introspective propensities, or the presence of personality rigidity (due to aging or other factors). To help such persons the minister must use other counseling methods to which they *can* respond. Another problem is that counseling which produces significant insight is usually a lengthy process requiring more training than most pastors possess and more time than they can invest without neglecting other responsibilities. In spite of the relative theoretical simplicity of the Rogerian approach, actual counseling relationships which go deep enough to produce liberating insight usually involve the counselor in the labyrinthian complexities of the human psyche. Pastoral psychotherapy (insight counseling) is a helpful and appropriate activity for a clergyman who has the time and training to do it with competence. (See Chapter 15.) It does not constitute a useful method and goal of counseling for parish clergymen in general.

Insight becomes a secondary and optional goal in the revised model. The master goal of relationship-centered counseling (see Chapter 1) is to enhance a person's ability to relate in mutually need-satisfying ways. Deep insight into one's feelings, motives, and relationships is not essential to the realization of this goal. In many cases it is unnecessary to achieve any radical changes in the personalities of a couple in order to help them learn to relate in more need-satisfying and fewer need-depriving ways.

Troubled people can receive genuine, lasting help on many levels of their lives, not just the deepest levels. The most useful counseling goal for the great majority of those who come to a minister is *to help them*

[7] In the early development of his approach, Carl R. Rogers set limits regarding those who could be helped by it. See his *Counseling and Psychotherapy* (Boston: Houghton Mifflin Co., 1942), pp. 61-80. More recently, he has reported success with a variety of types of psychopathology and has expressed reluctance about setting such limits in any arbitrary fashion. See Robert A. Harper, *Psychoanalysis and Psychotherapy, 36 Systems* (Englewood Cliffs, N.J.: Prentice-Hall, 1959), p. 91. My experience causes me to lean toward his earlier position.

improve the quality of their relationships. The achievement of this goal is often feasible within the limits of the minister's time and training *and is precisely what the person needs most.* Most counselees have aspects of their personalities which are healthier (more mature) than those which dominated their precounseling relationships. Many of these can learn, without depth therapy, how to utilize their healthier sides in their relationships.[8]

The pastor who uses the revised model is more apt to confront the person (within a strong counseling relationship) with the need to face his unconstructive patterns of living. Living in self-contradictory ways which violate one's sense of justice, integrity, and respect for persons is seen as a *cause* and not just a *symptom* of inner conflicts. Many people are capable of making constructive changes in this behavior whether or not their inner conflicts are resolved. Therefore, the person's guiding values and the behavior resulting therefrom should be examined, not just in terms of how he *feels* about these matters (although this is important), but also in terms of how they influence his relationships and sense of worth, and what he can *do* to live more constructively.

The revised model is more *action-oriented* than the older model. In Rogerian counseling behavioral changes are seen as the *result* of changes in feelings and self-perception. The new approach holds that the opposite is also true—constructive changes in relationships and behavior often produce significant feeling and attitudinal changes. Counseling, therefore, aims at helping a person deal constructively with his immediate problems, cope with a crisis, make a decision, face responsibilities, make amends for destructive actions, or do what he has been afraid to do. Within a counseling relationship he may be able to reverse destructive patterns and reestablish fractured relationships. *The part of the personality which copes with relationships and responsibilities is like a muscle. It grows stronger with exercise and atrophies with disuse. Counseling aims at helping a person exercise his coping abilities and thus gain strength, skill, and confidence in handling whatever life brings him.* Without ignoring feelings this approach stresses getting the person to *do* something positive, however small, about his situation.[9]

[8] Put in Eric Berne's terms, this consists of mobilizing or activating a person's inner Adult so that it can guide and control his inner Child and Parent. (See Chapter 7.)

[9] A report on the distinctive nature of "counseling psychology" throws light on pastoral counseling: "It focuses on *plans* individuals must make to play productive *roles* in their social

Interrupting negative, self-feeding patterns is an essential goal of the revised approach. These are the emotional and interpersonal "tail-spins" in which many people get trapped. Helping them pull out of the tailspin is often *all* that is necessary to help them get back on course and fly on their own. A "failure cycle" is present in many problems. Each failure increases the person's expectation of future failure, automatically reducing his chances of success. School dropouts are a case in point. Many marriage problems are the result of such a self-perpetuating cycle of mutual hurt and attack. Frequently, direct intervention in the form of confrontation by the counselor is required to interrupt the spiraling failure to cope and relate.[10]

The focus of counseling: The interlocking concepts of *unconscious factors in the motivation of behavior* and the *childhood roots of adult behavior* are a part of our legacy from the amazing discoveries of psychoanalysis. Both have influenced the self-understanding of our culture profoundly. A pastor's awareness of the crucial role played in behavior and relationships by unconscious forces inevitably impinges on his understanding of the nature of his counseling. The greater his psychological sophistication, the stronger this influence. Man is not the total master of the house of his psyche. The more emotionally disturbed a person is, the more pervasive the domination of his behavior by unconscious impulses, conflicts, and repressed memories.

The genetic emphasis holds that present behavior can be understood in depth only by exploring the complexities of a person's early relationships with need-satisfying adults. These relationships molded the individual's basic personality structure and therefore influenced all his subsequent relationships, including his relationship with God.

The minister who is knowledgeable concerning unconscious forces and the role of childhood experiences in creating these is confronted with a frustrating dilemma. The limitations of his time, training, and

---

environments. Whether the person being helped with such planning is sick or well, abnormal or normal, is really irrelevant. The focus is on assets, skills, strengths, possibilities for further development. Personality difficulties are dealt with only when they constitute obstacles to the individual's forward progress" ("The Current Status of Counseling Psychology," A Report of a Special Committee of the Division of Counseling Psychology [American Psychological Association, 1961], pp. 6-7).

[10] The ability to interrupt negative cycles was one of the values of the pre-Rogerian pastoral counselor's approach.

multiple roles consign him to deal in counseling mainly with current problems in living and with conscious and preconscious (out of awareness but recallable) material. Yet he knows that important causes of current problems (including theological problems) are in the parishioner's unconscious, tangled in his continuing conflicts from unsatisfied early-life personality hungers. Thus he may picture his counseling as superficial, dealing only with "surface symptoms," while the deep inner springs of behavior go untouched. Such an unfortunate self-image retards the development of a minister's unique and valuable functioning as *pastoral* counselor.

The revised model does not ignore early life or unconscious factors in current problems. In some cases exploration of a parishioner's formative years may illuminate the hidden roots of his troubled relationships.[11] This can be helpful provided he does not use his early life to excuse or justify his present irresponsible behavior. The counselor's awareness of the operation of unconscious influences can be very useful to him, even though he chooses not to deal with these factors directly. For example, a single dream may yield key insights concerning a counselee's underlying problem to a pastor trained in depth psychology. Diagnostically this can be invaluable, even though the counseling focuses on helping the person cope with here-and-now problems.

The primary focus of the revised approach is on conscious material and contemporary relationships. Many persons can be helped in significant ways on this level. Certainly in short-term counseling, the pastor usually achieves more constructive results by focusing on contemporary problems and realistic plans for the future than by searching (like a psychological archaeologist) for the past prototypes of current relationships. The revised approach is not necessarily second best. Many of those who come for pastoral help cannot utilize depth counseling because of their age or personality limitations. For them, a therapy which concentrates on present relationships and problems is the treatment of choice! Going back to the early life roots of problems usually is not essential (even if possible) in order to increase the constructive-

[11] For example, it may be perspective-giving to view a complex marital problem in terms of the childhood relationships of each person with the parent of the same and the opposite sex. Some people are helped by seeing the early roots of current behavior, particularly if they "work through" the related feelings.

ness of relationships. As William Menninger has said, in effect, "It isn't necessary to know how a fire started in order to put it out."

Those aspects of the past which are important are not really past. They are observable (to the trained eye) in the ways that they distort here-and-now relationships. If necessary, the still-living past can be dealt with as it is projected on the screen of current relationships.[12]

The primary focus of the revised model is on the *between* of conflicting relationships rather than the *within* of intra-psychic problems. The disturbed relationship, *per se,* becomes the patient. Focusing on relationships provides an approach to dealing helpfully with the theological dimension in counseling. The health of one's internal life and his relationships with people are inseparable from the health of his relationship with God. Inadequacies in the vitality and maturity of the latter can cause, as well as be caused by, interpersonal problems. The practical implication of this is that the pastor should be as open to dealing with religious and value problems in counseling as he is to dealing with interpersonal difficulties.

In summary, the older model of pastoral counseling, derived mainly from insight-oriented, uncovering psychotherapy, is inadequate for the minister's self-understanding of his counseling role. It tends to cause him to function faultily in ways for which he is ill-prepared, while neglecting the approaches to short-term counseling which lend themselves to the parish situation. The older model tends to cause him to judge his short-term counseling by criteria relevant only to long-term psychotherapy, leaving him with an unwarranted sense of the superficiality or failure of his efforts. The relationship-centered model provides more realistic goals and more effective methods for the pastoral setting. It can allow the minister to discover the unique and valuable forms of counseling help which he is in an ideal position to give.

PROBLEMS AND HAZARDS OF THE REVISED MODEL

For the theological student beginning his mastery of the counseling art, a multiple methodology approach may seem formidably complex. But if instead he acquires the erroneous impression that all pastoral

[12] A focusing on the past is justified in pastoral counseling *if* the person is unable to deal with present realities constructively because of residual feelings.

counseling is a unity methodologically, he will discover when he reaches the parish that he lacks the variety of counseling tools which are required there. It is much better to *begin* with the awareness that a multiple methodology is essential!

The most difficult problem in the pastoral counseling field is that a majority of clergymen in parishes today have had little formal training in this skill. Many attended seminaries prior to the recent robust emphasis in this area. Inadequacies in formal training make the need for a flexible model which will release one's *native* helping abilities all the more pressing. A methodological model which is directly related to the counseling one is doing encourages experimentation with new methods and stimulates learning from one's successes and failures. It helps one reflect critically on one's counseling by providing a conceptual framework for understanding these experiences. One reason many pastors have difficulty with a one-track counseling approach is that they need a differential approach.

The revised model has certain propensities for misuse at the hands of authoritarian, emotionally blocked, or overworked ministers. By encouraging the use of supportive, confrontational, educative, guiding, action-oriented approaches, it may *seem* to justify a return to certain pre-Rogerian abuses in counseling. The more active model carries the risk of stimulating the natural tendency of some ministers to be overdirective and moralizing, and to encourage unconstructive dependence and superficial adjustment when deeper changes are possible. One busy pastor, with considerable counseling training, stated his problem: "When I get in a big hurry, I give people instructions, even though I know better."

I believe that these risks are more than offset by the increased pastoral effectiveness which can result from using this model. Pastoral counseling must move into a post-Rogerian period if it is to come into its own in helping troubled persons fully. Such a period will be a time of constructive growth only if two things happen: (a) the insights of the Rogerian and psychoanalytic approaches are retained as valuable parts of our heritage to balance the more directive approaches, and (b) the availability of personal growth experiences for clergymen is rapidly expanded in seminaries and clinical training settings. The effectiveness of any form of pastoral counseling will always be contingent on one factor—the pastor himself.[13] To the degree that he is open, genuine, free, self-accepting, and growing, he will naturally foster these qualities in others, even if his counseling methodology is inadequate. The better his methodology, the more fully he will be able to utilize his personality resources. Whatever the model which guides pastoral counseling, it is imperative that theological education (during and continuing after seminary) become more effective in preparing ministers *to establish creative relationships* which can help make men whole.

THE NEW MODEL IN THE LIGHT OF OUR HERITAGE

It is important that the pastoral counselor see himself within the long sweep of the rich heritage of pastoral care.[14] With reference to this book, it is helpful to see both models of pastoral counseling as recent developments in the venerable tradition of shepherding. When a minister counsels with troubled persons, he is walking in the footsteps of a long line of sensitive, dedicated pastors stretching back through the centuries of Christian history to a young carpenter whose words and touch brought healing to troubled persons in the first century. A minister's counseling work will acquire another dimension if he senses that he is a part of a heritage including such great pastors as John Chrysostom (d. A.D. 407), Ambrose of Milan (d. 397), Martin Luther, Richard Baxter, Horace Bushnell, and Washington Gladden.[15] With Chrysostom, from the age of the church fathers, he will think of himself as a "physician of the soul." He will draw inspiration from the fact that he is a part of a counseling tradition which is the most ancient of any profession.

The contemporary flowering of this ancient ministry should not blind the minister to his heritage. As one dimension of pastoral care, pastoral

[13] A counselor who is a manipulative person finds subtle ways of manipulating, even in the most nondirective approach. Such manipulation is more difficult to resist than the overt variety, because it is harder to recognize and more apt to employ guilt feelings as the lever.

[14] Pastoral care consists of "helping acts, done by representative Christian persons, directed toward the healing, sustaining, guiding, and reconciling of troubled persons whose troubles arise in the context of ultimate meanings and concerns" (Clebsch and Jaekle, *Pastoral Care in Historical Perspective,* p. 4). Counseling is one vital facet of pastoral care.

[15] Albert L. Meiburg's "The Heritage of the Pastoral Counselor," in *An Introduction to Pastoral Counseling,* Wayne E. Oates, ed. (Nashville: Broadman Press, 1959), pp. 3-18, is an excellent synopsis of the place of counseling in church history. A detailed history of pastoral care is John T. McNeill's *A History of the Cure of Souls* (New York: Harper & Row, 1951).

counseling is a sturdy plant with deep roots in the past. Its present blossoming is due to the rise of the clinical training movement and the strong streams of new knowledge from the sciences of man and the psychotherapeutic disciplines, which have watered this ancient plant and given it new and unprecedented vitality. The counseling pastor should learn all that he can from these rich new sources, but, fundamentally, his self-image should be molded by his own tradition of shepherding, not from the recent model of the psychotherapist.

In their compendium of pastoral care source material from the pages of church history, William A. Clebsch and Charles R. Jaekle identify four pastoral care functions: (a) *Healing*—"a pastoral function that aims to overcome some impairment by restoring the person to wholeness and by leading him to advance beyond his previous condition." [16] (b) *Sustaining*—"helping a hurting person to endure and to transcend a circumstance in which restoration to his former condition or recuperation from his malady is either impossible or so remote as to seem improbable." (c) *Guiding*—"assisting perplexed persons to make confident choices between alternative courses of thought and action, when such choices are viewed as affecting the present and future state of the soul." (d) *Reconciling*—"seeks to re-establish broken relationships between man and fellow man and between man and God." [17] Historically, reconciling has employed two modes—forgiveness and discipline.

The older model of pastoral counseling emphasized healing (insight counseling) with secondary attention to guiding. The revised model aims at utilizing all four strands of the pastoral care tradition. *Each function has its counseling aspect* in that within each, one-to-one or small group relationships are used to help people handle problems constructively and improve their relationships. The breadth of the revised model is derived from taking seriously the full range of pastoral care functioning, including its neglected strands. The future health of both pastoral care and counseling depends on the vigorous development, interaction, and balancing of all four pastoral functions. This book is an attempt to describe the varied methods of pastoral counseling which

[16] Clebsch and Jaekle, *Pastoral Care in Historical Perspective*, p. 33. The authors acknowledge their indebtedness to Seward Hiltner for his delineation of the first three functions.

[17] *Ibid.*, pp. 8-9.

are modern means of fulfilling these ancient functions of the minister. In emphasizing sustaining, guiding, and reconciling, as well as healing, it moves toward a shepherding (or pastoral) model, and away from a predominantly medical or psychotherapeutic model. Here, in diagrammatic form, is what I mean:

Pastoral Care Function	*Historical Expressions*	*Contemporary Counseling Expression*
Healing	Anointing, exorcism, saints and relics, charismatic healers	Depth counseling (pastoral psychotherapy); spiritual healing
Sustaining	Preserving, consoling, consolidating	Supportive counseling; crisis counseling
Guiding	Advice-giving, devil-craft, listening	Educative counseling; short-term decision making; marriage counseling
Reconciling	Confession, forgiveness, disciplining	Confrontational counseling; superego counseling; marriage counseling; Existential counseling (reconciliation with God)

3

The Mission, Theological Foundation and Uniqueness of Pastoral Counseling

In our time we have been uprooted from our former homeland, adrift in a mobile and changing society. We are lonely in crowds who seem not to care, pushed to and fro by machines to serve and be served, until we too become mechanical and act like machines. We meet the other persons as strangers, but mostly by external contacts passing by or bouncing away as if we were rubber balls. We are hollow men who do not know the inner life of other persons, and so we give attention mainly to the external appearance. Estranged from them or used by them, we are empty within ourselves, lost souls for whom no one seems to care. The need has never been so urgent for someone to care. How can a pastor care for his people in such a world?

—Paul E. Johnson [1]

Pastoral counseling is a response to the need for someone to really care for the troubled within the church fellowship and those numerous persons who have no church, but who turn to a minister for help when crises strike. A significant percentage of those who seek a pastor's counseling help are not a part of *any* meaningful fellowship. They are the *alienated ones* of our society. Their need for pastoral care is acute. Less obvious, but often no less painful, are the needs of those "lost within themselves in our own congregations." [2] Thus, pastoral counsel-

[1] "Where We Are Now in Pastoral Care," *Christian Advocate*, September 23, 1965, p. 7.

[2] These are the words of a psychiatrist who is also a devoted churchman. He calls for "a more intensive *in*reaching mission" to these persons (C. W. Morris, "The Terror of Good Works," *Pastoral Psychology*, September, 1957, p. 25).

ing has both an *inreaching* and an *outreaching* mission to persons in conflict and trouble, wherever they may be.

THE CRUCIAL IMPORTANCE OF PASTORAL COUNSELING

When a pastor who is in touch with his people looks at his congregation on Sunday morning, he sees many in whose lives heavy burdens and deep wounds are hidden. Often he is the only human being who has been allowed to enter the troubled person's inner world. As he scans his congregation, he may see a high school boy whose girl friend is pregnant, a man who admitted his wife to a mental hospital the day before, an elderly woman whose family has rejected her, a man writhing in the tentacles of compulsive gambling, a young wife deeply depressed by the tragic death of her husband, a mother who knows that her child has leukemia, a young couple on the brink of divorce, an alcoholic struggling with his addiction, a couple whose son is failing in college, a teen-ager obsessed with guilt over his sexual fantasies, an ambulatory paranoid woman who has not responded to psychiatric treatment, a woman facing surgery for a condition she suspects is malignant, a man anticipating with near terror the emptiness which mandatory retirement will bring to his life.

Many of these people trust the very fabric of their lives to the counseling skills of their minister. Whether or not he deserves their trust, they open their hearts to him in their desperate need. They see him as a competent, trusted shepherd. They ask him to walk with them through their personal shadowed valleys. If he is lacking in skill, he may give them a stone when they ask for bread. As Wayne E. Oates puts the matter:

> The pastor, regardless of his training, does not enjoy the privilege of electing whether or not he will counsel with his people. . . . His choice is not between counseling or not counseling, but between counseling in a disciplined and skilled way and counseling in an undisciplined and unskilled way.[8]

In 1960, the results were published of an unprecedented study of the "normal" adult population of our country. University of Michigan investigators conducted extensive interviews with hundreds of Ameri-

[8] Oates, *An Introduction to Pastoral Counseling*, p. vi.

cans representing a cross section of the noninstitutionalized population. Their findings, reported in *Americans View Their Mental Health,*[4] gives a clear picture of the feelings and attitudes, problems and fears of adult Americans.

The extent of disturbances revealed by the study was impressive. Fewer than five out of ten Americans, for example, considered their marriages "very happy." Over half of those who did consider themselves to be very happily married felt inadequate as wives or husbands. Almost 25 percent of Americans admitted that they had felt themselves to be on the verge of a nervous breakdown at some point in their adult lives. The death of loved ones and job pressures were the two greatest factors contributing to this feeling. One person out of four admitted that he worries "a lot" or "all the time."

Nearly one person out of every four indicated that he had had a problem in which professional help would have been useful. *One out of seven* of all those interviewed had actually sought such professional help. Where had these persons gone for help? *Forty-two percent* had gone *to clergymen* and 29 percent to nonpsychiatric physicians. Only 31 percent had gone to a psychiatrist, psychologist, or marriage counselor, either in private practice or an agency setting.[5] Fifty-four percent of the Protestants who attend church at least once a week went to a minister when they sought personal help. Even among those who attend church less frequently, 33 percent who went for help chose a clergyman.[6] In the light of these findings, there is no doubt that *ministers occupy a central and strategic role as counselors in our society.*[7] It is obvious that clergymen are on the front lines in the struggle to lift the loads of troubled persons!

There is also evidence that the majority of church members regard counseling as an important function of ministers. A study by Murray H. Leiffer showed that 87 percent of the laymen surveyed believed that training aimed at skill in counseling should be included in ministerial education.[8]

[4] Gerald Gurin, Joseph Veroff, and Sheila Feld (New York: Basic Books, 1960).

[5] *Americans View Their Mental Health,* p. 307. (Some of the respondents had gone to more than one type of help.)

[6] *Ibid.,* p. 335.

[7] *Ibid.,* p. 319.

[8] Dean Johnson, "Self Understanding in Pastoral Counseling" in Wayne E. Oates, ed., *The Minister's Own Mental Health* (Great Neck, N. Y.: Channel Press, 1955-61), p. 133.

The amount of time spent in counseling varies markedly from minister to minister. In a study by Richard V. McCann, a group of clergymen was found to spend only 2.2 hours per week in this activity.[9] But a survey of thirty-four suburban Pittsburgh pastors showed that they spent 30 percent of their time in counseling.[10] The fact that the minister is a part-time counselor is, of course, no excuse for incompetence, any more than his being a part-time teacher and preacher excuses slovenly work in those areas. There is no other aspect of a minister's work in which lack of competence can have comparable negative effects. In counseling, the pastor often deals with people at the time of their greatest vulnerability and deepest need. His counseling skill, or lack of it, can have a decisive effect on their future.

It is important to obtain the best available training in counseling, not only to avoid doing harm but also to maximize one's abilities to be of genuine help to the disturbed and the burdened. If he is competent, a counselor frequently has the privilege of walking with another human being on his inner journey toward wholeness. A pastor's competence allows him to stand on the sacred ground where personality growth occurs. He is a catalyst in a healing-redemptive process, a pastoral midwife in the rebirth of persons to larger dimensions of their humanity. The minister who has paid the price of that disciplined study and training which leads to competence knows the joy and wonder that comes with the realization: "My personality, with all its flaws and frailties, has been used as an instrument by which the power of the universe brought healing to another human being." Counseling is both a highly demanding and highly rewarding pastoral function. Whatever a theological student or minister does to increase his skills in this area will pay rich, person-centered dividends.

J. F. T. Bugental's observation concerning the privilege of being a psychotherapist also applies to the pastoral counselor: "We are for our brief time hoisted on the shoulders of our fellows that we may catch some glimpse of the yet untouched reaches of what it means to be truly man." [11]

Training in counseling enhances a clergyman's effectiveness as a re-

[9] *Action for Mental Health* (New York: Basic Books, 1961), pp. 135-36.

[10] Joseph W. Eaton, *et al.*, "Pastoral Counseling in a Metropolitan Suburb," *Journal of Pastoral Care,* Summer, 1963, pp. 93-105.

[11] *The Search for Authenticity* (New York: Holt, Rinehart and Winston, 1965), p. 375.

newal agent in the noncounseling aspects of his work—preaching, teaching, calling, worship, administration, group leadership, evangelism, family life activities, social action, community leadership, and the many noncounseling dimensions of pastoral care.[12] Counseling skills are basically skills in *relating* and *communicating* in growth-stimulating ways. Since every facet of a clergyman's complex job has relationships and communication at its heart, his total ministry benefits from the sensitivities and skills acquired in counseling training. Learning to listen to feelings, for example, has a deepening effect on all one's pastoral relationships. The same principles of human dynamics and the same heart hungers are involved in counseling and in administration. As Harry and Bonaro Overstreet state: "The most important effect of psychological understanding is . . . to approach our people with a more sensitive and informed awareness." [13] This *awareness* is vastly more important in a renewal ministry than are the counseling *techniques per se*. The techniques are helpful only in the presence of awareness!

PASTORAL COUNSELING AND THE CHURCH'S PURPOSE

To grasp the mission and significance of pastoral counseling, a minister needs a clear picture of the relationship between counseling and the basic purpose of the church. The definitive study by H. Richard Niebuhr, Daniel Day Williams, and James M. Gustafson (reported in *The Purpose of the Church and Its Ministry*) concludes that the ultimate objective, the unifying goal of the church, is the "increase among men of the love of God and neighbor." [14]

As indicated in Chapter 1, a person who is emotionally disturbed is unable to establish mutually need-satisfying relationships. To a painful degree he is blocked or crippled in his *ability* to love deeply. This is the heart of his problem. He is *unable* to love God and neighbor fully. To say to such a person, "You need to love God and neighbor more," is like shouting to a man floating on a log in mid-ocean, "What you need is dry land." Nothing could be truer or less helpful. What he needs is some way of knowing where land is and some effective

[12] The application of pastoral counseling insights to the other functions of ministry is the aim of my earlier book, *Mental Health Through Christian Community*. Thomas W. Klink's *Depth Perspectives in Pastoral Work* (Englewood Cliffs, N. J.: Prentice-Hall, 1965) also applies counseling sensitivities to the broader fields of the pastoral ministry.

[13] "Like a Mighty Army," *Pastoral Psychology*, June, 1954, p. 33.

[14] (New York: Harper & Row, 1956), p. 31.

means of moving toward it. Counseling aims at helping a person increase his ability to love God, his neighbor, and himself more fully. Understood in this way, pastoral counseling techniques are recognized as invaluable methods *for implementing the basic purpose of the church.* All of us are limited to some degree in our ability to love. For those whose ability to love is markedly crippled, counseling can mean the difference between a creative, productive Christian life and one of inner stagnation and self-rejection. For such persons, a skilled counselor becomes the instrument of God's healing and growth, a channel for his liberating love.

A counseling relationship can help overcome that alienation from ourselves, other persons, and God which is the essence of "sin." In counseling a minister and his people struggle together with basic theological issues on a deeply personal level. Whether the issues are identified by theological labels or not, they are *there at the heart of counseling*—sin and salvation (i.e. reconciliation), guilt and forgiveness, judgment and grace, spiritual death and rebirth. In a real sense *rebirth* to wider worlds of meaning and relationship is the ultimate goal of pastoral counseling. Counseling is an effective response to the words of a young carpenter-prophet, "You must be born again." The ministry of counseling is one of the means by which the church helps people experience that truth about themselves, others, and God which alone can make them inwardly free. There is nothing about sound pastoral counseling which is alien to the church's mission.

Traditionally, the church's task has been divided into three categories—*kerygma* (teaching and preaching the gospel), *koinonia* (the establishment of a fellowship with a vertical dimension), and *diakonia* (the implementation of the faith in loving service). Although pastoral counseling is primarily an expression of *diakonia,* the ministry of service, it is also a means of communicating the gospel and establishing *koinonia.* For many people God is dead. The word "God" is an empty symbol for them. They are unaware of any relationship with him. They are unable to hear the good news. Counseling becomes a way of communicating the good news to some such persons by opening them to life and relationships. Until they have *experienced accepting love in a relationship, it cannot come alive for them.* Until they are grasped by grace in a life-to-life encounter, the Christian message can neither touch nor release them. A counseling relationship is one place where this incarnation of grace can occur.

Because of their crippled ability to establish need-satisfying relationships, many church members cannot contribute to the establishment of *koinonia.* Their presence is divisive not uniting, pathogenic not healing. As Ludwig Binswanger has observed, psychotherapy can help to prepare such persons for the life of genuine community, *koinonia.*[15] They become *able* to contribute to the vitality of the church's healing-redemptive fellowship.

It should not be surprising that Christian truths often come alive in pastoral counseling relationships. David E. Roberts once observed: "Whatever is valid in Christ's disclosure of God is universally operative in human life, and, therefore, is verifiable within experience."[16] To the degree that persons through counseling find release from the captivity of their neuroses, overcome their alienation, increase their capacity to love, and renew their relationships—to that extent the counseling experience illuminates the theological verities which are woven into the fabric of all relationships. A productive counseling relationship thus may become a part of the continuing incarnation of God in the world, an expression of the body of Christ—the incarnation of the love of God through service to suffering persons.

Jesus' critics probably felt that he spent a disproportionate amount of his time with the burdened, the disturbed, the sick. But the importance which *he* attached to this phase of his ministry was crystal clear. His parable of the shepherd who left the ninety-nine to help the one lost sheep showed his concern for the individual in need. His words, "Those who are well have no need of a physician, but those who are sick" (Mark 2:17), indicate unmistakably the orientation of his ministry. Parts of the quotation from Isaiah 61 which he chose to describe the nature of his ministry also undergird the importance of the task of pastoral counseling: "To proclaim release for prisoners and recovery of sight for the blind; To let the broken victims go free." (Luke

[15] Ulrich Sonnemann, *Existence and Therapy* (New York: Grune and Stratton, 1954), p. 343.

[16] *Psychotherapy and a Christian View of Man* (New York: Charles Scribner's Sons, 1950), p. 142.

4:18 NEB). In his counseling role, the pastor seeks to walk in the footsteps of one described as the "great physician."

PASTORAL COUNSELING AS A RELIGIOUS ACTIVITY

In what ways is pastoral counseling a "religious" activity? It should be religious in its *effects, philosophy, instrumentality, resources, personnel,* and *ultimate focus of concern.*

Effects: The result of successful counseling, as has been indicated, is growth in the ability to relate creatively, trustfully, and lovingly to others and to God. Such relationships constitute the heart of the religious life.

Philosophy: Pastoral counseling recognizes that all healing and growth are of God. Unless the God-given resources for healing within the person and his relationships are released by the removal of whatever has blocked them, no healing can occur. The counselor is a catalyst in a process which he does not create, but which he has learned to release and facilitate. This philosophy of counseling is both theologically valid and practically useful in that it helps the counselor keep his perspective. His effectiveness depends on his awareness that healing and growth take place *through* him rather than as a result of his psychological cleverness. He must accept in his heart the truth of Paul's familiar words: "I planted, Apollos watered, but God gave the growth" (I Cor. 3:6).

Instrumentality: The essential change force in any effective counseling relationship is the unearned, freely given acceptance which mediates divine grace. Only when something of an *agape* quality is experienced by the counselee will growth occur. The profound truth of the great affirmation, "By grace you have been saved through faith" (Eph. 2:8), is illuminated repeatedly in counseling. "Faith" is the trust which the person develops as rapport grows in response to experiencing a measure of accepting love which does not have to be merited or earned. (Accepting a person does *not* mean that the counselor accepts irresponsible aspects of his behavior.)

Resources: Pastoral counseling draws on the rich wisdom and authority of the Hebrew-Christian tradition, as these are available through prayer, scripture, sacraments, liturgical practices, and the disciplines of the church.

Personnel: Clergymen are "representative Christian persons"—representatives of the faith, tradition, life, and fellowship of the church, who "bring Christian meanings to bear on human troubles." [17] The pastoral counselor represents, in his person, his religious tradition and community, whether or not he chooses to use explicitly religious practices and words in particular counseling relationships. The fact that he is perceived by the counselees as the leader of a religious community influences all his counseling profoundly.

Ultimate Focus of Concern: Dietrich Bonhoeffer's familiar statement, "God is the 'beyond' in the midst of our life," [18] can be used to describe the religious focus of the pastoral counselor's concern. If the minister is vividly aware of this "beyond" element in every person and relationship, he will be sensitive to the religious-existential dimensions in all problems. Whether they are recognized or not, ultimate issues—the meaning of existence, the threat of nonbeing, existential anxiety—are present in every counseling situation. The minister knows that for many problems there are only philosophical and/or religious answers. This transpsychological element looms large in pastoral counseling and affirms the importance of the pastor's ultimate goal—increasing the adequacy of the person's relationship with God.

THE UNIQUENESS OF PASTORAL COUNSELING

The minister needs to understand his uniqueness as a counselor, *vis-à-vis* other professionals who do counseling, so that he can identify his unique contributions to helping the troubled. His uniqueness as a counselor is derived from his *training*, his social and symbolic *role*, the *setting* within which he counsels, certain *tools* he uses, and his *explicit goal of spiritual growth.*

The uniqueness of the pastoral counselor's **training** is his background in philosophy, theology, ethics, world religions, and his experience in relating these to counseling through the discipline of psychology of religion. He combines his knowledge in these areas with those aspects of his training which overlap the training of the other counseling professions. Ideally the latter should include developmental psychology,

[17] See Clebsch and Jaekle, *Pastoral Care in Historical Perspective*, pp. 4-5 for a perceptive discussion of this matter.

[18] *Letters and Papers From Prison* (New York: The Macmillan Company, 1953), p. 124.

abnormal psychology, group dynamics, and techniques of individual and group counseling. Ordinarily he has considerably less formal training in these areas than other counseling professionals (and often less than he needs!).

The minister's theological training equips him to be of unique helpfulness to those whose problems center in complex ethical dilemmas, interfaith relationships, religious conflict, and such ultimate concerns as developing a viable philosophy of life and handling the fear of death constructively. Paul Tillich describes pastoral care as a "helping encounter in the dimension of ultimate concern."[19] The clergyman's training should prepare him to counsel skillfully in this dimension. This is his ministry of meanings. He should strive to become an *expert in spiritual growth*—knowing how to stimulate it and how to help remove the things that block it.

The pastor is unique among counselors in his socially defined **role.** As indicated above, those who seek his help perceive him as a religious authority figure, the leader of a religious community, and a symbolic representative of the values and beliefs of his traditions. This means that he is a religious "transference figure"—i.e., one whose symbolic role stirs up in persons a rich variety of early life feelings and associations. In his presence people may reexperience a welter of these feelings, including feelings about such matters as parents, God, heaven, hell, sex, Sunday school, death, funerals, church, right and wrong, etc. A minister *who is aware of feelings* has an opportunity to help people correct old distortions and acquire more mature attitudes. If he is reasonably mature, emotionally and spiritually, he will exert a continuing constructive influence on these deep-level feelings through all aspects of his ministry. By giving his people an accepting but gently confronting experience of relating with a religious authority figure, he can stimulate their growth toward a more mature and satisfying relationship with God.

The **context and setting** of a minister's counseling contribute to its uniqueness. The context is pastoral care—his general ministry of nurturing and shepherding. The setting is the life of a gathered community of faith, a local church. His ongoing, day-to-day relationships

[19] Address at the National Conference on Clinical Pastoral Education, Atlantic City, New Jersey, November, 1956.

with a sizable group of persons of all ages, in light and shadow, provide him with innumerable opportunities to help. He may identify serious problems long before they reach the advanced crisis stage which eventually will bring the persons to social agencies or other counselors. The pastor's natural, continuing contacts with families, the seedbed where personality is formed and deformed, is a unique asset in his counseling. If the groups in his church are alive (i.e., need-satisfying), they can complement and multiply the effectiveness of his ministry to distressed individuals.[20] *No other helping profession has a comparable, supportive fellowship available year-in, year-out, to undergird its work.* Through his counseling the minister can become the bridge by which some of the lonely ones in our depersonalizing society can discover a warm sense of belonging in need-satisfying groups.

Another aspect of the counseling pastor's uniqueness is derived from the fact that he is expected and, hopefully, trained to use **religious resources** as a regular part of his counseling. Used in a disciplined and selective manner such resources can be of major value in a number of types of pastoral counseling—supportive, crisis, confrontational, depth, and existential counseling, in particular.

In addition to instruments such as scripture, sacraments, and prayer, the time-tested wisdom of his tradition is a vital religious resource in a pastor's counseling. Anton T. Boisen put the matter clearly:

> The priest or minister at his best brings to the task of helping the distressed in mind certain insights. He is versed in the utterances of the great and noble of the race, has traced the adventures of the human spirit both individually and collectively in its quest of the more abundant life. He understands the deep longings of the human heart and the significance of the constructive forces which are manifest alike in the religious conversion experience and in acute mental illness. He recognizes the fundamental need of love, the dark despair of guilt and estrangement from those we love, and the meaning of forgiveness through faith in the Love that rules the universe and in whose eyes no one is condemned who is in the process of becoming better. In such insights lies the important contribution of the competent minister of religion rather than in any particular techniques.[21]

[20] If his groups are not vital, the pastor's task is to find ways of renewing them or creating new, viable groups in the life of his church.

[21] *The Exploration of the Inner World* (New York: Harper & Row, 1936), p. 285.

Finally, pastoral counseling has a quality of uniqueness about it which stems from regarding **spiritual growth as an essential objective** in counseling. This goal should be explicit in the pastor's mind, although it may or may not be discussed in a particular counseling relationship. Pastoral counseling should enhance the meaningfulness of one's relationship with God as well as with people. It is true that whatever counseling does to increase a person's ability to relate openly and in depth will help to prepare him for a more mature and satisfying relationship with God. But many people continue to have immaturities and distortions in their religious lives after they have moved beyond these in other relationships. They need special help in the religious area. Most clergymen see the development of a growing, satisfying relationship with God as an indispensable aspect of total personality health. Holding to this orientation inevitably influences counseling relationships whether or not "religious" topics are discussed. If the person's spiritual life is a primary source of conflict and guilt, it must become a major focus of attention in counseling.

THE MINISTER'S LIMITATIONS AND ADVANTAGES AS COUNSELOR

In understanding his role as counselor, the minister needs to be aware of his limitations and advantages in this area of functioning. Here are his *limitations:*

(1) Time: As a general practitioner the parish clergyman must invest his time and emotional energies in a variety of functions which are essential to his total ministry. Most pastors cannot counsel more than five to ten hours per week without neglecting other important duties. Consequently a minister should concentrate on developing skill in short-term counseling and referral.

(2) Training: The minister's training must give him proficiency in a variety of functions. As part-time counselors, most parish ministers do not have an opportunity to acquire the high degree of expertness which full-time counselors and psychotherapists must have. Fortunately, many people *can* be helped within the limits of the counseling training of the typical clergyman. As ministerial training improves in this area, the circle of those who can be helped by pastoral counselors will become more inclusive. A pastor needs to be able to recognize those problems which are beyond his particular level of skill, so that he can make a wise referral. It is also important that he not *underestimate* his actual helping capacities, thereby missing opportunities to use the unique aspects of his training.

(3) **Role:** The fact that the minister is perceived as a representative of ethical values prevents some guilt-laden people from seeking his help. Their fear of his being judgmental makes him psychologically inaccessible to them. If, in fact, a minister is self-accepting and therefore nonjudgmental of others, he will spontaneously communicate acceptance through his total ministry. This helps to diminish the projection upon him of a judgmental image by guilt-ridden people. However, the fact that parishioners encounter their pastor in a variety of noncounseling roles makes some of them prefer to take embarrassing problems to other helping persons. This is one reason why members of other churches frequently seek a minister's help. As one man put the matter, "I like and respect my minister but I would rather *not* have him know about my affair."

(4) **Transference:** Counseling (particularly long-term counseling) often gives rise to the projection on the counselor of strong, archaic feelings of love and hate. These stem from unresolved conflicts in one's relationship with parents. Either positive or negative "transference" attachments can be emotionally demanding, even if they are not jeopardizing to the minister's reputation. The professional psychotherapist, because of his training and relatively protected position, can utilize intense transference relationship as a path to helping the person resolve his residual early life conflicts. But this is a complex and time-consuming process requiring great skill.

General transference projection occurs to some degree in all relationships with a minister. Within limits these can be useful in pastoral counseling, as indicated above. But transference is apt to occur with great intensity in long-term counseling. The woman counselee who "falls in love" with the pastor is mainly in love with the image of her father (or mother), with whom she had an unsatisfying relationship. The same process is operative in the case of the individual who develops irrational feelings of hatred for his counselor. Both are usually unaware of the true nature of their feelings.

To minimize this danger, a minister should not attempt long-term, depth counseling with anyone unless he is well trained in these methods and has himself had depth psychotherapy. Further, it is unwise to attempt such counseling with anyone who holds a prominent position in the power structure of his church. Ignoring this principle may cost a minister his job should negative transference feelings motivate attack. Furthermore, the fact that a minister knows that he is vulnerable to attack by such persons prevents him from being as fully open, honest, and "congruent" (in the Rogerian sense) as he must be to counsel effectively. Referral of such church leaders to other counselors is the only wise course to follow. The same is true in other counseling situations in which the pastor senses that a strong transference relationship is developing. Unless he is trained and prepared to work with such persons on a long-term basis, a referral is in their best interests and his.

(5) **Payment:** The fact that a minister ordinarily does not charge for counseling is a limitation on his effectiveness in some cases. The neurotic meanings of money (symbolizing the giving and receiving of love and power) are not immediately available for scrutiny in counseling. Remarkable self-understanding sometimes emerges where this is possible. Further, lacking the test of motivation which paying for counseling supplies, people tend to abuse the minister's time in unproductive ways. Some ministers allow or even expect persons receiving longer-term counseling to contribute to a designated fund within the church, especially if they are nonmembers and are not contributing to the support of the church in other ways. (The minister's counseling with regular *parishioners* is like prepaid medical care.) Allowing a person to pay for his counseling helps to strengthen his self-esteem and decrease his dependency feelings on the counselor. It makes it possible for him to *give* as well as *receive* in the relationship. Whatever plan one favors should be cleared with the governing body of one's local church.

A minister has *several strategic advantages as a counselor* which he should utilize to the full, in order to maximize his effectiveness.

(1) **Trust:** In our culture millions of adults have feelings of trust toward clergymen, often from early childhood. This is in sharp contrast to the widespread feelings of fear concerning psychiatrists and other psychotherapists. The term "headshrinker" carries overtones of emotional fears of being hurt by their "magic." Compare this with the feelings of warmth and confidence which many adults have toward ministers.

(2) **Established relationships:** Like the family doctor, but unlike most professional counselors, the minister normally has a wealth of ongoing, established relationships. In many cases these provide a solid foundation for counseling, allowing progress to be made by the person in much less time than would be required to "start from scratch" in a counseling relationship. The clergyman's many relationships also provide frequent opportunities to apply counseling insights and methods in informal contacts.

(3) **Family Contacts:** The minister's continuing contact with families in the normal course of his work is a major advantage over other counseling and psychotherapeutic disciplines. Not only does he have knowledge about disturbances of the family organism from which individual problems are derived, but he has direct access to the family as an object of help.

(4) **Crisis ministry:** The minister frequently is present in such crises as bereavement, sickness, and accidents. He is on the scene when persons are most vulnerable and when the need for counseling is most apt to develop.

(5) **Availability:** The fact that a troubled person can usually see a minister without waiting several days (or longer) and even without making an appointment is an obvious advantage in helping those requiring emergency counseling. The recent development of "walk-in psychiatric clinics," to which a distressed person can go without an appointment for help in a crisis, indicates that the mental health professions are becoming aware of a dimension of service which has been a normal part of the minister's approach for centuries. The minister's availability allows persons who would be too embarrassed to make an appointment for "counseling" to get help by coming to him, ostensibly for less threatening reasons. The fact that he does not have to charge means that he is available to help entirely on the basis of need. The present high level of fees for private practice counseling and the continuing shortage of help on an ability-to-pay basis highlight the importance of having one profession which provides counseling mainly on a prepaid basis.

(6) **Training:** As indicated earlier, the unique aspects of the minister's training give him advantages in dealing with philosophical, existential, and religious problems.

(7) Role: The fact that he is perceived as a representative of the value and belief structures of his religious community is a tremendous advantage in some counseling. Those whose consciences are cruel and unchristian often come to him wanting punishment to reduce their staggering load of guilt. If, instead, they enter into a counseling relationship with a minister who "accepts himself as being accepted" (to use Tillich's familiar phrase), their guilt will be reduced on a healthier, more lasting basis as their self-acceptance increases through experiencing grace in the relationship.

At the other extreme are persons who suffer from weak, faulty inner controls which leave them (and others) at the mercy of their impulses. By relating to the minister and the structures of the church, many such persons find ways of buttressing their inner guidance systems through identifying with the standards of the minister and the religious group. (See Chapter 13.)

In summary, both his limitations and his advantages point toward the minister's particular role as counselor. His limitations should steer him away from long-term, depth counseling. His advantages should direct him toward the types of counseling included in the "revised model." These optimal types allow him to utilize his unique advantages as counselor and thus maximize his effectiveness as a renewal agent.

4

The Common Elements in All Types of Counseling

I am done with Great things and Big things, with Great institutions and Big success, and I am for those tiny invisible molecular forces, that work from individual to individual, creeping through the crannies of the world like so many soft rootlets, or like the capillary oozing of water, but which, give them time, will rend the hardest monuments of men's pride.

—William James [1]

Mr. S. phoned the minister for an appointment. S. had appeared in church three weeks before the call and had not returned. He was not at his room at the local YMCA when the minister attempted to visit him. When he returned, he found the minister's card with a brief "Sorry to have missed seeing you. It was good to have you in church!" This seemingly unproductive call was what made S. decide to phone for help. The card, which he carried in his wallet for several days before phoning, communicated the minister's concern as well as his phone number.

Pastoral counseling actually begins when the first contact is made by a person seeking help. Here are some fragments of the phone conversation between S. and the minister:

MR. S.: Hello, this is Bill S. I found your card. Sorry I wasn't home when you came by. (His voice had a flat, heavy quality.)

[1] Quoted in Halford E. Luccock's *Christianity and the Individual* (New York: The Abingdon Press, 1937), p. 38.

MINISTER: Good to hear from you, Bill. I just stopped by to say "hello" and welcome you to the community. You're new in town, I understand.

MR. S.: Yes, I moved here to the coast from St. Louis last month. Decided I'd try making a new start out here.

MINISTER: Well, we're glad to have you among us. How are things going?

MR. S.: O.K., but it's a little rough getting acquainted in a new place. As a matter of fact, there are a couple of things I'd like to talk with you about. I don't want to take much of your time, but—ah. . . .

MINISTER: I'll be glad to see you. What's your schedule like? When would it be convenient for you to drop by my office?

MR. S.: Well, I'm between jobs at the moment, so anytime will be O.K.

MINISTER: Unfortunately, I was just about to leave for an out-of-town conference. But tell me a little about your situation.

MR. S.: Well, my wife divorced me three months ago and I've been lower than a snake's belly ever since. These last few days I've felt like I had to look up to see the bottom. Haven't been able to sleep much.

MINISTER: It sounds as though things are rough for you. Would you be free to meet me at the church in twenty minutes?

MR. S.: Yes, but I don't want to hold up your trip.

MINISTER: That's all right. I'd *like* to chat with you for a little while before I go. My office is on the Oak Street side of the church. There's an outside entrance. I'll look forward to seeing you at 1:15.

MR. S.: O.K., I'll see you then.

This brief phone contact accomplished the following things: (1) A counseling relationship was begun. (2) The minister's warmth and concern for S. were communicated. (3) The ice was broken from S.'s viewpoint with regard to talking about his problem with the minister. (4) The minister obtained a tentative impression concerning the nature and seriousness of S.'s problems. (5) On the basis of his impression that S. might be seriously depressed, the minister made a decision to delay his trip and see him briefly. His expressionless voice, the fact that he had experienced a major loss recently, his sleeplessness, and his statement about having to "look up to see bottom" all pointed to depression. The minister knew that the risk of suicide is high among deeply depressed persons, particularly those living alone.

Even if the minister had not been on the verge of a trip, it would have been important to discover, on the phone, something about the nature and urgency of S.'s problem. An open-ended question such as, "What seems to be the difficulty?" or "Tell me a little about your situation" usually opens the door for the parishioner to describe the way he perceives his problem. The fact that the minister knows something of his problem makes it less likely that the person will break his appointment because of anticipatory anxiety regarding opening the discussion of his painful situation. This approach usually allows the minister to separate emergency or crisis situations from those chronic problems in which counseling can be scheduled with less of a sense of urgency. It is well, of course, to see any new counselee as soon as is mutually convenient.

THE GROWTH OF A THERAPEUTIC RELATIONSHIP

During the first counseling session, the following should occur:

(1) The foundation is laid for a growing therapeutic relationship as rapport is established.

(2) Through disciplined listening to and reflecting of the parishioner's feelings, catharsis of bottled-up emotions begins.

(3) The pastor acquires a tentative understanding of the person's "internal frame of reference"—how life looks from within his personal "world."

(4) The counselor gains a diagnostic impression concerning the nature of the counselee's problems, the ways in which his relationships are failing to meet his needs, and his resources and limitations in coping with his situation.

(5) On the basis of this tentative diagnosis, the minister suggests an approach (or approaches) to obtaining help.

(6) If continued counseling by the minister seems indicated, the structuring of a counseling relationship should occur.

Counseling consists of the establishment and subsequent utilization of a relationship, the quality of which can be described as *therapeutic* [2] (healing), *maieutic* [3] (facilitating birth), or *reconciling* (restoring of

[2] It is noteworthy that the word "therapy" comes from the Greek *therapeutēs* meaning attendant or servant—i.e., the help given by a servant in illness. Its root meaning is essentially interpersonal—the beneficial effects of one person on another. (Robert C. Leslie, "Group Therapy as a Method for Church Work," unpublished Ph.D. dissertation, Boston University, 1948, p. 13.)

[3] From the Greek word *maieutikos*, "midwife," this term is used in group dynamics circles to describe a democratic type of leadership which tends to help a group release its creative potentialities by avoiding the extremes of autocratic and laissez-faire approaches.

ruptured relationships). This is the psychological environment in which healing, growth, and successful coping can occur. Such a relationship is the *sine qua non* of counseling. Counseling procedures and techniques are helpful only within such a context. Experiencing this quality of relationship is *in itself* healing and growth stimulating. The most important single objective of the first interview is the beginning of this relationship.

A therapeutic relationship grows as the counselor pours himself into being *with* the burdened person. This means concentrating on *listening*, *feeling*, and *relating*. These activities are important during all phases of counseling. They are absolutely indispensable during the early stages. Instead of worrying about what he is going to say or do next (as inexperienced counselors tend to do), the counselor should focus his energies on feeling and being with the person in an alive human relationship. This is what the existentialists in psychotherapy call "presence." Karl Jaspers has declared: "What we are missing! What opportunities of understanding we let pass by because at a single decisive moment we were, with all our knowledge, lacking in the simple virtue of a full human presence!" [4] All of us have known the empty, depersonalizing feelings which result from conversing with a person who isn't really *present*. The opposite of this experience is required to produce a therapeutic relationship.

As the parishioner senses, even vaguely, that the minister is really trying to listen deeply and to relate fully, a tiny fragile nexus as delicate as a spider web will begin to connect his aloneness with the minister's aloneness. This is the first, vital strand of what will become a sturdy bridge connecting the islands of awareness of two human beings. This bridge is called *rapport*. In a spirit close to that of Martin Buber, Rogers has stated:

> To enter deeply with this man into his confused struggle for selfhood is perhaps the best implementation we now know for indicating the meaning of our basic hypothesis that the individual represents a process which is deeply worthy of respect, both as he is and with regard to his potentialities.[5]

[4] Ulrich Sonnemann, *Existence and Therapy*, p. 343.

[5] *Client-Centered Therapy* (New York: Houghton Mifflin Co., 1951), p. 45. For a discussion of this view by a student of Buber see: Maurice Friedman, Martin Buber: *The Life of Dialogue* (New York: Harper and Brothers, 1960), p. 192.

The art of *reflective listening* is essential in counseling. The pastor attempts to listen to *feelings* as well as words. He listens for feelings that are "between the lines," too painful to trust to words. Now and again he responds to these feelings. Dietrich Bonhoeffer's penetrating indictment underlines the importance of learning the lesson of listening and learning it well:

> Many people are looking for an ear that will listen. They do not find it among Christians, because Christians are talking when they should be listening. He who no longer listens to his brother will soon be no longer listening to God either. . . . One who cannot listen long and patiently will presently be talking beside the point and never really speaking to others, albeit he be not conscious of it.[6]

A line from Shakespeare's *King Henry IV* describes the problem of unawareness, the cause of many failures in pastoral counseling: "It is the disease of not listening, the malady of not marking, that I am troubled withal."[7]

I shall always be grateful to a little white-haired woman in a mental hospital who, years ago, helped to teach me the danger of not listening. She had been in the hospital for over twenty years. We both knew she was dying. Before I delivered a little homily to "comfort" her, something told me to ask her how she felt about the experience she faced. Her wonderfully honest reply made my prefabricated sermonette absurdly irrelevant. She responded with intense feeling: "Chaplain, I'll be so glad to get out of this damned place!" I had made the mistake of assuming that I knew how people in general feel about dying. The reason I was so wrong was that there is no such thing as the way people in general feel about anything.

The beneficial effects of being listened to have long been recognized. Ptah-hotep, the vizier of Egyptian King Izezi of the Fifth Dynasty (about 2450 B.C.), gave this advice to his son and designated successor:

> If thou art one to whom petition is made, be calm as thou listenest to the petitioner's speech. Do not rebuff him before he has swept out his body or before he has said that for which he came. . . . It is not necessary that every-

[6] *Life Together* (New York: Harper & Row, 1959), pp. 97-98. (Quoted by Clebsch and Jaekle, p. 53.)

[7] Part II, Act I, Sc. I, l. 139.

thing about which he has petitioned should come to pass, [but] *a good hearing is a soothing of the heart.*[8]

As a counselor listens *in depth,* with all his faculties, to the multiple levels of communication, verbal and nonverbal, he reflects back to the person, in paraphrased form, what he hears, particularly the person's big (dominant) feelings. His listening is "disciplined listening" [9]—focusing on what seems to have the most meaning and significance. By centering attention on significant points, summarizing what is being communicated, and occasionally asking a question for clarification, the counselor helps the person begin to organize his confused inner world. Thus he gradually comes to understand his problems more clearly.

The process of listening and reflecting serves a variety of other important functions:

(1) It allows the minister to check the accuracy of his perceptions. If he is not on the counselee's emotional wave length, his reflections provide opportunities for his misperceptions to be corrected.

(2) It lets the counselee know that the minister is trying to understand his inner world of feelings and meanings.

(3) This awareness of the minister's concern and dawning understanding stimulates the growth of the counseling relationship.

(4) In some cases, responding to feelings lances the psychic wound, permitting the poison of powerful pent-up feelings to drain off so that normal healing can occur.

(5) As counseling progresses, the counselor's listening and responding provides the counselee with sensitivity practice or *training in relating.* Helen Flanders Dunbar once compared the listener in therapy to the practice board which a tennis player uses to perfect his strokes.[10]

The counselor's aim is to achieve the maximum degree of what Rogers calls "empathic understanding" of the person's inner world. The research findings of R. D. Quinn are reassuring to the counselor who is

[8] J. B. Pritchard, *The Ancient Near Eastern Texts* (Princeton: Princeton University Press, 1950), p. 413. (Italics mine.)

[9] I am indebted to Robert L. Brizee for this way of describing an important aspect of counseling. Undisciplined listening consists of allowing the counselee to ramble through his inner world, without helping him begin to find the pattern in what he is saying or to focus on what seem to be significant issues. For an insightful discussion of listening in depth see Klink, *Depth Perspectives in Pastoral Work,* pp. 20 ff.

[10] *Mind and Body: Psychosomatic Medicine* (New York: Random House, 1955), p. 249.

worried about not understanding fully or responding with consistent accuracy. Quinn found that the heart of "understanding" a counselee's meanings is an attitude of *desiring to understand*.[11] It is this desire that communicates caring acceptance to the troubled person, causing him to permit the counselor to establish a beachhead of understanding in his inner world. From this the pastor can move to fuller empathy. It is unnecessary for a minister to be highly gifted in his ability to empathize (feel with others) in order to counsel effectively. If he is really *with* a person in a nonjudgmental, accepting way, his attempts to reflect feelings may miss the person's exact wave length repeatedly without vitiating the therapeutic effect.

Three things block the counselor's sensitivity to counselee feelings—overconcern with personality theories and counseling techniques, premature attempts to think of "solutions," and anxiety which produces unawareness of feelings—one's own and the counselee's. Inexperienced counselors need to be encouraged to avoid trying to "cure" the person or find answers to his problems, and instead to concentrate on *understanding* the person and his world. It is essential that the early phases of a counseling relationship be devoted to this objective. After a reasonable degree of understanding has been achieved, whatever decisions are made, by the counselee or collaboratively, will tend to be reality-oriented and therefore sound.

Creative listening is active listening, demanding an emotional investment in the other and relative openness to one's own feelings. A participant in a reality-practice counseling session made this discovery:

> We can never feel the pain or struggle of another, only our own pain in a situation like his own. In listening to a counselee talk about his situation, the counselor feels. His response is the result of listening to his own feelings. . . . If his feelings are not those of the counselee's, he will correct him, and the counselor will have another chance on the level of his own feelings to get with it.
>
> When I discovered that the voice of my own feelings—what they said about his—were trustworthy, I could relax and reflect spontaneously.[12]

[11] "Psychotherapists' Expressions as an Index to the Quality of Early Therapeutic Relationships," unpublished Ph.D. dissertation, University of Chicago, 1950. Cited by Rogers, *On Becoming a Person*, p. 44.

[12] Lynn Bush, School of Theology at Claremont, June, 1965.

A counselor who cannot feel his own feelings because of the inner blocks is seriously handicapped. He will be unable to experience "resonance,"[13] the responsive chord between two personalities which makes therapy possible.

MOTIVATION, DIAGNOSIS, AND STRUCTURING

Without the counselor's forgetting the absolute priority of relating and listening responsively to feelings, there are certain questions of great importance which he should keep in mind during the first session or two. If he does not acquire answers to them in the course of the parishioner's discussion of his problems, the counselor may ask them directly: Why did this person come for help *now? To me?* What is his problem *as he sees it?* Is he hurting inside or did he come because others pushed him? What kind of help does *he* want? How does he feel *about being here?* These questions are crucially important! All of them have to do with the counselee's *motivation.* Neglect of these questions often results in failure to establish a counseling relationship.

Returning to the case of Mr. S., with which we began the chapter, we find the minister greeting him at his study door and after some initial small talk about the weather saying, "Tell me some more about your situation." This encouraged S. to focus on his problem *as he perceived it* (the "presenting problem"). There often are deeper problems of which the counselee may or may not be aware, but the rule of thumb in the first session is to *start with the presenting problem.* In the course of S.'s description, the minister gradually acquired some basic information concerning his significant relationships, in which he had failed to satisfy his personality needs. He found that he was thirty-seven, had been married for eleven stormy years before the divorce, had two children, and had worked at various jobs, mainly as an auto mechanic. The minister remembered his words on the phone about "making a new start," suggesting that the man's previous life adjustment had probably crumbled. As S. talked, the minister listened for the *big feelings* among the various feelings he expressed:

[13] This apt word is used by Edoardo Weiss in *Principles of Psychodynamics* (New York: Grune and Stratton, 1950). The essence of a counseling relationship is "the reverberating emotional impact of two personalities on each other" (R. R. Grinker, Sr., *et al., Psychiatric Social Work: A Transactional Approach* [New York: Basic Books, 1961], p. 303).

MR. S.: This divorce hit me like a ton of bricks. Sure, we had had our disagreements, and she had threatened to divorce me, but when it happened, I just couldn't believe it. I felt mad, naturally, but mostly I felt like something big was gone.

MINISTER: It made you feel crushed and empty; something that had been very important in your life was taken away.

MR. S.: Yeah, and the empty feeling is worse being so far away. I miss my kids something awful. My boy started scouts this year and that's a program where dads are supposed to be in it with their boys.

MINISTER: The distance makes your loss more painful since it makes it impossible for you to participate in his activities.

The minister, at this point, is attempting to hear and reflect the man's dominant attitudes and feelings.

MR. S.: Uh huh, I keep wondering if I made a king-size mistake moving out here. I wanna be a dad to my kids and yet I just felt like I had to get away from the old stamping grounds. I had had some bad luck on jobs—gotten in trouble on a couple of them because of my temper. I thought maybe it would be better to make a new start where I didn't have all my old tracks around. I suppose I also wanted to show Jean that I didn't need her—that I could get along without her just fine!

MINISTER: Both of these things—the job and the marriage situation—made you feel that a move was in order. But now you're having some serious doubts because of your loneliness for the children.

MR. S.: (Nods.) There's no hope for the marriage, but I don't want my kids growing up without me.

MINISTER: If I understand what you are saying, you feel pulled in two directions, which makes it very difficult to decide whether to go back or stay.

MR. S.: That's right, and the more I mulled this over in my mind the worse I felt. Just seemed to go around in circles. I lay there on my bed in the Y feeling lousier and lousier—like what's the use? It just didn't seem worth the struggle. Then I remembered your card and decided to give you a call.

MINISTER: I'm glad you phoned. Things must have been looking very black.

The minister now has a tentative picture of why the man came for help. He knows that the man came on his own because of the inner pain of his loneliness and his conflict about whether or not to return to St. Louis. Here is a later segment of the interview:

MINISTER: You mentioned on the phone that you aren't working at present.

MR. S.: That's right. But a fellow at a garage across from the post office said he could use me starting next Monday.

MINISTER: Make you feel better to know you will have a job?

MR. S.: Well, I've never had any trouble finding work—I'm a trained auto mechanic. But it *will* be good to be working again and get away from that room. It happens that I'm nearly broke. I couldn't afford the bus fare to St. Louis now, even if I decided that was the thing to do.

MINISTER: I'll be glad to work with you on that decision. I'll be out of town for two days at the conference I mentioned. Would it be convenient for us to get together on Friday at this same time?

MR. S.: That'll be O.K.

MINISTER: Fine. Let's work *together* on this.

MR. S.: O.K.

MINISTER: How are you feeling now—about your situation? [14]

MR. S.: Better. It does me good to get some of these things off my chest.

MINISTER: Let me give you the name and phone number of one of our laymen, Sam Turner. He's a friendly person and retired, so you can reach him during the day, in case you want to chat with someone in the next couple of days. I think you'd enjoy getting acquainted. If you decide to phone him, you might tell him I suggested his name to you.

The minister noted that S. became more animated as the interview progressed. Apparently his depression lifted as a result of a supportive relationship and an offer of help. S. had two important supports during the minister's absence—the availability of Sam Turner and the security of having a definite appointment with the minister three days hence. (Turner was a member of that church's lay "pastoral care team.")

If Mr. S. had come because of pressure by another person, it would have been essential for the minister to *get rid of that third party*, psychologically. This is done by:

[14] The purpose of this question was to ascertain how depressed the man still felt.

(1) attempting to discover how the person who comes sees his problem (if any);

(2) finding out if *he* is hurting and where;

(3) encouraging the ventilation of his feelings of resentment about being coerced to see the minister;

(4) accepting his right to feel this way;

(5) accepting his right not to enter into a counseling relationship;

(6) being warmly interested *in him* and emotionally available, in case he desires to accept help. Here are some responses which illustrate this general approach:

TEEN-AGER: My mother thought I needed to have a talk with you. She thinks I should make up my mind about a career.

MINISTER: Apparently your mother feels you have a problem, but what interests me most right now is how *you* see your situation. How does it look from your point of view?

OR

It sounds as though your mother has been putting some pressure on you to "get with it" on your vocational choice, including having a talk with the minister. How do you feel about all this?

The six procedures listed above constitute a method which is frequently effective in motivating coerced, reluctant, or recalcitrant potential counselees. Unless a person is *aware of a problem* in the handling of which he *desires the minister's help,* there will be no genuine counseling, even though they may go through the motions *ad infinitum.*

During the first interview the minister begins to form a tentative *diagnostic impression concerning the nature and depth of the person's problems in living.* As he listens intently he becomes aware of *certain patterns or motifs* in the person's problems, feelings, and relationships. These give clues to the underlying inadequacies in his relationships, of which the presenting problem may be only one manifestation. Perhaps the person possesses reasonably adequate resources for coping, but has been thrown into a temporary tailspin by a crisis. If so, short-term counseling may be all he needs. Or, perhaps his personality is so conflicted that some long-term form of therapy is essential. The crucial decision involves estimating the person's ego strength. (This will be discussed in Chapter 8.)

The minister should ask himself, "Is this person likely to benefit from the counseling which my time, training, and native abilities permit me to provide? Is there some agency in the community which is set up to provide the specialized form of help which this person needs? Am I able to feel reasonably accepting toward him?" On the basis of considerations such as these, the minister comes to a tentative decision concerning whether to offer a continuing counseling relationship or to refer him. In some cases, the effectiveness of pastoral counseling can be discovered only by attempting it. If no progress is made or the person is regressing after four or five sessions, it is wise to make a referral.

In the case of Mr. S., the minister sensed that there were at least two levels to his problem. His loneliness and indecision concerning returning to St. Louis were aspects of his problem with which the minister felt competent to help him deal. But behind these immediate problems were his basic inadequacies in relating in a need-satisfying way—in his marriage and on his jobs. The minister knew that he would learn more about this level as he helped the man with his immediate dilemmas. In the light of what he learned, he could then decide whether or not to refer S. for help with his deeper problems.

If one decides that pastoral counseling is likely to help the individual, he should do more than offer it. He should *recommend it* by saying, in effect:

> I believe that it would be helpful for us to *work together* on this problem for at least a few sessions. If I understand your feelings, you find your situation very perplexing. Our goal will be to discover together constructive ways of handling it. How do you feel about coming in regularly, once a week for a few weeks?

If the person is resistant to this recommendation, his resistances should be discussed openly and, if possible, reduced or removed. If he agrees to try counseling, a definite appointment should be made with a clear understanding that he will phone the minister if any change in his plans should occur. It is usually best to let the person know that counseling sessions will be approximately an hour in length. Most of us cannot listen deeply to another for more than an hour.

The matters discussed in the previous paragraph come under the general heading of "structuring" the counseling relationship. In addition to the formalities of time and place, such matters as assurance concerning the confidentiality of the relationship and a brief indication of what the counselee should expect from counseling should be included. The *collaborative* nature of counseling should be stressed, particularly if the counselor discovers that the person *expects* some sort of magical prescription or pat solution. The doctor-patient model, in the minds of many who come for counseling, is inadequate because it elicits expectations of external curative agents which involve the person only minimally. Counseling, to be effective, must involve the person actively in working out his own "salvation" with the help of the counselor. It is a venture in mutuality. The counselor is like an athlete's coach or a guide to a climber on a precipitous mountain.

THE IMPORTANCE OF CATHARSIS

Emotional catharsis is a crucial part of nearly all types of counseling. This experience is also called abreaction, emotional ventilation, and the "releasing expression." "Certainly one of the significant goals of any counseling experience is to bring into the open those thoughts and attitudes, those feelings and emotionally charged impulses, which center around the problems and conflicts of the individual."[15] Generally speaking, the various counseling methods are distinguished by what occurs *after* catharsis.

The accepting quality of a counseling relationship provides a safe environment in which burdensome feelings which most people hide in their relationships can be revealed and explored. In a relationship of trust the counselee can face (with another) such powerful feelings as guilt, anger, panic, sexual impulses, and by dealing with them, break their stranglehold on his life. A counseling relationship provides a unique opportunity to unburden one's spirit by discovering, verbalizing, expressing, clarifying, and resolving these forbidden feelings, in the presence of an authority figure who does not reject the person for having them. Even if counseling goes no farther than the stage of emotional catharsis it can be therapeutic, helping to remove the inner log jams which block creativity and self-acceptance. Frequently, after pouring out a painful story, a counselee will say, in effect, "I've been carrying

[15] Rogers, *Counseling and Psychotherapy*, p. 131.

this for fifteen years, afraid to talk with anyone about it. For the first time in all these years, I feel as if I can stand up straight."

How does the pastor encourage emotional release? In general, by listening and responding to feelings. More specifically, the following approaches tend to facilitate catharsis:

(1) *Avoid asking informational questions* beyond the minimum needed to obtain essential factual data. Informational questions tend to pull the person away from feelings.

(2) *Ask about feelings*—e.g., "How did you feel when the chairman ignored you?"

(3) *Respond to feelings rather than intellectual content.* Reflect feelings, using feeling words in doing so. "You really felt clobbered by what happened!" "This hurts down deep!" "Let's see if I catch what you're feeling here."

(4) *Watch for doors* which lead to the feeling level of communication. These include feeling words, emotion in the voice or face, protesting too much, self-contradictions (indicating inner conflicts), and discussion of parental or other crucial need-satisfying relationships. Responding to these often leads to deeper levels of feelings.

(5) *Be especially alert for negative feelings.* These are the most frequently repressed and the most in need of being brought into the psychological sunlight of a therapeutic relationship.

(6) *Avoid both premature interpretations* of why people function or feel certain ways and *premature advice.* Both of these are tempting traps since they offer the counselor ways of feeling useful, intelligent, in control, and thus less anxious. Both interpretations and advice tend to block the flow of feelings.

ACTION—ESSENTIAL INGREDIENT IN COUNSELING

Counseling in general aims at some degree of constructive change in the relationships, behavior, and functioning of persons. In addition to helping them deal with burdensome feelings, it helps them *do* something constructive about their problems and their disturbing behavior *per se.* This includes such functions as exploring alternative plans of action and helping to motivate the person to implement the most feasible plan. The latter may involve dealing with the person's inner blocks to action and even putting some judicious pressure on him to move off dead center.

The church can learn a vital lesson from Alcoholics Anonymous by recognizing that *service to others* is an important part of religiously oriented counseling. Such service has two functions. On the one hand, it is an *instrument* of healing, permitting self-trapped persons to break out of their isolation, form new relationships, and experience the satisfactions of worthwhile work and self-investment in others. On the other hand, it is one purpose of *pastoral* counseling to release blocked people so that their creativity can be used in spontaneous (freely chosen, noncompulsive) service to people in need. The ministering church aims at becoming a supportive community of faith in which people will find the motivation, insights, and strength to be powerful therapeutic agents to others in need, both within and without its fellowship. Counseling is an instrument in achieving this goal. Second Corinthians gives the theological basis for this: "Blessed be the God and Father of our Lord Jesus Christ, the Father of mercies and God of all comfort, who comforts us in all our affliction, so that we may be able to comfort those who are in any affliction" (II Cor. 1:3-4).

TYPES OF COUNSELOR RESPONSES

Psychologist Elias H. Porter, Jr. has described five different attitudes which are implemented in a counselor's responses:

E—*Evaluative*. A response which indicates the counselor has made a judgment of relative goodness, appropriateness, effectiveness, rightness. He has in some way implied what the client *might* or *ought to do,* grossly or subtly.

I—*Interpretive*. A response which indicates the counselor's intent is to teach, to impart meaning to the client, to show him. He has in some way implied what the client *might or ought to think,* grossly or subtly.

S—*Supportive*. A response which indicates the counselor's intent is to reassure, to reduce the client's intensity of feeling, to pacify. He has in some way implied that the client *need not feel as he does.*

P—*Probing*. A response which indicates the counselor's intent is to seek further information, provoke further discussion along a certain line, to query. He has in some way implied that the client *ought or might profitably develop or discuss a point further.*

U—*Understanding*. A response which indicates the counselor's intention is to so respond as in effect to ask the client whether the counselor understands correctly what the client is "saying," how the client "feels" about it, how it "strikes" the client, how the client "sees" it.[16]

Put in other terms, an *evaluative* response is one which carries the counselor's value judgment; an *interpretive* response is one which intends to teach or explain the dynamics of a person's behavior (the "why"); a *supportive* response is one which seeks to reassure, inspire, or undergird a person; a *probing* response is one which questions; and an *understanding* response is one which reflects the counselee's feelings and attitudes.

I have found the EISPU categories very useful in helping pastors and students to become sensitive to whatever lopsidedness exists in their counseling. The counseling of many parish ministers consists almost entirely of P (probing) and S (supportive) responses, without their being aware of it. Moralistic ministers tend to major in E (evaluative) and P (probing) responses. Clergymen who have some exposure to abnormal psychology and psychodynamic theory often emphasize I (interpretive) responses, demonstrating their theories about why people feel and act as they do. Those whose only training has been in the Rogerian approach tend to rely too heavily on U (understanding) responses. Ministers with no training in counseling seldom use U or reflective responses.

It is my view that *all five of these types of responses have a valid place in pastoral counseling*. A minister should be able to use them all with flexible selectivity, depending on the needs of the particular counseling relationship. In the early rapport-building phase of counseling, it is essential to major in U responses. In confrontational counseling, E (evaluative) and I (interpretive in the sense of teaching) responses are important. In crisis counseling, S (supportive) responses must be used frequently. In short-term educative counseling (premarital, for example), P (probing) and S (supportive) and I (interpretive or teaching) responses are indispensable. In all stages and types of counseling,

[16] *An Introduction to Therapeutic Counseling*, p. 201.

U (understanding) responses are important. The counseling of many parish ministers is weakest in its *lack of U responses.*

Let me suggest that the reader, using the EISPU system, try to identify the five responses listed after this statement by ***a girl, age nineteen:***

I tell you I hate my father. I hate him! I hate him! I hate him! And there's no reason for it. He is a minister—a good and righteous man. He has never laid a hand on me, but I have this terrific feeling against him—and it makes me feel so terrible because there is no reason for it. It's a sin to hate your father—especially if you don't have any reason for it. I—it worries me.

(1) Of course you feel guilt about hating him so, especially since you can't put your finger on what he has done to make you hate him. And then, too, . . . you'll find that underneath it all you have some love for him, and this plays a part in your feelings of guilt.

(2) I guess everyone at some time or another goes through a period when they hate one or both of their parents. It's really not at all uncommon. Most people find they can work out some way of getting along until things settle down.

(3) This is certainly something which you will want to get cleared up. Happy relationships with parents are too constructive a thing to a person. . . . You won't want to jeopardize what it can mean to you.

(4) It worries you that you should hate your father without reason and you feel sinful for hating him.

(5) I think we ought to get at the root of that worry. Tell me about your father—all about him.[17]

The key for scoring this exercise is in footnote 17.

The usefulness of the EISPU system is enhanced if two types of P responses are distinguished—PI (probing for information) and PF (probing for feelings). The system is a valuable tool for analyzing written verbatim reports or counseling tapes, helping to identify the blindspots in the counselor's responses. In reality-practice sessions, an experienced observer-evaluator can "keep score" on the counselor, help him recognize lopsidedness in his pattern of counseling. Otherwise, a counselor may go ahead blindly for years, totally unaware of his need for

[17] *Ibid.*, p. 12. Here is the key to the EISPU exercise above: (1) interpretive, (2) supportive, (3) evaluative, (4) understanding, (5) probing.

flexibility in relating with other facets of his personality. The EISPU system can be a mechanical gimmick of little value. But, when used as a self-confrontational device within the context of a dynamic understanding of the counseling relationship, it is a useful tool.

MECHANICS: PUBLICITY, SETTING, AND RECORDS

Some people in every church and community are not fully aware of the fact that the clergyman is a resource for help with problems. Many who *do* know that the minister is available for counseling are resistant to the idea of coming for help *themselves*. In the light of these reality factors, the minister needs to encourage persons to come by publicizing the fact that counseling is one of his normal functions and by making himself psychologically available.

The minister can inform his congregation by printing a statement such as this in his church bulletin or newsletter occasionally:

> All of us have problems in dealing with the normal pressures and perplexities of daily living. There are times when we would benefit from talking with a trained counselor about our problems. One function of the church is to provide such help when it is desired by our members or others in the community.
>
> Your minister is available to talk confidentially with those facing family problems, crises, difficult decisions, or personal problems. He is equipped by study and experience in the area of counseling. In problems requiring medical or psychiatric skills, he will be glad to assist you in finding competent help. Facing one's problems and seeking professional help is a sign of strength. It is as logical as going to a doctor for a physical problem or a checkup.
>
> It is best to phone the minister for an appointment, but if this is not convenient, or there is a crisis situation, it is unnecessary to have an appointment in advance. Your minister is regularly available for counseling sessions on Tuesday afternoons and Thursday evenings, and at other times as the need arises. If it is not convenient for you to come to his study, he will be glad to visit your home.
>
> Here are some of the problem areas in which a pastor may be able to give assistance or aid one in finding specialized help: marital problems, parent-child difficulties, vocational decisions, emotional illnesses, spiritual problems, hospitalization, bereavement, sickness, crises, alcohol problems, problems of aging, premarital guidance, youth counseling, handicaps, a sense of general unhappiness and meaninglessness.

Persons desiring to talk with the pastor may phone him at the church (611-3433). Counseling and guidance are a normal part of a minister's work. Feel free to call upon him.

It is easier to do effective counseling if one has a quiet place relatively free from interruptions. If one lacks a secretary who can insure privacy during counseling, a "Minister is in conference" sign on the study door and a phone bell that will turn off are helpful. It is well to schedule formal counseling sessions, particularly in continuing counseling relationships, with a definite time to begin and end. Simply saying at the outset, "We will have until ——— today," alerts the person to the time which is available, communicates the feeling of value which the minister attaches to time, and encourages the person to use the time in productive ways.

Keeping careful records is an essential part of a disciplined approach to pastoral counseling. Many ministers develop haphazard practices in this matter because they are so busy and because they underestimate its importance. How many of us would continue to go to a physician who was known to keep inadequate records? The clergyman should be no less disciplined in ministering to men's spirits than a doctor is rightly expected to be in ministering to their bodies. Careful records serve these important purposes: They provide a memory supplement which becomes increasingly important as the quantity of one's counseling grows. They encourage the minister to think systematically about particular counseling relationships and to plan his general approaches to them. They are useful for reference between sessions, encouraging the minister to become aware of the developmental process of a particular relationship. They are indispensable for future reference, if a person returns for counseling after an extended absence. They provide a means for learning from one's mistakes. They are useful in making referrals.

Counseling records should be kept *in a locked file,* a manila folder being maintained on each counselee. General information should include: name, address, phone, age, interpersonal resources (family members and others), presenting problem, psychosocial dynamics, spiritual dimension, tentative diagnostic impressions, tentative plan for helping person, physician's name, development of the problem (chronologically), crisis factors needing immediate action. After each counseling contact a summary of significant developments should be added to the counseling record.

Taking notes during counseling sessions has these *disadvantages:* It may interfere with the relationship by preventing one from listening deeply, raise anxieties in the counselee about whether the notes will be kept confidential, and place emphasis on content rather than on the relationship itself.

The *advantages* of note-taking are these: It says to the person that you value and want to remember what he communicates. It may reduce embarrassment resulting from persistent eye contact. It helps keep an accurate record of what transpires during a given interview. It saves time after the session. Most counselors find that they can remember and record the vital aspects of an interview if they do it immediately after its termination.

If one takes notes during sessions it should be done without sacrificing frequent eye contact. Jotting down key words or dates can be done unobtrusively. These provide a framework for post-session recording of the interview highlights. It is usually best not to request permission to take notes since the request itself tends to increase anxiety. It is better to say in a matter-of-fact tone: "I want to jot down a few notes so that I can keep the whole picture in mind." The same matter-of-fact approach should be used with respect to tape recorders: "I like to tape a counseling session occasionally so that I can avoid the distraction of keeping notes and reflect between sessions on what was said. It may be that we will want to listen together to a playback of part of a session, occasionally." Hidden mikes are inappropriate since they contradict the basic openness and honesty of the counseling relationship.[18]

Having considered some of the common elements in counseling, we will now turn to the variety of counseling methods used in the parish setting.

RECOMMENDED READING

Seward Hiltner, *Pastoral Counseling.*

Carroll A. Wise, *Pastoral Counseling, Its Theory and Practice* (New York: Harper & Row, 1951).

[18] For a helpful discussion of problems of taping see Joseph W. Knowles, *Group Counseling* (Englewood Cliffs, N. J.: Prentice-Hall, 1964), pp. 87-88. Taping is considerably more threatening to most counselees than note-taking.

The following should be read by those not familiar with the approach of Carl R. Rogers:[19]

Counseling and Psychotherapy (1942)—pp. 85-114, "The Creation of a Counseling Relationship"; pp. 131-73, "Releasing Expression."

Client-Centered Therapy (1951)—pp. 131-96, "The Process of Therapy."

On Becoming a Person (1961)—pp. 39-57, "Characteristics of a Helping Relationship"; pp. 107-24, "What It Means to Become a Person"; pp. 125-59, "A Process Conception of Psychotherapy."

If, after exposure to the EISPU system, you suspect that you are not utilizing the full spectrum of responses, it is strongly recommended that Elias H. Porter, Jr.'s *An Introduction to Therapeutic Counseling* (Boston: Houghton Mifflin, 1950) be used as a workbook. The "Counseling Procedures Pre-Test" (pp. 10-44) is very useful in self-evaluation.

REALITY-PRACTICE SESSION

PARISHIONER'S ROLE: Take the role of a person with whom you have counseled or whose problems you know intimately in some other way. Feel your way inside his "internal frame of reference," responding as you believe he would respond.

PASTOR'S ROLE: Practice listening to and reflecting (in paraphrased form) the feelings and attitudes expressed by the parishioner. Forget about trying to find answers to his problem or reasons why he feels and behaves as he does. Instead, concentrate on feeling *with* him and giving U (understanding) responses that will let him know you are with him.

OBSERVER-EVALUATOR'S ROLE: Be particularly aware of the U responses which the pastor gives. In your evaluation, call attention to the points at which E, I, S, or P responses were used.

[19] All three books are published by Houghton Mifflin.

Reality-practice sessions using these roles should be continued until each member of the team has an opportunity to become skilled in hearing and responding to feelings. This is such an essential ability in counseling that it merits whatever investment of time is required to achieve it. If no observer-evaluator is available, it is particularly important to record and play back the sessions.

5

Methods of Informal and Short-Term Counseling

The pastor and other religious workers . . . can never become so professional in their pictures of themselves that they underestimate the importance of informal relationships both as powerful ministries in and of themselves and as points of vital contact for beginning more formal counseling relationships.

—Wayne E. Oates [1]

The clergyman's position allows him to reach and help many *who will not come for formal counseling.* This is one of his strategic opportunities. If he is to maximize his ability to help the troubled, he must learn to utilize the host of unstructured, informal counseling opportunities which arise in the normal course of his calling, group contacts, and general pastoral work. Much of his counseling will be done in informal settings. Some will occur in his office, but without an appointment, when people "drop by for a chat." Effective counseling will frequently be done by phone. By allowing the sensitivities and skills of counseling to permeate his informal and chance encounters with people, he can become an instrument of help in the lives of many times the number of people he could reach through formal counseling alone. Reflecting on his parish experience a seasoned pastor observed:

The time allotted to what I would call formal pastoral counseling may amount to no more than 6 to 12 hours a week, depending on the nature of

[1] *An Introduction to Pastoral Counseling,* p. 69.

the church, the size of the congregation and the importance the minister attaches to this function. What I would call the more informal counseling relationships, which stem from the occasions when a minister meets people in his role as pastor or administrator or educator, may consume whole days out of each week.[2]

The minister should strive to recognize and utilize the pastoral care opportunity which is potentially present in every interpersonal contact.[3] If he approaches all his activities with "Good Samaritan" sensitivities, this will become a natural pastoral reflex. With this pastoral care orientation, he will discover frequent opportunities to do informal counseling during the ordinary interpersonal encounters of parish life. Occasionally these will become formal counseling relationships.

"Informal counseling" is informal in one or more of these ways—*setting, set, structure, sequence.* The setting may be anywhere—a street corner, a grocery store, a hospital room, the church lounge, a parishioner's office or living room, a union hall, at an AA meeting, on a plane or bus, or at the community swimming pool. The atmosphere is informal. The counseling happens in the context of some other relationship not identified as counseling—e.g., a chance encounter, a pastoral call, a hospital visit, following a meeting or Sunday service. The person's mind-set reflects this informal atmosphere. He probably thinks of what occurs as "talking over a problem with the pastor" rather than "counseling." The temporal structure and sequence of formal counseling interviews—appointments, stated time limits and an agreed-upon series of sessions—are usually lacking. Such counseling is frequently of single-interview duration.

CREATIVE PASTORAL CALLING AND COUNSELING

Informal counseling opportunities occur most frequently during a pastor's home and hospital visits. Much of what he does during these calls is general spiritual nurture—i.e., pastoral care. It becomes counseling when two factors—the *sine qua non* of counseling—are present: (a) a degree of awareness of a problem on the parishioner's part, (b) a

[2] Harry B. Scholefield, "The Significance of an Educative Analysis for the Parish Ministry," in *The Minister's Own Mental Health*, p. 326.

[3] Thomas W. Klink used the word "encounter" to describe the basic unit of pastoral work —"the distinctive moments of meeting which mark the life of ministry." See *Depth Perspectives in Pastoral Work*, p. 37.

desire for help of some kind from the pastor. Awareness of the *nature* of the problem may be vague and the desire for help minimal. All human motivation is mixed, including that which causes people to seek and accept help. In some cases the pain of a problem and the fear of telling another about it may be in balance, blocking action. Motivation is like a teeter-totter. Until the pain of a problem and the hope of getting help outweigh the fear of self-disclosure and the neurotic satisfactions accruing from the situation, a person usually will not seek help. But his motivational teeter-totter may be tipping back and forth long before this occurs decisively. He may be *open* to help before he actively *seeks* it. He may be receptive to informal counseling long before he takes the initiative in entering formal counseling. It is very difficult, if not impossible, for some people to make a formal appointment for counseling, even when nearly crushed by their problems. Unfortunately, they feel that to do so would be to admit failure and to damage further their feelings of self-worth. This is why the minister's ability to *go to people, make himself emotionally available, establish nonlabeled informal counseling relationships,* and perhaps *motivate them to accept formal counseling* is a priceless professional asset which he should use to the full!

How can the minister create opportunities, during his pastoral contacts, for spiritually significant conversations, informal and formal counseling? [4] First, he can *maintain a confidential, up-to-date "Special Help List,"* including the names of all whom he knows *or suspects* are in particular need of pastoral care—e.g., the bereaved, the sick, the unemployed, the depressed, the hospitalized, those in psychotherapy (and those who should be but aren't), the disgruntled, newlyweds, new parents, the handicapped, alcoholics and their families, the lonely, those with disturbed children, and those who face crises and perplexing decisions. An alert pastor often senses intuitively that a certain family is under extreme pressure. Such "pastoral care suspects" should go on his Special Help List. By devoting extra pastoral visitation time to these persons, the minister builds sturdy bridges of relationship with them. Such relationships bring pastoral care and informal counseling help to

[4] It should be emphasized that there are no sharp lines dividing general pastoral care and informal counseling, or precounseling and informal counseling. These pastoral activities tend to overlap. A relationship may move gradually from precounseling to informal counseling, as the person becomes aware of his need for help.

the troubled and make it easier for them to seek formal counseling. The building of relationship bridges with those who are likely to need help but are not yet motivated to obtain it comes in the category described by Seward Hiltner as "precounseling." [5] All a pastor's interpersonal contacts contribute to this objective, if they make people feel that he is accepting, competent, shockproof, not "too busy," and comfortably aware of his *own* humanity.

Second, the pastor's *sensitivity to the subtle signs of distress* is an asset in spotting potential counseling opportunities. Many ministers "walk by on the other side" of their parishioners' Jericho Roads simply because they lack awareness.[6] The pastor's emotional radar antennas should be tuned to the wave length of people, not just of "buildings, budgets, and bean suppers," in order to pick up their quiet cries for help, their often coded "mayday" signals. Here are some typical distress signals:

(1) Disturbed children (which usually reflect marital unhappiness).
(2) Veiled antagonism between husband and wife, sometimes hidden behind saccharine-sweet surface behavior.
(3) A frantic attempt to keep the conversation on the surface, avoiding all depth encounter.
(4) Unusual embarrassment at the minister's call.
(5) Depression—including such symptoms as sleeplessness, loss of interest in food and other pleasures, anxious agitation or heavy sluggishness, feelings of worthlessness, emptiness or helplessness, a phony gaiety.
(6) Frequent intoxication.
(7) A radical change in usual behavior, including church attendance.
(8) Irrational or frantically compulsive behavior.
(9) Affiliating with extremist groups or lunatic-fringe religious groups.
(10) Guilty avoidance of the pastor.

[5] For a discussion of precounseling, including the delicate issue of when the pastor should take the initiative and go to people offering help, see Hiltner's *Pastoral Counseling*, pp. 125-48.

[6] A minister who finds himself missing such clues regularly should arrange to have personal psychotherapy or clinical training to defog his perceptive apparatus.

When these or other distress signals are identified, the pastor should concentrate on making himself emotionally accessible by building relationship bridges to the persons involved.

A third element in discovering informal counseling opportunities is *the judicious use of "openers"*—statements designed to interrupt the superficial conversation which characterizes most social calls and to provide a chance for meaningful dialogue. Here are some samples: "How are things going in your situation?" "How are things going with you spiritually?" "How do you feel about . . . ?" "You seem to be tired (discouraged, upset)." "I get the feeling you have a burden on your mind." Although such openers may startle people initially, they express the pastor's concern and, by implication, offer his help. A well-chosen question, asked with empathy in a sound pastor-parishioner relationship, can open an infected wound, allowing it to drain. A minister should not be content with timid small talk during pastoral calls. Of course, he should "not expect that every call will produce a conversation about significant problems." [7] But he should help his people feel free to talk about burdening concerns when they need to do so. A question about one's spiritual and interpersonal condition should be no more startling from one's "spiritual physician" than is a question about one's physical symptoms from a family doctor.

Fourth, *listening and responding to feelings* during pastoral encounters help carry a conversation below the surface level to significant therapeutic interaction. By establishing genuine dialogue a pastoral visit can move into informal counseling in a natural, unthreatening way.

When people sense that their minister is emotionally available, counseling opportunities will occur during all sorts of pastoral contacts. While making a routine hospital call on a man convalescing from surgery, a minister ran into a heated family conflict centering on whether or not the man's daughter should remarry:

FATHER: Dorothy, why don't you tell the Reverend what we were discussing? Maybe he can help us out.

DAUGHTER: (Dorothy) Well, yes, maybe you can help us out, though I hesitate to bother you with my problem. I'm so bewildered and confused.

[7] Wise, *Pastoral Counseling, Its Theory and Practice*, p. 171

PASTOR: If you will tell me, I'll try to help.

DAUGHTER: (with halting speech and great uneasiness) Well, I hardly know where to begin or how. (Pause) I—well—for some reason I don't think I want to go through with my marriage. All of a sudden I have a feeling I don't love Ed anymore.[8]

As the pastor listened, the girl's confusion and the father's domineering nature became increasingly evident. He sensed that he should try to prevent the father from pushing his daughter into marriage and that he should see the girl individually so the she could make her own decision. This illustrates the type of informal counseling in which an ongoing, formal counseling relationship should be established or a referral made to a psychotherapist.

PREVENTIVE PASTORAL CARE

Because they involve people in some degree of crisis, hospital calls should have top priority in a minister's schedule. They are rich opportunities for both general pastoral care and informal counseling. Home visits help a minister establish strong bonds with his people by relating to the family in their natural setting. Furthermore, it is often helpfully revealing to observe a family "at home." This makes home visits a valuable aspect of marriage and family counseling, as nonministerial counselors are beginning to discover. There are also relationship-building values in informal contacts with parishioners at their work and at community functions.

Granger E. Westberg describes the following plan for "preventive pastoral care." The pastor aims at setting aside at least a half hour a year for a talk with each member *in his study*. These talks focus on the question, "What has it meant to you this past year to be a member of this Christian congregation?" In presenting this plan to new-member classes, the minister explains that he wants to know whether their church has been serving the spiritual needs of its people.[9] Such "pastoral conversations" have many values. In addition to the stated purpose, they deepen relationships, help accustom people to coming to the pastor's study, and give them an opportunity to open up personal problems.

[8] For a full verbatim account of this interview see Newman S. Cryer, Jr., and John Monroe Vayhinger, *Casebook in Pastoral Counseling* (Nashville: Abingdon Press, 1962), pp. 276-83.

[9] *Minister and Doctor Meet* (New York: Harper & Row, 1961), p. 138.

William E. Hulme describes a similar plan for use with youth in *How to Start Counseling.*[10] These approaches complement a pastor's routine home visitation, which is also a form of preventive pastoral care.

THE GOALS OF SHORT-TERM COUNSELING (FORMAL AND INFORMAL)

As Wayne E. Oates points out, "Much of the help which a pastoral counselor renders to his people is given in a single interview." [11] Certainly most of his counseling will be short-term—one to five and seldom more than a dozen sessions. Therefore a minister should develop his ability to give *significant* help in a few interviews.

To do this, a minister needs an inner conviction that short-term counseling *can* produce significant results. From experience in a walk-in psychiatric clinic in Los Angeles, psychiatrist Louis Paul states that these attitudes are essential for one who is working in such a setting: "That something eminently useful—and not second best—can be done in one, two, up to six, interviews; that the explicit time limit . . . can mobilize constructive efforts." [12]

The short-term nature of most pastoral counseling does not mean that its results are necessarily superficial. If short-term counseling is judged by its own goals and not those of long-term counseling and psychotherapy, it is clear that highly significant help *can* be given in many cases. Here are some *realistic goals of short-term counseling,* not all of which apply in every case:

(1) Provide a supportive, empathic relationship.

(2) Help restore functioning by reducing the pressure of pent-up, blocking feelings through emotional catharsis.

(3) If a person comes with a specific decision or interpersonal conflict, help him deal directly and responsibly with this.

(4) Mobilize the person's latent resources for coping. Help him discover and learn to use them.

[10] (Nashville: Abingdon Press, 1955), pp. 43-45.

[11] *An Introduction to Pastoral Counseling,* p. 108.

[12] "One Walk-in Clinic Technology" (unpublished paper. A revised version of this paper entitled "Treatment Techniques in a Walk-in Clinic" appeared in *Hospital and Community Psychiatry,* February, 1966). A walk-in clinic is a psychiatric facility where disturbed persons may go without an initial appointment for brief crisis-intervention help.

(5) Assist the person in achieving a broader and more constructive perspective on his situation by objective review of it.

(6) Interrupt panic reactions and regressive snowballing by helping the person face and deal with immediate, here-and-now problems.

(7) Help him to clarify the issues and explore the alternative approaches to his problem.

(8) After alternatives have been explored, help him choose the most promising and then to take at least small steps toward implementing the choice.

(9) Provide guidance in the form of useful ideas, information, and tentative suggestions. These can become useful tools which the person employs between sessions and after counseling terminates.

(10) Stimulate the person's self-reliance and functional competence by suggesting a limited number of sessions.[13]

(11) Establish an accepting quality of relationship which will make it easy for the person to return for additional counseling later. "The door of the relationship should always be left ajar so the person can feel free to come back again if he chooses to do so." [14]

(12) Ascertain whether the person is deeply disturbed or for other reasons is in need of medical, psychiatric, or other specialized help. Make a referral if this appears to be the case.

Counselors who *expect* to give genuine help in brief counseling are likely to do so. The following evidence is cited to show the realism of this expectation. Psychoanalysts Franz Alexander and Thomas Morton French report: "Both the theoretical survey of the psychodynamics of therapy and the impressive evidence gained from actual observation require us to abandon the old belief that permanent changes of the ego cannot be accomplished through shorter and more intensive methods." [15]

Five years of experience with nearly two thousand patients at the Cleveland Center on Alcoholism was summarized as follows:

> Many alcoholics do require treatment that may last from six months to a few years but this does not apply to all or even most. Many of our patients have been seen in one to five interviews and the rate of success is about the

[13] Experience at walk-in clinics confirms this.

[14] Oates, *An Introduction to Pastoral Counseling*, p. 111.

[15] *Psychoanalytic Therapy*, p. 164.

same as it is for those treated over much longer periods. . . . One alcoholic may need a hundred therapy sessions while another may be quite adequately helped in two or three counseling hours.[16]

At the marriage counseling service of the Court of Conciliation in Los Angeles, 60 percent of the four hundred couples who apply for help each month have already filed for divorce. The head counselor there calls the service "an emergency receiving hospital for sick and dying marriages." [17] Couples are seen for only one to three interviews. *For about one third of them, this is enough* to bring an off-balance marriage back to a functional balance! These are usually families in which crises such as illness or loss of job have knocked the marriage off stride. The problems snowball. Brief help, *in an authority-centered structure,* interrupts the vicious cycle which otherwise would probably end in divorce. About two thirds of the couples are more severely disturbed and require a referral for extended counseling. However, the fact that one third are helped significantly in three or less sessions is impressive indeed.[18]

Many people come to a pastor for help with specific decisions or concrete problems. When these are resolved, or are discovered to be insoluble, such persons often have no further desire for counseling. One to three sessions will often suffice in such cases. Some counselees can "turn the corner," to use Seward Hiltner's phrase, in a few sessions:

Turning the corner means that the direction has been changed. Many of the problems that come to the pastor's attention are life-situation problems. . . . They are . . . made worse because the point of view, which the person assumes is the only one he can take toward the situation, is narrow and inadequate. If he can turn the corner, clarify the conflicting forces involved, gain a bit of insight into why he feels as he does, then he has a new point of view or a new place on which to stand. Even brief counseling can often do just enough to bring a slightly new perspective, hence altering the approach to the situation and giving a chance for spontaneous successful handling of it by the parishioner.[19]

[16] *News of the Cleveland Center on Alcoholism,* September-October, 1961, p. 2.

[17] Lecture by Meyer Elkin, School of Theology at Claremont, April 5, 1963.

[18] Of every one hundred couples who come to the service, sixty decide to attempt a trial reconciliation. Follow-up studies a year later showed that three fourths of these marriages were still intact.

[19] Hiltner, *Pastoral Counseling,* p. 83.

It is amazing how much help a single interview can give in certain cases. As psychiatrist Lewis R. Wolberg states, "Problems which do not yield to short-term measures are those that have persisted a long time and perhaps date back to early childhood."[20] In my experience those who do not profit to some degree from short-term counseling usually are persons with weak or rigid personal structures.[21]

A particularly fruitful form of short-term pastoral counseling is *fork-of-the-road counseling* with persons possessing reasonably adequate ego strength. A bright young man, as a result of brief vocational guidance by his pastor, decided to go to college, in spite of his parents' indifference. By helping this lad choose the path which led to the fulfillment of his potentialities, the minister, in three sessions, had a constructive influence on the next forty years of his life. As John Dewey showed clearly, serious thinking often begins at the fork in the road in one's life when it is unclear which way leads to one's desired goal.

In counseling with a man in the throes of deciding between his family and his paramour, the minister confronted him with the probable consequences of choosing the latter. Thus he helped him avoid a destructive path which would have darkened his entire future. The path he chose made reconciliation through marriage counseling possible. This case, and many others like it, recall the sign at one end of a muddy dirt road: "Choose your track carefully. You'll be in it a long time." Some decisions are like that. Having wise guidance at such times can save one from years of suffering. It is noteworthy that "guiding" of this sort is a time-honored part of our pastoral tradition.[22]

THE PROCESS OF INFORMAL AND SHORT-TERM COUNSELING

What approach is most helpful in one-to-five-interview counseling? These elements are usually part of such a process:

(1) *Listen intensively and reflect feelings* (U responses). The pressure of time in short-term counseling tempts the minister to spend too little time listening. If he yields to this temptation, he deprives the person of the salutary effects of emotional catharsis and himself of an all-important awareness of the person's "internal frame of reference."

[20] *The Technique of Psychotherapy*, p. 105.
[21] See the discussion of ascertaining ego strength in Chapter 8.
[22] See Clebsch and Jaekle, *Pastoral Care in Historical Perspective*, pp. 49-56.

Wayne E. Oates recommends that, in one-interview counseling, the pastor give two thirds to three fourths of the time to concentrated listening.[23] Certainly, at least one half of the session should be used in this way.

(2) *Use questions carefully to focus on conflict areas rapidly* (P responses). If the minister is to be a guide through the wilderness of a complex problem, he must have a relatively clear map of that wilderness. In short-term counseling there isn't time to wait for all the essential segments of the map to emerge spontaneously. After giving a person an initial opportunity to present his picture of the problem, a few key questions can fill in the major gaps in essential information. They can also encourage the person to explore neglected dimensions of his problem and to look in new directions for solutions. The use of selected questions permits *focused listening* in crucial problem areas.

Pastoral counselors can learn from the growing experience at walk-in psychiatric clinics, where one of the aims is "to actively assist the consultee *as quickly as possible* in identifying and getting in contact with his most preconscious, most highly charged emotions, thoughts, purposes, and conduct (. . . the focal conflict, the main presenting 'problem,' the precipitating stress situation, the problem area)." [24]

Mrs. D., a middle-aged woman, consulted her minister for guidance in deciding whether or not to leave her alcoholic husband. Through disciplined listening the pastor began to grasp the broad outlines of the situation—many years of excessive drinking, a series of job losses and repetitive unfulfilled promises to stop drinking excessively. To be of help as a *pastoral guide,* the minister had to know whether the man had any awareness of his need for help, the nature of the marital interaction (e.g., was the wife pampering him unwittingly?), and the dynamic role of other members of the family. The only efficient way to acquire this knowledge is to ask questions aimed at key issues.

(3) Help the person *review the total problem.* This tends to produce a clearer perspective and prepare the person to make an enlightened

[23] *An Introduction to Pastoral Counseling,* p. 112.

[24] Paul, "One Walk-in Clinic Technology," p. 2. It should be made clear that sizing up a problem quickly and recognizing the key conflict requires a considerable degree of clinical sensitivity. It often takes more skill to move quickly than to move slowly in counseling. For this reason, it is erroneous to assume that because most of a pastor's counseling is short-term, he therefore needs relatively little training. Effectiveness in brief counseling is contingent on solid skills in the general area of counseling.

decision. It also helps him mobilize his inner resources. Under protracted stress a person often becomes confused about the real nature of the problem and loses sight of his own resources for coping. He bogs down in the swamp of his own hopelessness, neglecting the very things which he needs to meet this problem constructively. Mrs. D. had become so obsessed with her husband's drinking that she had neglected her friendships in the church which she now needed desperately. Through counseling she discovered this and began to rectify the situation.

(4) *Provide useful information.* By explaining certain well-established facts about the nature and treatment of alcoholism, the minister helped Mrs. D. to abandon her futile attempts to shame her husband into controlled drinking. This knowledge helped her "turn the corner" and walk in a more realistic and constructive direction in her relationship with him. Such "educative" elements in brief counseling can provide the person with information, ideas, and perspectives which he uses as tools to improve his situation, long after counseling terminates.

(5) *Focus on the major conflict, problem, or area of decision with the aim of clarifying viable alternatives.*[25] The minister asked Mrs. D., "What do you see as the paths that are open to you?" He then helped her explore the consequences of each alternative. If she left her husband, he might intensify his drinking or even commit suicide. Could she face these possibilities? On the other hand, the shock of her leaving might confront him with reality and for the first time open him to help. What would be the probable effects on the children if she didn't leave and he continued excessive drinking? Without leaving, could she alter her ways of relating so as to insulate herself and the children from the full impact of his destructive behavior? Before counseling she had,

[25] Psychologist Robert L. Brizee has suggested that the "decision-making model" is very useful in counseling. It focuses on the implicit decision which is present in the crucial conflict, seeking to help the person formulate his dilemma clearly so that he can then begin to face it. This approach works on the level of decisions. It looks at the past only when the person is unable to make and implement the decisions he must make to cope with his situation constructively. By discussing the past *in the context of current decisions,* the past is kept in dynamic relation with the present. Leona E. Tyler in *The Work of the Counselor* (New York: Appleton-Century-Crofts, 1953) has a helpful chapter on "Decision-Making Interviews" (pp. 228-42), which is relevant to short-term pastoral counseling. She points out that in the decision-making process a person first needs to achieve a sense of the general direction in which he wishes to go and "the purposes that the decision must serve for him." Unless he has this, his specific choices are unlikely to be satisfying. Along with this the person needs to become aware of the limits of his situation, within which he is free to choose.

in her words, "muddled around in the problem," never really thinking clearly about the implications of her live options.

(6) *Help the person decide on the "next step" and then take it.* Getting a person to act constructively, on a tentative plan, usually results in the strengthening of his inner resources. Even if the decisions and actions are on minor matters, they help break the paralysis of chronic indecision. In Mrs. D.'s case, the minister helped her plan the steps she would take *the next day* to discover job possibilities or other sources of temporary financial support. She needed to do this before she could make her larger decision. Practice in taking small steps strengthens the person's self-confidence and his "psychological muscles," enabling him then to take larger steps.

(7) *Provide guidance when it seems useful.* The minister recommended certain things that Mrs. D. should do, including attending the local Al-Anon group and obtaining psychotherapy for their disturbed adolescent son. These recommendations were based on the minister's general knowledge and experience in counseling and his partial but increasing awareness of the dynamics of the D. family. He made his recommendations in a form that would allow her to reject them *without rejecting him.* He respected her right not to implement them, and he encouraged her to discuss her reactions to them. All this is radically different from dispensing facile, off-the-cuff advice. Implicit in the careful use of suggestions is the view that the role of the pastoral counselor is modeled as much on the image of the *guide* and the *coach* as on the professional *psychotherapist.* The use of the minister's knowledge and authority is often essential in brief counseling.

(8) *Give the person emotional support and inspiration.* The familiar line, "Walk softly, for every man you meet is carrying a cross," is poignantly and repeatedly illustrated in a counselor's experience. Many crosses are hidden. If a person comes for counseling, it is safe to assume that his cross is, from his point of view, a heavy one. He needs someone to walk with him and put a shoulder under the load. The most vital support offered in counseling is the relationship, *per se.* But, within the relationship, it is often appropriate to give the person verbal encouragement for his efforts to carry his burden.[26] The careful use of religious instruments—prayer, scripture, sacraments—can deepen and enrich

[26] The danger here is that such encouragement may register with some persons as a form of manipulation or emotional coercion.

brief counseling by reestablishing contact with resources beyond the human relationship. The pastoral counselor *confronts*, but he also *comforts!* He *challenges*, but he also *cares.* It is the bringing together of these two paradoxical dimensions (judgment and grace) which produces growth in counseling.

(9) *Move into longer-term counseling* if brief counseling does not prove adequate. This may involve continued counseling with the pastor or making a referral. Mrs. D. came with the initial intention of seeing her pastor for one session to get specific advice. But that session made her aware of her need for longer-term counseling. The pastor offered this help, explaining how counseling could complement the group support and help of Al-Anon.

THE TRANSITION FROM INFORMAL TO FORMAL COUNSELING

Following a commitment service at a summer youth institute, a minister noticed a sobbing girl (Miss G.) and offered his help. She poured out her guilt feelings (apparently aroused by the service) about her hatred of her stepfather. Emotional catharsis and the minister's concern allowed her to experience a sense of forgiveness. Although this brief, informal counseling was obviously helpful, the minister failed at a crucial point. He did not attempt to relate the girl to her own minister for continued counseling to deal with her complex, conflicted family problem. He should have sought her permission to contact her pastor and/or encouraged her to do so as soon as she returned home.[27]

A man lingered in the church narthex after the Sunday service to inform the minister that he had decided to leave his wife. This was the minister's first knowledge of their trouble. He said, "Let's step back to my study where we can talk without being interrupted." The man indicated that an urgent obligation would prevent an adequate discussion then, so an appointment was made for three o'clock that afternoon. Many people will move from informal to formal counseling, if they are encouraged to do so and are offered a definite appointment.

[27] For a verbatim account of this informal counseling see Cryer and Vayhinger, *Casebook in Pastoral Counseling*, Case No. 28, pp. 157-61.

REDUCING PREMATURE TERMINATIONS

Much counseling is unproductively brief in that the counselee terminates before the helping process has had a chance to be effective. Here are some ways of reducing this premature attrition.

The counselee's experience of the counselor's warmth, understanding, and acceptance is basic.[28] In addition, terminations can be reduced by:

(1) Expressing *active interest* in working with the person in resolving his problem.

(2) Explaining *why* multiple-session counseling is necessary.

(3) Voicing whatever hope is realistic concerning how counseling may reduce the person's suffering and increase his satisfactions.

(4) In addition, it is important to *give the person something definite during the first interview.* This can be an understanding summary of his situation as the pastor sees it, a pamphlet to read, or the "assignment" of something to discuss, reflect on, or do.

(5) Near the close of each early-stage session, the counselor should ask, "How do you feel about our discussion during this hour?" If the counselee feels disappointment and does not have an opportunity to verbalize these feelings, he may act out his unrecognized and unexpressed feelings by terminating.

(6) If a person seems likely to terminate, the possibility should be discussed openly. Predicting it helps to prevent it.

(7) If a counselee's initial expectations about counseling are grossly unrealistic, they should be altered gently and gradually rather than abruptly.

(8) It is wise to say at the outset, "Let's plan on meeting for four or five sessions. After that we'll evaluate our work together to see how helpful it has been, and then decide whether to continue." This tends to reduce initial fears about the imagined interminability of counseling. It also encourages the person to work hard from the start.

THE USE OF THE TELEPHONE IN COUNSELING

The telephone can be a highly useful instrument in pastoral care, informal counseling, and even formal counseling. An experienced minister reports that he could not begin to handle the pastoral care load of his church without its frequent use. He writes:

[28] Warmth does not mean effusiveness, of course. People who are afraid of being overwhelmed by others will retreat from the effusive pastor's aggressiveness.

> Surely I don't believe in using the telephone as a substitute for personal contacts. But sometimes the telephone is an excellent supplement. There are times when it can do—and do as effectively—what a personal call could do, and when a personal call is impossible. Much use of the telephone is in the area of administration. However, even as we call on an administrative matter, we must remember that the one to whom we talk is the one whose son we just buried, whose daughter we just married, whose grandson we just baptized, whose daughter's marriage is crumbling, and whose heart is breaking because of it.[29]

Following a discussion of a controversial issue at his official board, there were several "No" votes. The next day he phoned those persons and simply inquired, "What were your reactions to the board meeting?" This was person-centered administration—the kind which often leads to counseling. This minister also uses the phone to supplement his in-person hospital calls now that most patients have bedside phones. He reports that this is deeply appreciated.

The telephone can be very useful in precounseling and informal counseling, allowing a minister to keep in close touch with his Special Help List and to become aware quickly of the need for counseling. In emergency or crisis situations, effective supportive and stopgap counseling can be done by phone. In longer-term counseling, the phone can be used between sessions to increase the frequency of contacts.

RECOMMENDED READING

Franz Alexander and Thomas M. French, *Psychoanalytic Therapy* (New York: Ronald Press, 1946), Chapter 9, "Efficacy of Brief Contact."

Heije Faber and Ebel van der Schoot, *The Art of Pastoral Conversation* (Nashville: Abingdon Press, 1965).

Seward Hiltner, *Pastoral Counseling*, "Precounseling Methods," pp. 171-83; "Brief Counseling," pp. 81-85, "Strategic-Problem Therapists," pp. 105-11.

Reuel L. Howe, *The Miracle of Dialogue* (New York: Seabury Press, 1963).

Wayne E. Oates, *An Introduction to Pastoral Counseling*, "Informal Pastoral Relationships," pp. 69-80; "Pastoral Visitation and Counsel-

[29] Letter from Warren A. Nyberg, July 5, 1965.

ing" (by J. L. Elder); and "The Exploratory or Short-Term Interview," pp. 108-16.

Helen H. Perlman, *Social Casework: A Problem-Solving Approach* (Chicago: University of Chicago Press, 1957).

Lewis R. Wolberg, *The Technique of Psychotherapy,* " 'Brief' or 'Short-term' Psychotherapy," pp. 103-5.

REALITY-PRACTICE SESSIONS

PARISHIONER'S ROLE: You are Miss G., the teen-ager at the youth institute, described earlier in this chapter. Your problem is a generally unhappy home situation and guilt about your hatred of your stepfather. (See *Casebook in Pastoral Counseling,* 157-61, for a full account.)[80]

PASTOR'S ROLES: First, you are the minister at camp who notices the girl crying and tries to help. Then you are the minister of her home church to whom she has been referred by the minister at camp.

OBSERVER-EVALUATOR: Your function is to help Miss G. and the pastor increase their awareness of what is happening during the counseling. Be aware of the feeling tone and be candid in your suggestions for improving the counseling.

[80] Other cases for use in reality-practice of informal and short-term pastoral counseling: the cases described in this chapter, plus these from Cryer and Vayhinger, *Casebook in Pastoral Counseling:* Case No. 2, pp. 24-31 and Case No. 55, pp. 298-301. Counseling opportunities during pastoral calls: Case No. 47, pp. 257-62 and Case No. 43, pp. 235-40—cases involving difficult decisions.

6

Role-Relationship Marriage Counseling

Therefore a man leaves his father and his mother and cleaves to his wife, and they become one flesh.—Gen. 2:24

Marriage represents for most people a central life adjustment area. . . . Being married or not married is an all-pervasive life condition which sets up . . . certain channels for the gratification of important human needs, and certain inevitable blocks to these needs. Furthermore, the marriage role can . . . set the pace for other important life roles—friendship, parenthood, work.

—*Americans View Their Mental Health* [1]

Proficiency in marriage and family counseling is the pastor's most indispensable counseling skill. In this area he should be among the best informed, most skilled persons in his community. A reasonable degree of proficiency in other types of counseling is essential. But in family life counseling his opportunities are so frequent and so crucial that a degree of competence approaching *expertness* is required to meet the needs.

Two factors make it imperative that a clergyman work to acquire the highest level of family counseling skill of which he is capable. First, *more than half* of a typical parish minister's counseling opportunities involve family problems! In the nationwide study reported in *Americans View Their Mental Health*, *59 percent of the persons who had sought pastoral counseling did so because of a marriage or family problem.*[2] This included 46 percent who had gone for help with mar-

[1] Pp. 91-92.
[2] P. 309.

riage problems, 8 percent for problems with children, and 5 percent for other troubled family relationships. Think of the implications of this fact—*nearly six out of every ten persons seeking pastoral help are motivated by the pain of family conflicts!*

The second factor which makes it essential that a minister maximize his abilities in this area is the matter of the human values at stake. A growing, need-satisfying family relationship is like a cold spring on a hot dusty journey. It is a fountain of rejuvenation, a place of renewal, a garden of growth. A healthy, maturing marriage, studded with occasional moments of agony and ecstasy, is as close to heaven on earth as human relationships come.[3] Conversely, a "fractured family," the product of a mutually destructive marriage, is a painfully close approximation of hell on earth. In family counseling the stakes are very high!

Here is what I mean by a "good marriage" (or a "good family"): *A marriage (or family) in which all those involved have maximum opportunity, through mutual need-satisfaction, to grow toward the fulfillment of their God-intended potentialities as persons.* In no type of counseling are long-range personality values more crucially involved. Through skilled marriage counseling, the pastor contributes to the long-range mental and spiritual health of the marital partners, their children, their children's children, *ad infinitum*. Parents are the "architects of the family." [4] If a marriage is disintegrating, the family as the fundamental *nurture group* fractures, producing gradual emotional starvation and, consequently, personality deformation. Marriage and family counseling focuses a healing light on the root of all personality pathology. As such, it is an effective form of *prevention* of mental and spiritual illness, now and in the unborn future.

All marriages and all families have problems! Psychiatrist Harry Stack Sullivan expressed this with a touch of humor:

> I have yet to find a marriage which has only satisfactions and only securities. . . . If a person tells me his home-life is perfect, I take off my glasses, which means I can't see him, and gaze at him, and say, "Extra-ordinary!" I then pass on to some other topic but I return to this later.[5]

[3] Otis A. Maxfield writes: "Marriage can be a tangible model on the human level of what all spiritual relationships can be like." Quoted in Robert A. Blees, *Counseling With Teen-Agers* (Englewood Cliffs, N.J.: Prentice-Hall, 1965), p. 17.

[4] This is Virginia M. Satir's apt phrase.

[5] *The Psychiatric Interview* (New York: W. W. Norton Co., 1954), p. 171.

Family-centered counseling helps to reduce the blocks to personality growth which exist in some families to a paralyzing degree. Skilled counseling would increase the creativity of many reasonably adequate (i.e., need-satisfying) marriages. In "sick" and "dying" marriages it is indispensable.

Counseling can increase the abilities of families to "live their religion." [6] Family life offers our best opportunities for "covenants of intimacy" [7] in our culture; it is important, therefore, that the Good News come alive in the dailiness of family relationships. A healthy marriage is the most psychologically intimate of all human relationships. This makes it at once the most demanding and the most potentially rewarding.

A clergyman is in a strategic position to do family counseling. His professional activities give him a network of deeply meaningful relationships with families. Thus he has a natural entrée to family circles when the need for counseling arises. The minister's presence during many family stress periods creates counseling opportunities. His role as an educator permits him to plant seeds which germinate and flower as counseling opportunities. To illustrate, an insightful sermon on family life almost always produces at least one counseling opportunity.

THE NATURE OF MARITAL CONFLICT

A man and a woman are attracted to each other because each senses that the relationship will be a means of satisfying a variety of needs. Each party brings a unique pattern of personality needs to the marriage. These needs must receive at least minimal satisfaction if the person is to be capable of satisfying his partner's and children's needs. A "happy marriage" is one in which there is a relatively high degree of mutual need satisfaction. Conversely, an "unhappy marriage" has a high degree of mutual need frustration. If a relationship produces chronic, unmet emotional hungers, it will diminish the self-esteem of those involved, resulting in rejection, anger, and aggression.

The particular need-pattern which one brings to his marriage depends

[6] From the title of a book by Regina Wescott Wieman, *The Family Lives Its Religion* (New York: Harper & Row, 1941).

[7] For a discussion of the concept see Gibson Winter's *Love and Conflict* (Garden City, N.Y.: Doubleday & Co. 1958), pp. 71-95.

on the personality-molding experiences with need-satisfying adults in his early life. The needs whose satisfaction determines the relative strength of a marriage are of two kinds—personality needs and sexual needs. The basic personality needs were described in Chapter 1.

Carl G. Jung held that maleness and femaleness complement each other psychologically. A man is attracted to a woman, and vice versa, for many reasons. On a deep level, there is the desire to complete one's unfinished identity by joining one's maleness to the femaleness of another. Closely linked to this is the desire to fulfill one's biological creativity by literally becoming "one flesh" in the new life of a child.

Marital conflict is fundamentally the conflict of two need systems—the needs of one person collide head on with the needs of the other. For example, Joan and Larry, married three years, have an incompatible need to "parentify" each other. Each wants to be the "child" in a child-parent dependency relationship.

Because of severe, chronic early life need deprivation, many people bring *neurotic needs* (as contrasted with "normal" needs) to their marriages. A neurotic need has two characteristics: (a) It is an *exaggeration of a normal need*—so much so that no one could possibly satisfy it. (b) It is *ambivalent* or conflicted. On a conscious level the person desires one thing; on a nonconscious level he wants just the opposite! This inner contradiction makes interpersonal conflict inevitable. The person is always frustrated because he can't "eat his cake and have it too." The counselor's awareness of self-contradictory need patterns will help him understand many chronic marital battles.

Carl was raised by a cold, nongiving mother who could not feed her children's personality hungers. As a result Carl, now in his late twenties, has an insatiable need for reassurance, warmth, and emotional feeding. Normal amounts of affection from his wife, Patricia, would seem to him to be a starvation-level emotional diet. Unfortunately she finds it difficult to give Carl even moderate amounts of emotional food. In spite of a warm exterior, she is remarkably like his mother in her underlying personality. Why was Carl attracted to a person who could not meet his needs? Because he has other, conflicting needs. He needs to be dependent, but he also needs to feel hyper-manly. His powerful dependency needs make him feel weak and unmasculine. To protect himself from these intolerable feelings, he must deny his dependence and strive for an exaggerated "self-made-man" independence. His fear of his dependency prevented him from marrying someone who could give him generous mothering. On an unconscious level, Patricia has a parallel conflicted need system which drew her to Carl.

As Lawrence S. Kubie has stated:

> No one has ever married himself out of a neurosis. Instead, when two young people are drawn into marriage by the lure of the other's illness, one will add the weight of his own neurotic infirmity to that of the other, with growing pain and resentment.[8]

Three useful tools for helping disturbed marriage and family relationships will be presented in this chapter and the next: *role-relationship marriage counseling, family group therapy,* and *Eric Berne's transactional approach to therapy.* Each method is pregnant with possibilities for pastoral use. Each will add significantly to the pastor's relationship-centered counseling armamentarium.

THE FOCUS AND GOALS OF ROLE-RELATIONSHIP MARRIAGE COUNSELING

Two persons meet, begin to relate, and eventually marry. Their interaction before and during the course of their marriage results in the creation of a new psychological entity—*their relationship.* This new entity, called the "identity of the marital pair" by psychiatrist Nathan W. Ackerman,[9] includes what each brought to the relationship—his needs, problems, personality patterns and resources, expectations and hopes—but much more. The "more" is *their interaction*—what each becomes in the process of responding to what the other becomes in the process of responding to him, and so on. Out of the reciprocal intricacies of relating on many levels (from the physical to the deepest strata of their psyches) emerges an original creation—their marriage relationship. We are dealing here with what Martin Buber describes in discussing the potentiality which exists when two people meet as the "dimension of the between." [10] Every human relationship that is mutually meaningful

[8] Victor W. Eisenstein, ed., *Neurotic Interaction in Marriage*, p. 18.

[9] *The Psychodynamics of Family Life*, p. 22.

[10] This is discussed in *Between Man and Man* (New York: The Macmillan Company, 1947), pp. 203-5; see also Antonia Wenkart, "Betweenness and Transition," *Journal of Existential Psychiatry*, Spring, 1960, p. 127. Buber wrote: "A soul is never sick alone, but always through a betweenness, a situation between it and another existing being" (Maurice Friedman, *Martin Buber, The Life of Dialogue*), p. 191.

(need-satisfying) creates something of this "betweenness." The longer and the more intense the interaction, the more vivid the identity of the relationship.

Role-relationship counseling focuses on improving the marriage relationship, not (as in the case of uncovering psychotherapy) on resolving intrapsychic personality conflicts. Addressing psychotherapists in training, Harry Stack Sullivan once declared: "If you are to correctly understand your patient's problems, you must understand him in the major characteristics of his dealing with people."[11] It is true that disturbed relationships reflect *inner* conflicts and unhappiness. But the distortions in the relationships perpetuate and intensify these inner conflicts, and produce new layers of psychological disturbance. In role-relationship counseling, the "sick" marriage relationship *per se,* becomes the object of treatment. It is the "patient." As a relationship becomes more constructive, the individuals who compose it become *free to change.*[12]

The master goal of this approach to marriage counseling is *to make the relationship more mutually need-satisfying.* To accomplish this, certain *operational goals* should be in the pastor's mind during the process of counseling. Their listing tends to make this counseling seem complicated and highly ambitious in its objectives. Actually, the full list represents the *optimal* possibilities of this approach. The achievement of even a few of these goals will improve the need-satisfaction capabilities of most marriages. Here are the goals; the counselor helps the couple:

(1) Reopen their lines of communication.
(2) Interrupt the vicious cycle of mutual retaliation.
(3) Face the need to work together in strengthening the relationship.
(4) Become aware of the nature of their interaction, particularly the ways in which it produces pain in both parties, and the roots of their interaction in their role images.
(5) Learn how to learn from their conflict.
(6) Have experiences of thinking together about sources of pain and pleasure in their marriage, followed by planning and working together toward mutually set goals.

[11] *The Psychiatric Interview,* p. 13.

[12] It should be noted that this is the opposite of the usual way of changing a *relationship* in conventional psychotherapy by first changing the individuals who compose it.

(7) Face the futility of their campaigns of mutual reformation, and begin to "release" [13] each other, and accept the unchangeable aspects of their relationship.

(8) Begin to do something about their own areas of irresponsibility in the marriage.

(9) Begin to discover and experiment with new ways of relating which produce more mutual satisfaction of personality and sexual needs. Experience the satisfaction cycles of more mature relating.

(10) Find a focus of concern outside the family and a more satisfying relationship with the "extended family."

It should be made clear that these goals overlap. Some are fulfilled spontaneously as a marriage relationship improves. Except for the first three, there is no typical sequence involved in their fulfillment.

ROLE-RELATIONSHIP METHODOLOGY

These goals will become clearer when viewed operationally in the following case.

Mrs. Blackright, age thirty-two, phoned her minister to ask if he would see her about a marital problem. He said: "Yes, of course, I will be glad to be of whatever help I can. How would your husband feel about coming along to talk with me?" She replied that he was worried about their marriage, but felt they could work out their own problems. The minister replied: "I see. Do you suppose he would be willing to come at least this time so that both sides of your relationship will be represented? I'd like to know how each of you feels about it." She responded in the affirmative and a tentative appointment was made, to be confirmed after she talked with her husband.

Marriage counseling aims at treating a disturbed relationship; it is important, therefore, to make every effort to involve *the couple* in the helping process.[14] The longer a counselor sees one partner without the

[13] This refers to a letting go, emotionally, of the futile attempt to run the other person's life. See Chapter 9 for a discussion of this useful concept.

[14] A direct invitation, by phone or a note, often accomplishes this, if the antagonism between husband and wife makes it likely that the approach used above will fail. William L. Carrington, in *The Healing of Marriage*, gives his procedure. With the permission of the spouse he writes: "Dear Mr. ———: Your wife has been to see me for help in the marital situation that has arisen between you. I think I could be of more help if I could have the opportunity

other, the more difficult it becomes to establish rapport with the other. If one has been seen alone, it is wise to schedule at least one individual appointment with the other in order to establish rapport and give him the feeling of having "equal time." Should the person who initiated the counseling resist telling his spouse that he is coming, these feelings should be examined and challenged (after rapport is established). Frequently this is a form of resistance to dealing with the realities of the marriage relationship and/or a desire to have a private relationship with a parent figure.

If the absent spouse will not come, counseling with one person is difficult, but possible, provided the counselor: (a) avoids the trap of allowing the sessions to be spent analyzing and criticizing the absent person, (b) focuses on the present party's side of the interaction and what *he can change in himself;* (c) helps that person "release" the other emotionally as a way of interrupting the neurotic interaction; (d) makes generous allowances for the unavoidable distortions in either spouse's perception of the marriage relationship, and (e) avoids taking sides. This last point constitutes a pitfall in all marriage counseling since taking sides blinds the counselor to the couple's neurotic interaction, awareness of which is the heart of the helping process.

When the Blackrights came, the minister began to reopen the lines of meaningful communication by asking each to describe the problem as he saw it. This produced spirited negative interaction between the Blackrights, which the pastor observed carefully. He noted that they talked to each other *through* him. Since they couldn't *communicate* directly, except for the mutual recriminations stemming from their suffering, they lacked the basic instrument for resolving their own conflict. "Communication" includes all the verbal and nonverbal ways in which persons transmit feelings, attitudes, ideas, desires, and hopes. Communication skills are the pathways by which people relate and thereby satisfy personality hungers. The "sickness" of the Blackrights' marriage could be understood as pathology in its communication system.[15] Marriages in which there has been no real communication for

of hearing how you feel about it. If you can manage to come for a talk I would be glad if you would make an appointment at a mutually suitable time. Yours faithfully" (pp. 156-57).

[15] Carl R. Rogers illuminates the communication problem when he writes: "The whole task of psychotherapy is the task of dealing with a failure in communication. The emotionally maladjusted person . . . is in difficulty first, because communication within himself has broken

many years are not a rarity. The need-deprivation of such marriages produces intense, though often quiet, suffering.

The presence of the minister allowed the Blackrights to talk about the issues which caused their suffering. Their marital "two-party group," paralyzed by mutual attack, became a three-party group with one member taking the role of mediator and communication-facilitator. As in a deadlocked labor-management dispute, a neutral third party changed the nature and interaction of the Blackrights' "group," enabling communication to be reopened.

The presence of the pastor, symbolizing social and religious authority, also began to interrupt the vicious cycle of mutual retaliation in which the Blackrights were caught. Speaking from the perspective of long experience in marriage counseling, Hilda M. Goodwin and Emily H. Mudd observe:

> When the marital relationship does not afford an acceptable degree of satisfactions for each spouse's needs, or if conflict develops, several processes are set in motion which undermine personal identity and promote failure of each partner to alleviate the anxiety of the other.[16]

These processes include spiraling resentment, feelings of rejection, and the progressive breakdown of problem-resolving communication. The more personal identity is undermined, the faster the rejection-anxiety spiral whirls; the stronger the momentum of the vicious cycle, the more difficult it is for the couple to interrupt it unassisted. The Blackrights' spiraling negative interaction brought out the witchy, withholding sides of each which multiplied the need for mutual attack.

Basic to interrupting this vicious cycle is draining off the intense feelings of hurt, resentment, and rejection which feed it. The pastor does this by encouraging emotional catharsis, usually in separate sessions (one

---

down, and second because, as a result of this, his communication with others has been damaged. . . . In the "neurotic" individual, parts of himself which have been termed unconscious or repressed, or denied to awareness, become blocked off so that they no longer communicate themselves to the conscious or managing part of himself. As long as this is true, there are distortions in the way he communicates himself to others, and so he suffers both within himself, and in his interpersonal relations. The task of psychotherapy is to help the person achieve, through a special relationship with a therapist, good communication within himself. Once this is achieved he can communicate more freely and effectively with others. . . . Good communication . . . within or between men, is always therapeutic." (*On Becoming a Person*, p. 330.)

[16] *Marriage Counseling in Medical Practice*, Ethel M. Nash, *et al.*, eds. (Chapel Hill: University of North Carolina Press, 1964), p. 278.

or more) with each party. Often the reduction of the explosive "head of steam" must be accomplished *before* helpful communication can occur in couple counseling.

The initial session with the Blackrights together gave the minister a valuable opportunity to discover how they related, as well as to offer and interpret the help which was available if they both desired it. Near the end of the first hour, he summarized:

If I understand the way you feel about your marriage, Mr. Blackright, it is. . . . And your feelings, Mrs. Blackright are these. . . . Do I have an accurate picture of how you each feel?

Receiving affirmative responses, he continued:

Each of you is suffering acutely as a result of the inadequacies of your ways of relating. You feel your problems are beginning to disturb your children. A lot has happened between you during the ten years that you've been married. So I'm sure you can see that it will take some time to untangle the things that are causing you both unhappiness. If I sense your feelings accurately, you both would like to try to improve your marriage, although you're discouraged and not sure it is possible. I am quite willing to work *with* you in helping *you discover* more mutually satisfying ways of relating to each other. Mr. Blackright, would you be willing to meet regularly for a while to see what can be done to improve your relationship? (The same question was then directed to Mrs. Blackright.)

This statement recognized the pain which they were feeling, pointed to its source in their dysfunctional relationship, recognized their desire to change, offered help, and indicated the goal of counseling as a more mutually satisfying relationship. It carried a recognition of the difficulties involved in constructive change and the fact that they would have to be active participants in the process.

During the initial interview the minister concentrated on establishing rapport, listening with all his faculties, reflecting feelings, watching for patterns in their relationship, and trying to grasp *their* inner pictures of their problems. In addition, he formed a tentative impression concerning the depth of their disturbance and their ego resources for learning to cope more constructively. Because he sensed that they both possessed considerable personality strength, had had some past success in their relationship, and were adequately motivated [17] to work at improving it, he decided to attempt ongoing counseling with them.

A basic principle of couple counseling is *to give each party a comparable opportunity to express his views on each topic*. In the case of the Blackrights this required a referee function. Occasionally the minister would interrupt the more aggressive Mrs. Blackright by a statement such as, "I think we have a picture of how you see the argument you had last night, Mrs. Blackright. Now, let's hear how it looked from your perspective, Mr. Blackright." After rapport was firmly established, the pastor felt free to call the Blackrights' attention to what he observed in the dominance-submission pattern of their relationship during the counseling sessions. Such live, here-and-now material offers valuable doors to awareness.

During the initial hour, the pastor concentrated more than half of his attention on Mr. Blackright, letting him feel his empathy, understanding, and support. The principle being implemented was that of *focusing on the less strongly motivated spouse* in order to establish a bond of rapport with him. Because Mr. Blackright had come with some reluctance, the pastor asked him *first* whether he would be willing to meet regularly to work together on the marriage.

During the first hour the pastor encouraged the Blackrights to reconstruct a chronological picture of their relationship. He asked: "How long has the trouble been going on, as you see it, Mr. Blackright?" (followed by the same to Mrs. Blackright). "How were things before this?" This helped to remind them of their pre-children "golden age," during the first three years of their marriage. If such a happily remembered predisturbance period had been absent, the prognosis for counseling would have been less favorable. The Blackrights' realization that they had once had a better relationship gave them hope of recapturing it.

The individual sessions with the Blackrights (two with each person)

[17] It is unnecessary for both parties to be wholehearted about counseling. What is essential is a willingness to participate in the process and to remain in counseling long enough to allow it to have beneficial effects. If, as often is the case, one party is resistant to counseling, the pastor's objective must be to discover where that person is hurting and is therefore motivatable; e.g., Mr. Blackright's concern about the negative effects of the marital conflict on their children and his desire to reduce his own pain in the marriage were points at which his motivation to participate in counseling could be activated.

were used to give each a chance to share confidential information,[18] strengthen rapport, drain off anger, interrupt the negative cycle, and reduce projection of responsibility on the other. To ascertain their degree of projection, the pastor asked each person, "What do you see as the ways in which *you* have contributed to the problem in your marriage?" At first the Blackrights, like most early stage counselees, gave only vague, generalized, halfhearted answers. But as their resentment and anger were reduced, their ability to be more honestly self-aware increased. If this had not occurred and the need to project total responsibility on the other had continued unabated, the pastor could have reasonably suspected the presence of severe personality disturbance in one or both parties.

After the individual sessions, the remainder of the Blackrights' counseling was *couple counseling* in which both were seen together.[19] The focus was kept on specific incidents, "vignettes of interaction." [20] When one engaged in generalized complaints against the other, the pastor would say, "Let's look at a 'for instance' of that problem." He guided the couple to stay with a particular disagreement or (later) satisfying incident until they had discovered what was really happening in terms of feelings and the meaning of their behavior. After asking for each person's view of the incident, the minister continued to ask questions of clarification to make them look in detail at that incident, rather than hop from one to another. He pointed out that recent incidents are preferable, since memory of details is fresher, but remote incidents which are still festering should be brought up to discover *why the person has held on to them.* Depth exploration of a single incident seemed tedious at first to the Blackrights, but they gradually found it to be a helpful approach. The implicit working hypothesis is that the depth understanding of a single incident often reveals the basic patterns and dynamics of the relationship.

[18] In the first individual session with each person, the pastor indicated that nothing communicated by that person would be shared with the spouse (by the pastor) unless explicit permission to do so had been obtained. Unless the principle of confidentiality is enunciated, crucial material (e.g., regarding a paramour) is likely to be kept hidden.

[19] With adequately motivated couples who communicate meaningfully in the first hour, it is not essential to have separate sessions, although they do help to strengthen rapport with the less-motivated party.

[20] R. W. Speers, "Marriage Counseling and the General Practitioner," in *Marriage Counseling in Medical Practice*, p. 9.

From the beginning the minister kept asking, "What can we learn from this incident (hassle, misunderstanding, happy experience)?" or "What was really going on?" Gradually, by imitation, the Blackrights began to ask the same kind of questions *between sessions*. This orientation allowed them to learn from their conflicts. It also helped them to interrupt their negative cycles sooner. As the minister put it, with a smile, "If you have an argument and don't learn from it, you've wasted a good fight!"

In this way the Blackrights gradually became aware of the nature of their interaction—the ways in which the feelings, attitudes, and behavior of each person produced suffering and need-hunger in both himself and the other. Early in counseling the pastor emphasized the *self*-hurting nature of their ways of relating—the ways in which their own needs were being deprived by the response which their negative behavior elicited from each other. This appeal to enlightened self-interest is more effective in reversing a negative cycle than is an appeal to altruism. As their awareness increased, they tended to interrupt the self- and other-damaging interaction which had dominated their relationship.

An essential ingredient in the Blackrights' dawning awareness was their discovery of the conflicting role images which each had held unconsciously for himself and for the other. As he grows up, every person forms inner pictures of what constitutes "right" behavior for a husband, father, wife, mother, keeper of finances, church member, etc. Scores of these images concerning appropriate roles are internalized unconsciously as a result of his experiences in the childhood family. These influence him profoundly throughout his life, usually without his being aware of what is happening. If those around him conform to his images of "right" behavior and attitudes, he feels comfortable; if not, he feels anxious.

In the case of the Blackrights, the role images which they brought to their marriage were very different. Mr. Blackright was reared by an aggressive, quick-tempered father and a passive, overly self-sacrificing mother. His mother and two sisters waited on the "men of the family"—himself and his father. In reacting to his father's authoritarianism Mr. Blackright identified with his mother. Like her, he is "easy going." In Mr. Blackright's family, the males did the yard work; the women did the inside housework. Mrs. Blackright came from a home where the father was the nominal head of the house, but her mother really exercised major control. Mrs. Blackright described her father (in an obvious dig at her husband) as "not *too* good to do the grocery shopping and even help with the dishes now and then," even though he was a busy accountant. Although Mrs. Blackright consciously rejected identification with her mother, her behavior revealed that her model of "normal" wifely and motherly behavior was cut from the cloth of her mother's controllingness. She was also like her mother in being relatively ungiving emotionally with her husband and their three children. Mrs. Blackright viewed Mr. Blackright's mother as a "martyr," and Mr. Blackright saw her father as "henpecked."

In response to the minister's query, "Mr. Blackright, what do you see as the things you'd like to change in your relationship?" he protested, "She pushes me too hard! I salute her when she gets too pushy." Mrs. Blackright responded that she had "more drive" than her husband, comparing his job and income unfavorably with her father's. After several sessions, the Blackrights began to see the pattern of their relationship—her pushing, pressuring, and manipulating him to do what she desired, and his *passive aggressive* form of fighting back by procrastinating, avoiding discussion of differences, evading her questions, and letting her take responsibilities in which she was sure to fail. The response of each tended to make the response of the other more extreme.

In one session this "vignette of interaction" was analyzed in detail. That evening Mr. Blackright had spilled a pitcher of orange juice on the kitchen floor.

PASTOR: What happened then?

MRS. BLACKRIGHT: I came charging in, yelled at him to be more careful, and then cleaned up the mess.

PASTOR: Why did *you* clean it up?

MRS. BLACKRIGHT: I knew he'd take hours to get around to it, and he'd make another mess in cleaning up that one!

PASTOR: (To Mr. Blackright) How did you feel about her cleaning up the mess?

MR. BLACKRIGHT: She's a perfectionist! Always after me to do something! I can never do anything well enough to please her! She wouldn't have liked the way I cleaned up the floor.

PASTOR: Anything else?

MR. BLACKRIGHT: (with a sly smile) Well, I suppose I knew that if I waited a little while she'd do it.

This final insight was a bright ray of hope to the counselor. The same was true of Mrs. Blackright's admission, in an early interview, that sometimes she pressured Mr. Blackright just to see how far she could push him, not because she particularly wanted what she was pushing for. These admissions, *in the presence of the other,* showed a capacity for honesty and an abandonment of the use of projection, indicating basic areas of personality health in the Blackrights. Gradually Mr. Blackright began to recognize his procrastination and his "forgetting" as countermanipulative mechanisms to resist Mrs. Blackright's aggressive manipulation. Mr. Blackright's maladaptive coping devices proved to be almost identical with the ones used by his mother to cope with his "perfectionistic" father. When this became apparent, the minister introduced the concept of the role image which "all of us bring to our marriages."

The self-defeating consequences of the Blackrights' power struggle gradually became obvious to them. They saw that the more Mrs. Blackright nagged and pushed, the more Mr. Blackright tended to retaliate by passive-aggressive bungling, forgetting, and procrastination. This made her need to control him all the more frantic, and so the vicious cycle whirled on. In the spilled juice incident, the minister pointed out that the way each responded brought out the very side of the other which each disliked most.

The Blackrights' division of labor had produced a continuing battle. Her unconscious image of the "good" husband who helped with the dishes (her father) and his image of the husband who avoided all housework as "unmanly" (his father) brought them into head-on conflict. His refusal to help with the dishes registered with her as lack of love. Her interest in working in the yard registered with him as criticism of his competence as a male and an invasion of his area of responsibility. In each other's presence they gradually connected their feelings with role images derived from their childhoods. As a result, the pressure of these feelings gradually diminished and they were able to experiment with new divisions of labor. A major breakthrough occurred when Mr. Blackright, without thinking about it, *washed his own cup and saucer!*

Finances had been another battleground for the Blackrights. In contrast with his passive stance in other areas, Mr. Blackright was irrationally authoritarian in this area. He would criticize her severely for making a "foolish" seventy-five cent purchase. A major explosion occurred when he discovered that she had a secret bank account.[21] The function in Mr. Blackright's psychic economy of his attempted domination was that of preserving a sense of manliness modeled after his father. During a counseling session, while reflecting on his financial authoritarianism, he mused, "When I feel that she is dominating me, I hear my father saying, 'My son is a weakling. He's let himself be dominated by a woman.' " Mrs. Blackright, at this point, admitted that her aggressiveness probably was related to her fear of being dependent on a man. Yet, she continued, "I want him to be stronger and more responsible." These flashes of insight, as they brought awareness of their *inner* conflicts, had a gradual liberating effect in their relationship. Their need to force each other into the mold of one or the other of their parents was lessened. They began to change as the pressure of the other to *make* them change was reduced. Furthermore, they began to face and accept the fact that some inadequacies in their spouses probably were not going to change ("So why fight it?" Mrs. Blackright said) and that they could have a good marriage in spite of these. It should be emphasized that the *value* of the Blackrights' new understanding of themselves and their relationship was increased by the fact that *both* were participating in the discovery process.

The minister was not at all timid about *confronting* them with the effects of their manipulative and (in the case of Mr. Blackright) irresponsible behavior. This direct approach helped them to recognize and interrupt their negative cycles. The minister encouraged each person to decide what constituted *responsible behavior* on his part, in particular situations. Occasionally they were given "homework" as a form of action therapy. In the early stages this consisted of such suggestions as a certain pamphlet or book chapter to read (which was later discussed in counseling) or a list (of things they had once enjoyed doing together, for example) to be worked out *jointly* between sessions. Later in counseling, the "assignment" tended to consist of encouragement to experiment between sessions with the new ways of handling their

[21] This was a way of defeating his control in the area of finances and of reducing her fear of dependency on a male figure.

problems which they had discussed during the sessions. Such assignments tend to make for the implementation of a healthy emphasis on working to *change behavior as well as feelings.* Psychologist O. Hobart Mowrer has put the matter clearly:

> In one sense, feelings do control behavior; but it is equally true, in another sense, behavior controls feelings. It is probably too much of an oversimplification to assume that, for example, merely *acting* happy *makes* one happy; but it can hardly be denied that acting in certain ways brings gratifying reactions from others, and that acting in other ways has the reverse effect. Certainly in our generation there has been a too primal emphasis on how we *feel,* rather than upon how we *do.*[22]

Gradually Mr. Blackright became able to take a stand for what he wanted, instead of using covert aggression. Mrs. Blackright became less dominating as she discovered that she liked his new strength, that it was safe to depend on him, and that it "feels better not to have to run everything." Both were beginning to experience the satisfactions of *positive* reciprocity in their behavior. As their healthy needs were better satisfied, they tended to relinquish their relationship-damaging behavior.

Their sex life improved as they began to affirm their masculinity and femininity, respectively, and as they gradually abandoned the power struggle which had also dominated that area of their relationship. The minister encouraged them to discuss with each other what gave each particular pleasure and to develop a playful, mutually gratifying sex life. Improvement in this area made sex a positive, fulfilling force in their entire relationship. A *glow* replaced the *shadow* which had been over their marriage.

The maturing of the Blackrights was evident in their increasing ability to plan *together* and make compromises between their respective desires, without feeling they had lost their identity by "giving in" to the other. They were able, for the first time in their marriage, to decide on and implement a mutually agreeable vacation plan.

It is significant that the disciplining of the Blackrights' three young children, which had been a major battleground, was the area which responded most slowly to the role-relationship changes in the parents. Relationship with one's children is an area in which archaic feelings

[22] From *Critical Incidents in Psychotherapy,* ed. by S. W. Standal and Raymond J. Corsini (Englewood Cliffs, N.J.: Prentice-Hall, 1959), p. 81.

from relationships with one's parents often exercise powerful unconscious influences. This was the case with the Blackrights.

Maturation of the Blackrights' relationship allowed them to develop richer relationships within their "extended family"—the circle of those relatives and friends to whom a couple spontaneously turns in crisis. They broke out of their ingrown, family narcissism and became more interested in the neighborhood, community, and the world around them. Their church participation became less compulsive but much more satisfying in terms of interpersonal relationships. By achieving greater independence from their internalized parental images, they were freed to establish more meaningful contemporary relationships. To a considerable extent the Blackrights had "put away childish things" in their marriage and had become "sensitive and responsive to the needs of others." Their negative, self-perpetuating cycles of mutual frustration were being replaced by positive, self-perpetuating cycles of mutual need-satisfaction.[23]

THE COUNSELOR'S ROLE

In this type of counseling the minister must take an active role. I agree with the view that "if joint interviews are to be constructive, the counselor must assume responsibility for establishing limits, structure, balance, and focus during the interview." [24] Dean Johnson has pointed to one of the dangers of counselor passivity:

> If by being passive, the counselor allows the client to talk without direction, and thus fails to guide the interview, the client may anticipate that by pouring out his difficulties he will be able to shift the burden of them onto the counselor, who will then arrive at solutions for him.[25]

The Blackrights' minister was, in Sullivan's phrase, a "participant observer," but more, an "observant participant." He was a *referee* who saw that each person had a fair chance to express his feelings and views, and a *coach* who helped them learn how to play a more constructive game of "marriage." He was *teacher* and *advisor* who recommended things they should do to hasten their progress toward a more mature

[23] The counseling in this case took place on a once-a-week basis for about three months, biweekly for another four months, and then on an occasional basis for about a year.

[24] Goodwin and Mudd, in *Marriage Counseling in Medical Practice*, p. 279.

[25] *Marriage Counseling: Theory and Practice*, p. 62.

relationship. He was a *communicator* who by his own openness concerning his feelings helped them to deal honestly with theirs. He was a *communication-facilitator* who helped them practice the art of effective, meaning-transmitting communication. He was an *accepting authority figure* who confronted them with the consequences of their immaturities and irresponsibilities. He was a *pastor* supporting them by his empathic concern. By his understanding of what was happening dynamically between them, he was an *awareness stimulator*. He was a *reality tester* for them, allowing them to check their perceptions of the realities of their relationship against his. He was a *detective of behavior*, arousing their curiosity about the deeper meaning of their feelings and behavior by his concerned, penetrating curiosity. He was a *guide* who helped them explore the intricacies of their relationship. Most of all he was a *warm human being*, a friend who was reaching out, *not* down, to help them.

Being actively involved as a participant does *not* mean making decisions for the counselees, doing for them what they could do for themselves, or pushing them toward prefabricated "solutions" to their difficulties. To illustrate, if a person asks, "Should I get a divorce?" it is important to accept his feeling of desiring authoritative advice, but then (gently but firmly) make it plain that this is a decision that is too complex and personal for *anyone* else to make. The counselor's role, as it is then interpreted, is to help the person examine alternatives, face the consequences of various paths, and gain a greater degree of objectivity so that *he* can make a wiser decision.

In marriage counseling the counselor's function is not to "save the marriage" in every case, but rather to help the parties discover and do whatever gives the greatest promise of maximizing the personality values involved. In some cases, a relationship is so irreversibly destructive to personality values that a divorce is the only hope of salvaging anything interpersonally constructive. Divorce represents a failure, but there is no reason to compound the harm by continuing the person-damaging interaction (which is a marriage in name only), after repeated and strenuous efforts to revive the marital corpse fail. In such cases, the pastor should make himself readily available for pre-divorce and post-divorce counseling, aimed at minimizing the destructive effects on both children and adults.[26] Hopefully, such counseling will help prepare the persons for more constructive (need-satisfying) relationships when remarriage occurs (as it does for two thirds of divorced women and three fourths of divorced men).

Unlike the Blackrights, many people come to the minister after their relationship has disintegrated beyond repair or nearly so. Seeing the minister is a kind of last resort, a way of salving their consciences by "having counseling" or by playing the Bernian game, "See How Hard I've Tried." When things have moved far along toward a divorce, the minister should try to interrupt the process by asking for a moratorium on all legal procedures. It is usually futile to attempt reconciliation in the midst of lawyers' maneuverings.[27] If necessary, the minister should try to block a couple's headlong plunge toward divorce by confronting them with the fact that they are proceeding without discovering whether their marriage *can* be reconstructed on a basis that will be more satisfying to both parties. A postponement of legal procedures can sometimes be obtained by pointing out: "You can always go ahead with a divorce, if we discover that your relationship is not reconstructable. You may feel little hope, but I strongly recommend that you participate in at least six months of *serious* counseling in order to give yourselves a fair chance to receive the benefits of counseling." In cases where "emotional divorce" has already occurred, it is well to use the extended "reconciliation session," recommended by Charles Stewart, to see if the parties can come to a mutual decision to make a "new start" and attempt reconstruction of their relationship.[28]

SHORT-TERM MARRIAGE COUNSELING VERSUS MARITAL THERAPY

The case of the Blackrights was presented to illustrate the rich possibilities of the role-relationship approach. In the light of its duration and intensity the counseling which occurred should probably be de-

[26] See Chapter 11 for a discussion of minimizing the emotional trauma to children. For a full discussion of "divorce counseling," see Charles W. Stewart's *The Minister as Marriage Counselor,* pp. 114-31. J. G. Emerson, Jr.'s *Divorce, the Church, and Remarriage* (Philadelphia: Westminster Press, 1961) deals with the positions of the churches on this matter. Walter T. Winter's *Divorce and You* (New York: Crowell-Collier, 1963) summarizes a wealth of information regarding the legal aspects of divorce.

[27] This is one of the "ground rules" for marriage counseling recommended by Charles Stewart, *The Minister as Marriage Counselor,* p. 106.

[28] *Ibid.*, pp. 94-113.

scribed as "marital therapy." Fortunately for busy pastors, many couples can be helped by briefer counseling aimed merely at restoring communication and helping them pull out of tailspins of destructive interaction. This is particularly true of moderately sound marriages that have been thrown off keel by severe family crises. Extreme frustrations lead to personal attacks, which produce counterattack and spiraling resentments. As indicated in the discussion of the Court of Conciliation Counseling Service (see Chapter 5), the intervention of a firm, accepting authority figure can often help such marriages in a relatively few sessions.

There are some people who seek pastoral marriage counseling whose underlying personalities are so disturbed that a role-relationship approach (brief or extended) is bound to fail. If the minister discovers that certain persons are incapable of responding to his use of the role-relationship method, he may shift to individual counseling aimed at resolving intrapsychic conflicts, or he may refer them to a Family Service Association center for more extended family therapy. If he is convinced that they need individual psychotherapy, he may refer them to a mental health clinic or competent psychotherapist. Intensive psychotherapy on an individual and/or group basis may eventually help such persons rejuvenate or abandon their sick marriages.

The Blackrights illustrate a successful counseling case. Many marriage counseling relationships do not have such happy results. Marriage is a complex human relationship and marital problems are often exceedingly difficult to treat. Even the well-trained minister frequently faces his finitude in being confronted with the fact that there are many people he cannot help. In other cases he can help in only limited ways—e.g., assisting them in achieving a more constructive perspective on a situation which defies major alteration.

THE ROLE-RELATIONSHIP VERSUS THE PARALLEL APPROACH

The role-relationship method of marriage counseling is better adapted to the work of the counseling pastor than is the other major approach—*parallel counseling* of each partner with the goal of resolving neurotic inner conflicts. The role-relationship *orientation* can, of course, be applied with profit to both couple and parallel individual counseling. Some combination of the two methods is often necessary.

The approach which aims at helping a marriage by resolving inner conflicts in individual sessions has these drawbacks:

(1) It is time consuming.

(2) The more strongly motivated party can achieve significant insight without its producing a more need-satisfying relationship.

(3) Counseling may produce personality changes in one or both persons which drive a wedge between them.

(4) Seldom are both parties motivated strongly enough to stay with insight-oriented counseling long enough to allow it to be effective.

(5) The partners often continue to act out their inner conflicts in the neurotic interaction of the marriage in a way that blocks constructive personality changes. Direct focus on the interaction tends to interrupt this acting out.

(6) If the two persons are seen on a continuing basis in separate sessions, they may use what the minister says (in distorted form) to attack each other. This can have disastrous effects on the counseling relationships. When distortions or misunderstandings occur during couple counseling, they can be rectified directly in the presence of all three parties.

The goals of role-relationship are more achievable in short-term pastoral counseling. This approach tends to avoid many of the pitfalls of the counseling-for-personality-change approach.

RECOMMENDED READING

Charles W. Stewart, *The Minister as Marriage Counselor.* (Nashville: Abingdon Press, 1961). A role-relationship oriented approach. The place to begin one's reading in this area.

Additional Books on the Techniques of Marriage Counseling

W. L. Carrington, *The Healing of Marriage* (Great Neck, N.Y.: Channel Press, 1961)

R. Lofton Hudson, *Marital Counseling* (Englewood Cliffs, N.J.: Prentice-Hall, 1963)

Dean Johnson, *Marriage Counseling: Theory and Practice* (Englewood Cliffs, N.J.: Prentice-Hall, 1961)

J. K. Morris, *Marriage Counseling, A Manual for Ministers* (Englewood Cliffs, N.J.: Prentice-Hall, 1965)

Emily H. Mudd, *The Practice of Marriage Counseling* (New York: Association Press, 1951)

Books on Marital Interaction

Nathan W. Ackerman, *The Psychodynamics of Family Life* (New York: Basic Books, 1958)

Victor Eisenstein, ed., *Neurotic Interaction in Marriage* (New York: Basic Books, 1956)

Books on the Sexual Aspects of Marriage

Dorothy W. Baruch and Hyman Miller, *Sex in Marriage, New Understandings* (New York: Harper & Row, 1962)

Jerome and Julia Rainer, *Sexual Pleasure in Marriage* (New York: Julian Messner, 1959)

———, *Sexual Adventure in Marriage* (New York: Julian Messner, 1965)

REALITY-PRACTICE SESSIONS

PARISHIONERS' ROLES: (Two persons are required. Invite one or more wives to join the group for this session.) You are Mr. and Mrs. Blackright, prior to counseling. Try to feel your way into their problems in relating. Mrs. Blackright contacts the minister by phone for counseling. Let your roles develop naturally rather than trying to follow the development described in this chapter. If you prefer, take the roles of a couple whose marital problems are well known to you personally.[29]

[29] The following cases from Cryer and Vayhinger, *Casebook in Pastoral Counseling* will be found useful as starting points for reality-practice sessions on marriage counseling: Case No. 15, "Unfaithful Husband," pp. 93-98; Case No. 17, "Marriage Breaking Up," pp. 103-9; Case No. 18, "Post-divorce Counseling," pp. 108-13; Case No. 14, "Protestant-Catholic Marriage," pp. 89-93; Case No. 52, "Deserted Wife," pp. 283-88; Case No. 16, "Conflict with Drinking Husband," pp. 98-102.

PASTOR'S ROLE: Practice the couple counseling approach, concentrating on understanding how each feels, giving both opportunities to express themselves on each topic. Then try to summarize the big feelings of both on the major points of conflict.

OBSERVER-EVALUATOR: Be aware of the interaction during the counseling, with particular reference to the "minister's" success in eliciting the feelings of both parties and in avoiding preferential responses.

Give each member of the reality-practice team an opportunity to master the couple counseling method.

7

Family Group Therapy and Transactional Analysis

The family therapist would seem to be arguing thus: psychopathology in the individual is a product of the way he deals with intimate relations, the way they deal with him, and the way other family members involve him in their relations with each other. Further, the appearance of symptomatic behavior in an individual is necessary for the continued functioning of a particular family system. Therefore, changes in the individual can only occur if the family system changes, and resistance to change in an individual centers in the influence of the family as a group. Most techniques of Family Therapy center in shifting the focus from the identified patient to the family and then resolving the problems in family relationships. At that point the individuals in the family undergo change.

—Jay Haley [1]

Family group therapy—the simultaneous treatment of an entire family—is one of the most promising developments in current methods of helping troubled persons. During the last decade there has been within the counseling professions, a virtual explosion of interest in this approach. The impact of family therapy methods has caused a radical shift in the practice of many counselors and therapists, changing the primary focus from individual to family-organism therapy. A variety of distinctive methods or styles of family therapy have been developed within the span of a few years.[2]

[1] "Whither Family Therapy," *Family Process,* March, 1962, p. 70.

[2] *Ibid.,* pp. 69-100. Haley described eight different schools of family therapy, applying humorous and perceptive labels.

RELEVANCE FOR THE MINISTER

Family therapy offers rich possibilities for use by the counseling pastor. Few, if any, of the emerging counseling methods are so directly relevant to the clergyman's setting, role, and function. For the following reasons family therapy can be used effectively in the minister's counseling:

(1) It is often helpful on a relatively short-term basis. Within six to twelve sessions many families can acquire skills which they then use on their own to improve their life together.

(2) It is often more efficient and effective than individual counseling since it deals directly with the family source of individual problems.

(3) It functions on a role-relationship level, thus avoiding many of the complications of counseling focused on intrapsychic conflicts.

(4) It is a natural approach for the pastor since he normally has ongoing relationships with whole family units. By means of family therapy methods the mental health professions are now using a therapeutic opportunity which clergymen have had, but not utilized fully, through the centuries. Family therapy approaches give the minister new ways of using his natural pastoral advantages as a family-centered professional with a direct entrée to many family circles.

THE RATIONALE FOR FAMILY THERAPY

The family is a *social organism*, for better or for worse. Nathan W. Ackerman suggests that the term "organism" connotes the biological core of the family, its qualities of living process and functional unity, and its natural life history—"a period of germination, a birth, a growth and development, a capacity to adapt to change and crisis, a slow decline, and finally, dissolution of the old family into the new." [3] Whatever affects one part of the family organism automatically affects all parts, just as an infected, injured, or well-functioning hand influences the entire body. Ackerman declares:

> The family is the strategic center for understanding of emotional disturbances and also for intervention on those psychic forces in human relations that have to do both with health and illness. In other words, the family group can make

[3] *The Psychodynamics of Family Life*, p. 17.

or break mental health. It has this power, insofar as it influences every aspect of human development, and of human relations. [4]

As an organism a family has its unique psychological identity. The marital pair identity becomes the core for the expanding "family identity" as children are added.

It is the interaction, merging, and redifferentiation of the individualities of the partners of this marital pair that mold the identity of the new family. Just as a child's personality internalizes something of each parent and also evolves something new, so too the identity of a new family incorporates something of the self-image of each marital partner and the image of their respective families-of-origin and also develops something unique and new. . . . The psychological identity of the marital pair shapes the child, but the child also shapes the parental pair to his needs.[5]

The personality health or disturbance of an individual is to a considerable extent an expression of the emotional climate of the family and the quality of its need-satisfying network of interaction. An individual's symptoms are the product of a total family organism which is not meeting the personality needs of its members. As Virginia Satir has observed, the pain of the "identified patient" (the one who is "sick," "neurotic," "delinquent," etc.) is an overt expression of the covert pain which the whole family is suffering in its relationships. The "negative complementarity" of a disturbed family organism has been observed by many clinicians. Psychoanalyst Martin Grotjahn describes the complementary neuroses which often obtain among members of a family,[6] producing mutual reinforcement of neurotic behavior. Apparently all members in a disturbed family derive crucial emotional gains from the identified patient's sickness. The interpersonal balance in such families appears to be based on this unconscious family contract: "We all agree that this one of us will be 'sick' ('delinquent,' 'alcoholic') so that the rest of us can continue to function." These are cases in point—the alcoholic's wife who becomes disturbed when he achieves sobriety, the "good family" which has chosen, unconsciously, a black sheep to

[4] "Emergence of Family Psychotherapy on the Present Scene," in *Contemporary Psychotherapies*, p. 231.

[5] Ackerman, *The Psychodynamics of Family Life*, pp. 21-22.

[6] See *Psychoanalysis and the Family Neurosis* (New York: W. W. Norton, 1960).

act out the family's forbidden impulses, and the schizophrenic's family in which the relative adequacy of the other members' functioning is contingent on the sick member staying sick. These are examples of extreme negative family complementarity. Negative complementarity obtains in all disturbed families, to some degree, even though it may appear that only one member is disturbed. Families usually seek outside help only when the member who bears their collective conflicts comes to the attention of persons outside the family.

Since families interact as organisms, it is logical to help dysfunctional families [7] as units. This is precisely what family therapy does. The pastor who grasps the profound implications of the family organism point of view will find that it makes a dramatic difference in his marriage and family counseling. For example, he will tend to focus on *total family interaction* rather than simply on the ways in which parents influence their children. Parents often are threatened, in traditional parent-child therapy, by being reminded by implication that the sins of the fathers are visited on their children psychologically. As Bell states, "In family therapy we have to think, also, that the sins of the children are visited on the parents." [8] Any minister who has observed the ways in which some parents are manipulated by their children can vouch for the accuracy of this statement. Family therapy helps the whole family become responsible for improving its interdependent web of need-satisfying relationships.

In all counseling the minister is actually dealing with an interlocking network of persons, whether or not he is aware of this fact. In individual counseling he has access to only one facet of the total interpersonal network. The limitations of this are roughly analogous to those which a physician would face if he attempted to help an ill person by examining and treating only his arm.[9] Couple counseling and family counseling are methods which give direct access to larger portions of the total network, permitting more comprehensive understanding and help to be given to the persons involved.

[7] Families which are failing to meet the normal personality needs of their members, to a pronounced degree.

[8] *Family Group Therapy*, p. 49. Bell states: "What each parent and each child may be is the result of the family totality" (p. 4).

[9] In spite of the limitations of this analogy (the person obviously has more functional autonomy and ability to form new relationships than does an arm), it communicates a fundamental truth—the *essential* interdependence of persons.

THE GOALS OF FAMILY THERAPY

The goals of family therapy are almost identical with those of role-relationship marriage counseling. The master goal is to reduce negative complementarity (mutual frustration) and to enhance positive complementarity in family interaction. This means making the relationships more mutually satisfying of personality needs. The *operational goals* of family therapy include:

(1) Reopening the lines of intrafamilial communication so that feelings, wishes, goals, and values can be discussed.

(2) Interrupting the self-perpetuating spiral of mutual need-deprivation and attack.

(3) Increasing the family members' awareness of the roles which various ones play and are expected by others to play in their interaction.

(4) Becoming aware of their essential interdependence and identity as a family.

(5) Having practice in thinking together about sources of pain and pleasure in family interaction.

(6) Beginning to experiment with more flexible and mutually satisfying roles and with more responsible ways of relating.

This approach focuses simultaneously on *feelings* and *functioning*, seeking to enhance both meaningful communication and constructive behavior. It keeps asking, "What can be done to help this family change relationships within it so that individuals may be free to change?"

BELL'S APPROACH TO FAMILY THERAPY

From the various family therapy methods, I will present a synopsis of two which lend themselves to use by ministers—the approaches of John E. Bell and Virginia M. Satir.[10] Bell holds weekly sessions with the parents, children age nine and older,[11] and with any other persons who are living with the family. In his experience family therapy tends to move through these stages:

> 1. The treatment begins with an *orientation phase*. Two orientation interviews are held: one with the parents alone, . . . the other with the whole family present at the first conference attended by the children.

[10] Bell, a psychologist, is Acting Chief, Mental Health Services, Region IX of the Public Health Service. Haley calls his approach the "dignified school." Satir, a social worker, is Director of Training, Family Project, Mental Research Institute, Palo Alto, Calif.

[11] Some family therapists include younger children, down to age five.

2. Treatment proceeds into a *child-centered phase*. During this period the child is held in the center of the family group, and he is given the chance to air his complaints and to suggest the changes in family procedure that he would regard as desirable.

3. The *parent-child interaction* emerges next. This phase is characterized by an examination of the dimensions of the parent-child relationships, especially of much previously unverbalized emotion associated with the ways in which children experience the parent and vice versa.

4. The center of therapy shifts to the *father-mother interaction.* In the presence of the children, toward the later stages of the treatment, the parents begin to discuss openly their own emotional interrelationships and problems.

5. As the parents approach resolution of their difficulties, emphasis gradually shifts to the *sibling interaction,* a stage in which the relationships between the children in the family are subjected to examination.

6. Finally, we observe what has been called the *family-centered phase.* In this concluding stage, there is evidence of two forms of family functioning: family activity in which all members of the group participate according to the commonly accepted and generally approved roles for each; and family support for each member in the activities that take him away from the family.[12]

According to Bell the stages of this pattern tend to emerge in the natural flow of therapy. They do not represent an agenda to be imposed on the process by the therapist. In my experience it has been impossible to predict the order in which the stages will emerge. Families often go back and forth among several focuses of interaction, so that even the term "stage" is somewhat misleading.[13]

During the first session with the parents alone, Bell works out such practical details as time and frequency of meeting, obtains their descriptions of the problem, and orients them to the goals of family therapy. He emphasizes the importance of allowing the children to talk freely, particularly during the early sessions. He asks the parents to limit their own talking and to grant whatever changes they feel are feasible in response to the children's requests.

The therapist functions as a coach and referee. He stays outside the psychological boundaries of the family by not taking over decision-

[12] Bell, *Family Group Therapy,* p. 6.

[13] Focusing on sibling problems often occurs during the child-centered stage, rather than later, in my experience.

making roles, which rightly belong to the family, or becoming a parent-substitute, which would weaken the parents' position in the family. He facilitates communication, supports those who have difficulty participating, helps the family explore communication blocks and become aware of the multiple roles each is playing. He helps them express hidden feelings, wishes, hopes, fears, in order to free themselves from communication paralysis. He may interpret what has been said or comment on the interaction during the sessions, in order to extend the limits of the family's awareness of its patterns of relating. He makes sure that everyone has an opportunity to participate fully. The therapist aims at strengthening the family group as a group by facilitating healthy interaction. He does not give interpretations of depth, intrapsychic material. Instead, his interpretations are of four kinds: *reflective* of what the family is doing or saying; *connective*—pointing to unrecognized, causal, or reciprocal links in their interaction; *reconstructive*—providing a context for present behavior by recalling the history of family relationships; and *normative*—commenting on parallel or contrasting relationships or behavior in other families to give perspective.

In my use of family therapy I have found it helpful to employ judicious *confrontation* of the whole family by holding up my perception of the realities of their relationships. This is a constructive procedure only after strong feelings of trust in the counselor have developed. I also use *action therapy*, recommending certain things which the family might do together, on an experimental basis, between sessions.

SATIR'S CONJOINT FAMILY THERAPY

Virginia M. Satir's approach emphasizes the marital relationship as the axis around which all other family relationships are formed. The "identified patient"—e.g., a disturbed child—is the family member who is most obviously affected by the pained marital relationship. Relationships are pained because they are dysfunctional. The distorted communication patterns of a family reveal the nature of its underlying problems. Dysfunctional persons did not learn in childhood to communicate effectively because of low self-esteem and distorted parent-child communication. Dysfunctional "parenting" produces dysfunctional families, which perpetuate distorted communication patterns.

The touchstone of Satir's therapy is the concept of *maturation*, defined as "the state in which a given human being is fully in charge of himself." [14] A relatively mature person characteristically behaves in ways which are "functional" in that they enable him to deal with the world in which he lives in a competent and precise way. Functional or mature persons can resolve conflicts, solve problems, and compromise different-ness because they are able to communicate effectively. Making families more functional is the goal of Satir's form of therapy. The functional or mature person will:

(1) Manifest himself clearly to others.
(2) Be in touch with signals from his internal self, thus letting himself know openly what he thinks and feels.
(3) Be able to see and hear what is outside himself as differentiated from himself.
(4) Behave toward another person as someone separate from himself and unique.
(5) Treat the presence of different-ness as an opportunity to learn and explore rather than as a threat or a signal for conflict.
(6) Deal with persons and situations in their context, in terms of "how it is" rather than how he wishes it were or expects it to be.
(7) Accept responsibility for what he feels, thinks, hears and sees, rather than denying it or attributing it to others.
(8) Have techniques for openly negotiating the giving, receiving and checking of meaning between himself and others.[15]

In contrast, a dysfunctional person will deliver conflicting messages, be unable to perceive the "here and now" accurately because of distortions from the past, and will not be able to "check out" his perceptions to see if they tally with the actual situation or the intended meaning of another. He will lack the communication tools for handling conflict constructively.

During the first session of conjoint family therapy, Satir describes their task:

As you know, we work with families here. And we have found that when one member has pain, all share this pain in some way. Our task is to work out ways

[14] *Conjoint Family Therapy, A Guide to Theory and Technique*, p. 91.
[15] *Ibid.*, p. 92.

> in which everyone can get more pleasure from family life. Because I am sure that at one time this family had better times.[16]

By making increased family satisfaction the explicit goal, she increases motivation and hope and decreases fear of therapy.

Satir holds that family therapists must be active in structuring and guiding the sessions, otherwise they become "one of the family" or a "ping-pong ball." She recommends that the therapist structure the first two sessions (held either with or without the children) by taking a detailed "family life chronology." This serves several functions:

(1) It reduces the fear with which families enter therapy by giving a sense of direction.

(2) It helps to lessen their despair and revive hope by reminding them of past successes.

(3) It gives the therapist his first clues concerning how dysfunctional the marital relationship is.

(4) It takes the attention away from the identified patient where it has been lodged unproductively.

(5) It allows family members to talk about the pain in their relationships and permits the therapist to gradually introduce key concepts in the process of being a family chronicler. In other words, therapeutic change *begins* during this family history taking.

> If illness is seen to derive from inadequate methods of communication (*by which we mean all interactional behavior*), it follows that therapy will be seen as an attempt to improve these methods. . . . The emphasis will be on correcting discrepancies in communication and teaching ways to achieve more fitting joint outcomes.[17]

The therapist helps families to take the risk of looking clearly at themselves and their actions, often for the first time. He does this by reducing their fears,[18] building self-esteem (e.g., "You have feelings,

[16] *Ibid.*, p. 117. The final sentence of this statement reminds the family that they were able to cope more effectively at some stage in the past and, by implication, that they *can* do it again.

[17] *Ibid.*, p. 96. Italics mine. All interpersonal behavior is an attempt to communicate.

[18] The threat element in therapy is reduced in various ways, including the therapist's statement that at the end of five sessions they will reevaluate what has been accomplished and decide where they need to go from there. He also indicates that the total process will not drag on indefinitely, but that they will have a certain number of sessions within which to work together.

too, you know"), labeling assets, and encouraging each person to communciate his feelings (e.g., "We need your reactions and experiences. Only you can tell us what you saw and heard"). The therapist helps the person to see how he looks to others, tries to make sure that no one speaks for anyone else, relates silence to covert control, interprets anger as hurt, and helps the parents see how past models (their parents) influence their current behavior. He helps the family members unscramble garbled messages, complete gaps in messages, and attempts to make his own communication a model of openness, honesty, and undefensiveness. Fundamentally, the therapist is a teacher of need-satisfying, conflict-resolving communication.

THE PASTOR'S USE OF FAMILY THERAPY

Family therapy is not an approach for ministers with little training in counseling. To be effective it requires a substantial degree of interpersonal awareness and skill in counseling. It is not, however, beyond the potential reach of a pastor who possesses good native aptitudes, has had some training in counseling (especially clinical training), and has the capacity to learn from his experience. Here are some steps by which such a minister can acquire the family therapy method as a usable tool:

Step 1: Strive to increase your skill as a role-relationship couple counselor. Family therapy is an extension of the same basic approach but is more demanding because it involves additional people.[19]

Step 2: Master the theoretical material contained in Bell's monograph and Satir's book (see Recommended Reading). Both contain case material which helps to bring family therapy methods alive. Only a sketchy introduction to these approaches has been presented in this chapter. It is my hope, however, that enough has been said to whet the reader's interest in exploring these important new methods further.

Step 3: Begin with a three-member family which is not severely disturbed and which does not occupy a crucial position in your church's power structure. The need to succeed (and the fear of failure) with pillar-of-the-church types tends to arouse more anxiety in the coun-

[19] Couple counseling involves three interactional axes (pastor-husband, pastor-wife, husband-wife) of which the pastor must have some awareness. Family counseling with a couple plus one child doubles the interactional axes (six). A couple plus two children increases the axes to ten, and a couple plus three children raises it to fifteen.

selor than is compatible with the level of awareness required in effective counseling, especially with families.

Step 4: If possible, establish a continuing relationship with a consultant from one of the mental health professions who is experienced in family therapy.[20] Check the development of your family counseling relationships regularly and in detail with this person. This practice will accelerate growth in this skill.

Step 5: Tape family group sessions (with their permission) for your study and reflection between sessions and for use with your consultant. You may be able to recognize some of your mistakes by hearing a playback.

BERNE'S APPROACH TO THERAPY

Eric Berne, a California psychiatrist, has developed a conceptual system for understanding and improving interpersonal relationships which has aroused widespread interest among psychotherapists and marriage counselors. It offers the pastor a set of new tools which are useful in many types of counseling, particularly in marriage counseling. His therapy has two dimensions—*structural analysis,* the identification of the three basic "ego states," Parent, Adult, and Child; and *transactional analysis,* the analysis of interaction between persons including their "pastimes," "games," and "scripts."

When the Bernean approach is used in marriage counseling, the basic concepts should not be presented until strong rapport is established and the presenting problems explored in a preliminary way.[21] Here is an example of how this approach may be presented:

PASTOR: We're beginning to get a clearer picture of some of the patterns in your ways of relating that have caused pain in your marriage. I believe it would be helpful, at this point, for me to share some ideas which I have found to be useful to couples like yourselves. We may be using them in our talks together, and you may find them helpful between sessions, too.

[20] Many competent psychotherapists are not familiar with or adept at family therapy.

[21] A pastoral counselor who uses Bernean tools regularly in both individual and marriage counseling reports that he endeavors to have each person "become aware of the various parts of himself and how they interact *before* I show the pictures of PAC." This is usually done in the third or fourth session.

COUPLE: (Indicates interest.)

PASTOR: These ideas can help all three of us understand your relationship more fully. First, let me draw a diagram. (Takes a sheet of paper and draws the circles as in figure 1.[22]) This represents the three sides of your personalities or mine. The P in the top circle stands for our inner "Parent." Each of us has a Parent part of his personality, which is the way we saw one or both of our parents as children. Our inner Parent has two sides—the *nurturing* side which lets us take care of our children (or our spouse when he is sick), and the *prohibitive* side which says "No" and sets limits much as our parents did. This prohibitive or prejudicial side is the part of us that gets witchy and dominating occasionally. Know what I mean?

WIFE: Yes, I catch myself using the same shrewish tone with my children, when they get in my hair, that my mother uses when she is annoyed with me because I don't drop everything and run when she calls.

PASTOR: That's your prohibitive Parent voice. We all have a whole set of attitudes, feelings, and behavior patterns that resemble our parents as we perceived them early in our lives.

HUSBAND: Yeh, and do I get the witchy treatment when I get slightly loaded and fool around a bit at a party!

PASTOR: I'm glad you mentioned that.[23] It has to do with the bottom circle —with the C. Each of us has a playful, creative, pleasure-seeking side of his personality. Eric Berne, the psychiatrist who devised this approach, calls this the "Child ego state." The everyday way of saying it is that "everybody has a little boy or girl inside him." When this side of us is activated, it is as though we are in the same state of mind as we were at a certain age. Our feelings and ways of responding to others are like they were at a certain stage of childhood. Did you ever notice how you feel and behave when

[22] Figure 1 — Figure 2

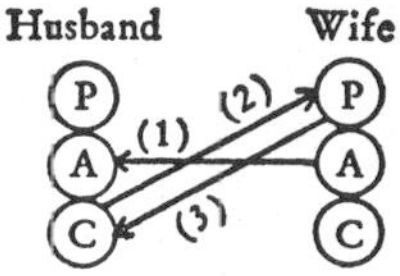

Figure 1: (P) Parent; (A) Adult; (C) Child

Figure 2: Husband — Wife; (P) (A) (C) — (P) (A) (C); (1), (2), (3)

From Berne, *Transactional Analysis in Psychotherapy*, pp. 31, 93.

[23] The pastor chose not to reflect the husband's anger at this point, but rather to attempt to use the response to illustrate the Bernean approach. The man's anger continued to rise, as the next response shows.

you're called on the carpet by the boss or a policeman gives you a ticket? That's your Child side in action.

HUSBAND: Yeh, I stutter and stammer like a five-year-old—feel about two inches high. But (annoyed) what's that got to do with Jean's witchy side when I enjoy myself at a party?

WIFE: Is it that the parental side of me gets upset when Joe's child side runs wild?

HUSBAND: Aw, come on now! There you go exaggerating again!

PASTOR: You feel that Jean is making too much of the party incidents.[24]

HUSBAND: Damn right! She makes a federal case out of having a good time!

PASTOR: I wonder if you could tell me how you felt when she used the words "runs wild." [25]

HUSBAND: Made me burn! Felt like, "There the old lady goes again criticizing me unfairly!"

PASTOR: In Bernean terms, what came through to you as her nagging Parent side got a strong response from your inner Child. I might point out that the opposite happened in our last session when your inner Child, Jean, responded to Joe's "making like big daddy," as you put it. Remember that?

The pastor encourages them to express their reactions and to think of other examples of Parent-Child "transactions" in the vignettes of interaction they had discussed previously. To stimulate their thought he gives an example of P-C interaction from his own marriage: "My wife and I find that my inner Parent gets turned on when ——— and this tends to turn on her inner Child. Like the other night. . . ." Although autobiographical examples should be used sparingly, they do serve to show the counselees that the pastor is not talking *down* to them from some pedestal of mental and spiritual health.

The Child ego state is a still influential relic from our childhood. It is most apt to be activated by the presence of someone else's energized Parent ego state.

PASTOR: Most marital conflicts are variations on the Parent-Child and Child-Parent interaction themes. We could diagram what occurred a minute ago when you got mad at Jean's use of the words "runs

[24] At this point the pastor responds to the here-and-now feelings of anger.

[25] Here, the pastor is attempting (unsuccessfully at first) to activate the husband's (Adult) awareness of which ego state is dominating his feelings and behavior.

wild," Joe. (Draws another set of circles as in figure 2 in footnote 22.) The arrow (2) between your Child, Joe, and Jean's Parent shows what happened when you responded. What would have happened if I hadn't intervened by asking you to look at what was occurring?

WIFE: My parental side would have snapped back at him that I wasn't exaggerating and that he *was* behaving in an irresponsible way. (Pastor draws arrow (3) from wife's Parent to husband's Child.)

HUSBAND: And that would have turned on my Child side some more, and we would have been off to the races for two days of fighting.

PASTOR: Uh huh. The side of your personalities which lets you stand off and become aware of what was going on is represented by the middle circles—your Adult ego states. This is the part of your personality which can deal objectively and realistically with the way things are—making decisions on the basis of probable consequences. Adult to Adult relationships tend to be in line with present reality and with how it can be handled in the most satisfying and satisfactory way. Incidentally, your observation about your response to Joe's activities at parties, Jean, may have been intended as an Adult to Adult communication, as indicated by line 1, but your choice of words turned on Joe's inner Child.

WIFE: (Laughs) Maybe it *was* my Parent that chose those words!

HUSBAND: (Also laughs) Could be!

PASTOR: Well, in any case, it was your Adult sides which allowed you to interrupt the Parent-Child fight.

WIFE: Should we try to get rid of our Parent and Child sides so that our marriage will be Adult?

PASTOR: No, I can understand how you might have received that impression from what I've said. Actually, all three ego states are permanent and valuable parts of our personalities. Each has an important role in a good marriage. The Child in us is very important—it brings enjoyment and spontaneity to a relationship. Sexual enjoyment is a Child to Child relationship. Our Parent sides enable us to *be* adequate parents to our children and to nurture each other when we need help. They also provide guidelines in thousands of routine matters by giving us the "this is the way it's done" feeling. The goal of counseling is to strengthen the Adult side so that it can regulate the activities of the Parent and Child. When one's Adult is weak or inactivated, the inner Parent and/or Child usually runs things—

into the ground, I might add. Having a robust inner Adult in charge most of the time lets one keep a healthy balance among the ego states. How does all this strike you?

The above case (in condensed form) shows how the basic concepts of structural analysis can be presented in marriage counseling by using the live interaction of the session. As in this case, some couples begin to use these conceptual tools almost immediately. Others come back to them later with the counselor's encouragement. Still others simply do not respond to this approach. The counselor should be guided by the clues given by counselee responses. If a couple grasps the tools immediately, counseling progress is usually rapid.

Here is the way one couple used Bernean tools to interrupt their spiral of negative interaction. They had had a violent argument on the way to see the minister and were still seething with anger as the session began.

HUSBAND: (Pointing angrily at his wife) Let me tell you something, dear. (The word "dear" was snarled as his wife sat cowering in a semi-fetal position.)

At this point he suddenly interrupted himself and said: "That was my Parent giving your Child the business." His wife straightened up and agreed with his insight.

PASTOR: I might point out that it was your Adult which made you able to recognize and interrupt your Parent-Child interaction. You were able to get your Adult back in operation.

The practical effect of introducing this couple to the Bernean approach was to gain the cooperation of their inner Adults early in the counseling process. Their Adults became the active allies of the pastor's Adult.

TRANSACTIONAL ANALYSIS

In Berne's terms interactions between persons consist of "transactions," including *pastimes*, *games*, and *scripts*. A pastime is a transaction without ulterior motive. Common pastimes include "General Motors" (comparing cars), "Do You Know?" (so-and-so), PTA (deals with delinquents), and "Who Won?" (sports). Berne defines a game as "an ongoing series of complementary *ulterior* transactions progressing to a well-defined, predictable outcome." [26] Games are profoundly serious matters, their functions being to provide psychological "stroking," preserve psychic equilibrium, and avoid psychological intimacy. Games are essentially manipulative. They operate unconsciously. Children learn their dominant games in early relationships. "Family life and married life, as well as life in organizations of various kinds, may year after year be based on variations of the same game." [27] Almost any game can provide the scaffolding for married life, but certain games tend to be more prevalent in this setting.

The all-time favorite marriage game, "If It Weren't for You," is present in most marital wrangles. Another marital game, "Look How Hard I've Tried," is often played with an unsuspecting counselor. "Frigid Woman" is played by a wife who is sexually provocative and then rejects the husband's ardent advances. Although the husband blames the wife (part of his "payoff"), he is usually as frightened of sexual intimacy as is she. Unconsciously he chose her to protect him from facing his fear of sex. "Uproar" is a popular game for escaping sexual intimacy by pre-bedtime fights. By provoking mutual rejection both parties can avoid the feared intimacy without loss of self-esteem. "Courtroom," a three-handed marital game involving a plaintiff, a defendant, and a judge (e.g., wife, husband, counselor), begins with the plaintiff saying, "Let me tell you what he did." [28]

The usefulness of the Bernean approach in understanding family dynamics is shown in this fragment of a family group therapy session:

WIFE: For years I've had a terrible time getting him (husband) up. It takes about an hour each morning to get him out of bed. When I finally succeed, he's angry because I haven't gotten him up sooner.

HUSBAND: You have no intention of getting me up sooner.

WIFE: You really don't want to get up sooner. You just want to gripe.

HUSBAND: I just can't get up. I've always been that way.

[26] *Games People Play*, p. 48. (italics mine.) A game involves a structured series of moves (transactions) leading to a predictable prize or "payoff."

[27] *Ibid.*, p. 17.

[28] As Berne observes, some marriage counseling is a perpetual game of "Courtroom." Unless this is interrupted, nothing constructive can be accomplished.

The Parent-Child nature of this interaction is obvious. By assuming responsibility for getting him up, the wife allowed the husband to defeat her and play "If It Weren't for You" (I'd get up sooner). The husband was also playing "Wooden Leg" ("You can't expect me to run a race with a wooden leg") in his statement about having always been unable to get up. The payoff of the "I Can't Get Him Up" game, for the husband, included the abundant attention he received from his wife each morning and his avoidance of responsibility in this area of his life, which allowed him to make her fail and yet blame her for her failure. The game also enabled him to avoid facing his fear of getting out into the competitive world each day. By blaming her for his late starts he could avoid responsibility for his business failure. The payoff for her was a neurotic sense of being needed by him which helped keep her fragile self-esteem intact. It was not until the counselor could help her give up all responsibility for getting her husband out of bed that the futile game was interrupted.

Games are segments of more complex groups of transactions called *scripts,* which are unconscious master plans which determine the overall direction of a person's life. A script is a game which becomes a lifetime career. Awareness of the existence of such unconscious determinants can alert the counselor to the magnitude of the problem involved in changing the behavior resulting from them.[29]

THE GOALS AND VALUES OF BERNEAN THERAPY

The goals of Bernean therapy are on several levels. The first is social control—the interruption of destructive Child-dominated behavior by helping the person learn how to keep his Adult activated and in control most of the time. Everyone has a potentially mobilizable Adult, even the psychotic whose Child has acquired almost total control. The alcoholic, whose problems root in the domination of his behavior by his grandiose, demanding Child, can learn to keep from decommissioning his Parent and Adult by avoiding alcohol.[30]

The additional goals of Bernean-oriented marital counseling include: (a) helping the couple to give up destructive Parent-Child games; (b) making their games optional instead of compulsive; (c) adopting

[29] Script analysis is discussed in Berne's *Transactional Analysis in Psychotherapy,* pp. 116-27.

[30] Berne regards alcoholism as a five-handed game. See *Games People Play,* pp. 73-81.

more constructive and satisfying games; and (c) making their transactions complementary instead of crossed.[31] The ultimate goal, which is extremely difficult to achieve, is *game-free intimacy,* the ideal form of human living described as "autonomy." This is characterized by *awareness, spontaneity,* and *intimacy.* To the degree that a couple achieves these in their marriage, it will be a profoundly creative and fulfilling human relationship.

Here are some of the values of this approach for the pastoral counselor:

(1) It provides a fresh way of understanding human relationships—husband-wife, parent-child, pastor-parishioner, counselor-counselee, etc.—and the dynamics of individual behavior.

(2) It uses nontechnical terms (on its simpler levels) which can be readily understood by the counselee and are less threatening than technical jargon.

(3) It provides a rapid means of interrupting runaway (Parent-Child) cycles of interaction.

(4) It provides tools with which the counselee's Adult can cooperate with the counselor's Adult, during and between sessions.

(5) It encourages the conscious effort to become aware of one's ego states and games, which effort tends to strengthen the Adult through exercise.

(6) It provides a way of discovering how early life experiences continue to influence one's relationships—i.e., through one's inner Child and Parent.

(7) It is a useful adjunct in role-relationship marriage counseling and in family group counseling.

(8) It has a sane, whimsical quality which is appealing to most people.

(9) It can be used effectively in both short-term and long-term counseling.

In short, Berne is a boon to pastoral counseling. Both transactional analysis and family therapy offer remarkably rich resources for use by the skilled pastoral counselor in a relationship-centered approach.

[31] A complementary transaction is one in which both parties are responding on the same axis—Child-Child, Parent-Child, etc. Breakdowns in communication are produced by crossed transactions in which one person initiates a conversation on one axis and the other responds on a different axis.

RECOMMENDED READING

Family Group Counseling

Nathan W. Ackerman, "Emergence of Family Psychotherapy on the Present Scene," *Contemporary Psychotherapies*, Morris I. Stein, ed. (New York: The Free Press of Glencoe, 1961), pp. 228 ff.

John E. Bell, *Family Group Therapy*, Public Health Monograph 64, 1961.

Family Process, the journal on family therapy published by the Mental Health Research Institute, Palo Alto, California.

Virginia M. Satir, *Conjoint Family Therapy, A Guide to Theory and Technique* (Palo Alto, Calif.: Science and Behavior Books, 1964).

Bernean Therapy

Eric Berne, *Transactional Analysis in Psychotherapy* (New York: Grove Press, 1961) and *Games People Play* (Grove Press, 1964).

REALITY-PRACTICE SESSIONS

Family Group Counseling

PARISHIONERS' ROLES: If three or four persons are available, take the roles of a family with whose problems at least one member of the reality-practice group is thoroughly familiar.[32]

PASTOR'S ROLE: Practice family group counseling methods, using the approaches of Bell or Satir, or a combination.

Bernean Therapy

PARISHIONERS' ROLES: Two people take the roles of a couple with whose marital problems one member of the group is familiar.

PASTOR'S ROLE: Use Berne's PAC analysis in helping the couple to understand their interaction.

Observer-evaluators should be used in both these sessions.

[32] These cases from Cryer and Vayhinger, *Casebook in Pastoral Counseling*, will lend themselves to the family group counseling approach: Case No. 22, manipulative mother, passive father,. disturbed son, pp. 127-31; Case No. 23, a woman attempting to use the minister to control her family, pp. 131-35.

8

Types of Supportive Counseling

The sustaining function of the cure of souls in our day continues to be a crucially important helping ministry. . . . Everywhere today busy pastors are called upon to sustain troubled persons in, through, and beyond a plethora of hurts that brook no direct restoration. . . . Tightly knit communities once furnished friends and neighbors who could stand by in moments of shock, whereas in a society on wheels the task of providing such sustenance to urban and suburban people falls heavily upon the clergy.

—William A. Clebsch and Charles R. Jaekle[1]

Psychotherapeutic theory and practice draw a distinction between *uncovering, insight-oriented methods* of therapy on the one hand, and *supportive methods* on the other. This distinction is of major importance to the self-image and effectiveness of the counseling pastor. An understanding of its implications awakens a new appreciation for the person-helping potentialities of supportive pastoral counseling. It encourages him to develop his skill in using supportive counseling methods—methods which lend themselves naturally to the shepherding stance and to pastor-parishioner relationships. By mastering these methods a clergyman acquires the instruments for helping, during the years of his ministry, scores of persons who do not need or cannot respond to uncovering counseling approaches.

In supportive counseling the pastor uses those counseling methods which *stabilize, undergird, nurture, motivate, or guide* troubled persons, enabling them to handle their problems and relationships more

[1] *Pastoral Care in Historical Perspective,* p. 80.

constructively within whatever limits are imposed by their personality resources and circumstances. The nature of supportive counseling becomes clearer when contrasted with uncovering, insight-oriented approaches to counseling. The latter aim at basic personality changes through growth in self-awareness and self-acceptance, which occur by means of uncovering and dealing with previously hidden aspects of oneself and one's relationships. Such approaches usually focus on "depth" factors—unconscious material and early life experiences as well as current relationships. In contrast, supportive counseling does not employ uncovering methods and does not aim at depth insight or radical personality transformation. Instead, the goal is to help the person gain the strength and perspective which will allow him to use his personality resources (however limited) more effectively in coping with his life situation. Supportive counseling methods focus on here-and-now problems in living, helping the person to handle or accept these in reality-oriented ways, and thus strengthening his ability to cope in the future. They seek to help a person avoid self- or other-damaging patterns, and to increase mutual fulfillment (need satisfaction) in his relationships. Gradual personality growth often occurs in and following supportive counseling, *as a result of* a person's success in handling his problems and improving his relationships.

Both insight-oriented and supportive counseling methods depend on a strong, empathic pastor-parishioner relationship. Insight counseling uses the relationship as the *foundation* on which uncovering methods are based. The trustful quality of the relationship permits the person to deal with repressed, threatening feelings, fantasies, and memories. In supportive counseling the relationship *per se* is the primary instrument of change. Maintaining a dependable, nurturing relationship is the heart of the methodology. The specific methods, described later in this chapter, are seen as subsidiary. By relating to the pastor the parishioner is able to draw on his inner strength. This vicariously acquired ego strength allows the person to cope with his reality situation more constructively, and thereby strengthen the "muscles" of his coping abilities.

The distinction between insight-uncovering and supportive counseling is, in actual practice, usually a matter of emphasis and a choice of *primary* goals, rather than a rigid dichotomy. All effective counseling has a strong supportive dimension. "Supportive counseling" is that in which this aspect is central. In general, supportive methods are more action-oriented and involve a larger degree of counselor activity and careful use of authority than does insight counseling. In supportive counseling the pastor makes more use, than in depth (insight) counseling, of guidance, information, reassurance, inspiration, planning, asking and answering questions, and encouraging or discouraging certain forms of behavior.[2] Supportive methods are used in various types of pastoral counseling. For example, they play a key role in short-term, informal counseling, as described in Chapter 5. The present chapter will deal with supportive methods in a more comprehensive and systematic way than was possible in that context.

How does supportive counseling relate to general pastoral care—the network of sustaining, nurturing relationships which a pastor has with his congregation? Supportive pastoral relationships are certainly not peculiar to supportive counseling. They are integral to the entire pastoral ministry. A pastoral relationship becomes "supportive counseling" when *the methods of supportive counseling are employed to help an individual, couple, or family cope with a particular problem or crisis.* Like the reinforcing steel in concrete, these methods are used at stress points to strengthen and enhance the helpfulness of an ongoing supportive relationship.

METHODS OF SUPPORTIVE COUNSELING

Psychiatrist Franz Alexander [3] described five procedures which are used in supportive psychotherapy. They are also basic tools in pastoral counseling:

(1) *Gratifying dependency needs.*[4] The supportive counselor is a "good parent" figure upon whom the parishioner can lean. There are two forms of dependency gratification—"mothering," which includes comforting, sustaining, feeding (emotionally), and inspiring; and "fathering," which includes guiding, protecting, instructing, and setting

[2] In terms of Porter's EISPU categories, supportive counseling usually employs more P (probing), E (evaluative), and S (supportive) responses than does uncovering, insight counseling, which majors in U (understanding) responses, with the occasional use of I (interpretive) and P (probing).

[3] *Psychoanalysis and Psychotherapy*, pp. 55-56.

[4] The term "anaclytic therapy" is used by psychiatrist S. Margolin to describe the physical and mental nurturing care, encouragement, and companionship which are used in certain severe disorders. "Symposium on Psychotherapy in Medical and Surgical Hospitals," *Bulletin of the American Psychoanalytic Association*, 1952, p. 170.

dependable limits to prevent self- or other-damaging behavior. Both can communicate caring (in both senses) for a troubled person and are valuable pastoral functions in supportive counseling.

(2) *Emotional catharsis.*[5] As Carl Rogers has emphasized, the acceptance of a person's burdensome feelings is one of the most supportive things a counselor can do. Pouring out one's feelings in an understanding relationship not only drains the poison from the wound of the spirit but also reduces the paralyzing tensions which inhibit the use of judgment and problem-solving abilities. To sense that a respected authority person *knows* and *cares* about one's inner pain gives a troubled person powerful feelings of having his life undergirded.

(3) *Objective review of the stress situation.* The supportive relationship allows the counselee to gain enough objectivity to view his problem with a wider perspective and to explore feasible alternatives. This helps him make a wiser decision concerning what can and should be done.

(4) *Aiding the ego's defenses.* Methodologically, this is the opposite of uncovering, confronting, or probing.

A middle-aged salesman was at the wheel of his car when it was involved in an accident resulting in the death of his wife. In ministering to him during the bereavement period, the pastor listened as the man went over and over the grim events of the accident. The minister noted that he was minimizing his own responsibility by ignoring the excessive speed at which he was traveling and blaming the driver of the slow-moving truck which his car struck from the rear. The minister respected the man's present need for the ego defenses of *repression* (of the memory of his speeding) and *projection* (of blame). To face the gigantic remorse which awareness of his responsibility in the accident would bring, would probably have overwhelmed the man at that point, or perhaps precipitated self-destructive behavior. Eventually, as the severity of the crisis began to diminish, the man was gradually able to face his enormous guilt and, with the minister's help, to work it through constructively, to some extent.

(5) *Changing the life situation.* The pastor may either help the parishioner change or, if this is not possible, arrange to have changed the circumstances (physical, economic, or interpersonal) which are pro-

[5] Franz Alexander used the psychiatric term "abreaction" rather than "catharsis" in point 2; "manipulating the life situation" was his way of stating point 5.

ducing debilitating disturbances and frustrations in his life. To illustrate, a minister assisted a distressed family in finding an adequate nursing home for an aged, senile father. He also helped them resolve their neurotic guilt feelings regarding this necessary action. The practical help which a minister renders as a part of counseling—helping a handicapped person to find a job or driving him to a rehabilitation center,[6] for instance—has a strong supportive effect.

Two other methods of supportive counseling can be added to Franz Alexander's list.

(6) *Action therapy.* When a person is stunned or paralyzed by feelings of defeat, fear of failure, damaged self-esteem, or tragic loss, it is often helpful for the pastor to prescribe some activity[7] that will keep him functioning and in touch with people. This diminishes the tendency to retreat into depression and to withdraw from relationships. At the Suicide Prevention Center in Los Angeles it has been discovered that taking a battery of psychological tests is, in itself, often beneficial. This activity gives temporary structure to the suicidal person's chaotic world, offers hope of diminishing his pain, and an opportunity to please the authority figure who requested the activity.

The prescribed "homework" should have a bearing on the achievement of the goals which the person had in coming for help. A distressed person can be asked to write, between sessions, a list of the ways in which the problem might be resolved. Writing a brief autobiographical statement between the first and second sessions can be helpful to both counselor and counselee. Reading assignments which are relevant to one's problem can be very valuable. In fact, the use of "bibliotherapy," as an adjunct to various types of pastoral counseling, has much to commend it. The supportive effects of recommending certain forms of action can be reinforced by the device of writing out the "prescription." Like all supportive methods this should be used selectively, in cases where the person requires the support of an authority-centered device to carry out an activity which is necessary or promising for his well-being.

(7) *Using religious resources.* Prayer, scripture, devotional literature, Communion, etc., constitute valuable supportive resources which are

[6] Lay members of a pastoral care team (Chapter 16) can be used to give such practical services as a part of their ministry.

[7] This is not helpful, of course, in cases in which the person responds to a trauma by hyperactivity, another way of attempting to avoid facing one's pain.

unique to pastoral counseling. When employed appropriately they may give a counselee a fresh awareness that his life has meanings which transcend its tragedies and injustices. They may help him feel a sense of support which does not stop with the counseling relationship. In the moment of spiritual openness, elicited by the meaningful use of these resources, counselor and counselee can become aware of the transcendent supportive power which is available to both, through and beyond the counseling process.

SUPPORTIVE OR UNCOVERING COUNSELING?

How does the pastor decide whether a particular person is more apt to be helped by supportive or uncovering counseling methods? This is a crucial issue in selecting approaches to counseling and in making appropriate referrals. The most useful criterion is *the person's degree of ego strength.* Those with weak, rigid, or defective ego development usually do not respond to uncovering, insight-oriented approaches. With such persons supportive methods constitute the treatment of choice.

The "ego" is the executive branch of the personality. Its function is the integration of one's inner life and the handling of interaction with the outside world of persons and things. Its skills include reasoning, problem-solving, reflection, imagination, and motor activities such as walking and speaking. The ego also includes the sense of personal identity and worth. The person with a sturdy ego has firm, positive answers to two questions: "Who am I?" and "What am I worth?" In Eric Berne's terms, he is one whose Adult is able to direct his inner Child and Parent.

One or more of these characteristics may indicate the presence of ego weakness:

(1) *Inability to handle ordinary adult responsibilities and everyday relationships constructively.* The fact that a person has been chronically unable to meet the adult demands of holding a job or maintaining ongoing relationships usually indicates a lack of ego strength. Conversely, the fact that a person has held a job or remained married to the same person for a considerable time usually indicates inner strengths upon which counseling can build.

(2) *Inability to tolerate frustration and control impulses.* The weak-

egoed person is pushed about by his impulses. His frustration tolerance and willingness to postpone gratifications in the interest of long-range goals are markedly limited.

(3) *A low degree of ability to organize one's life, plan ahead realistically, or learn from experience.* The weak-egoed person often suffers from chronic economic chaos, repetitive mistakes, and general disorganization. His "executive department" is no match for the demands of economic reality or interpersonal relations. He is afflicted with what Roger Price calls "copelessness." His ability to focus and integrate the various aspects of his life is impaired.

(4) *Pronounced and chronic dependency.* His life is characterized by a pattern of parasitic dependency relationships which he forms with those who will take care of him, protect him, or give him a vicarious sense of importance or strength.

(5) *A considerable degree of perceptual distortion.* Since perception is an ego function, the degree to which a person's receiving apparatus distorts reality is an indication of the ego's relative strength. Distortions result from inner pressures and conflicts. The accuracy with which the counselee "sees" the counselor is a reliable index of ego strength.[8] Does he, for example, see the counselor as a stern judge or magical protector when, in fact, he is neither? If under ordinary life stresses a person regresses to the denial of reality, faulty ego functioning is present. The psychotic individual is an example of extreme perceptual distortion.

(6) *Pronounced personality rigidity.* This lack of "spring" or resiliency in the way the person relates can often be sensed by the counselor. Rigid theological or political views, held with a kind of drowning-man-clutching-straw tenacity, are frequently present. The person who holds obsessively to a peace-of-mind cult may be using this repressive mechanism to hold off inner chaos. Efforts to alter the views of such persons by rational, logical means are usually either futile or unwise. The only humane approach is to respect the person's need for his immature or neurotic theology, and not to attempt to deprive him of it unless one is reasonably sure that he can function without this defense. An immature theology may be a person's only source of consolation in a grim, chaotic existence. It is cruel for a counselor to take this away

[8] From Dean Johnson, *Marriage Counseling: Theory and Practice*, p. 29. Johnson discusses ego strength (pp. 28-33) in an illuminating manner.

unless it is apparent that the person is capable of a more mature theology.

People have defenses[9] because they need them. They function automatically to protect one from unbearable threats to self-esteem, stemming from either interpersonal or intrapsychic sources. In a relatively healthy person they operate with a certain amount of flexibility. For example, a student who fails an exam may defend his sense of self-worth by the temporary use of *rationalization* ("It's because I'm a well-rounded person and not a bookworm that I flunked"), *projection* ("It was the teacher's fault for giving such a hard exam"), or *denial* ("Passing exams isn't really important"). But as his sense of self-esteem recovers, he will become aware of his own contribution to the failure and take appropriate action to better his situation. In contrast, the weak-egoed person's defenses operate constantly and inflexibly, limiting his capacity for creative change, insight, or problem-solving. The goal of counseling with such a person is to give him support and esteem-enhancing experiences in order to *lessen the need* for rigid, relationship-damaging defenses—e.g., projection and denial of reality.

(7) *Inability to benefit from an insight-oriented counseling approach,* as indicated earlier, is characteristic of ego weakness or rigidity. The person lacks the ability to engage in the prolonged self-scrutiny leading to self-understanding and the modification of basic attitudes. His capacity to order his life, control his impulses, and learn from his experience by reflecting on it is so limited as to vitiate the effectiveness of insight-uncovering counseling methods. When counselees do not respond to a pastor's attempt to use an insight-oriented approach, it is usually wise to shift to a supportive approach, or to attempt a referral.

Insight-uncovering counseling is more apt to benefit those who use neurotic rather than "acting out" or psychotic ways of attempting to handle their inner problems.[10] Unlike the acting-out type ("character

[9] Freud used the term "ego defenses" to describe the unconscious mechanisms which a child's ego adopts early in life to protect itself and deal with conflict. These defenses operate automatically, outside conscious control. They include repression, regression, projection, rationalization, fixation, denial of reality, introjection, dissociation, reaction formation. See Anna Freud's *The Ego and the Mechanisms of Defense* (New York: International Universities Press, 1946).

[10] There are three categories of personality problems—neurotic, psychotic, and character problems. The neurotic internalizes his conflicts, whereas the character problem type externalizes his, acting them out in relationships. The psychotic's fragile defenses have collapsed, to some extent, allowing portions of his ego to be overwhelmed by impulses from his unconscious.

problem" or sociopathic personality), the neurotic person experiences a high degree of guilt and anxiety. The neurotic individual may have considerable ego strength but his defenses are very heavy and costly, producing exhaustion and painful symptoms by their inefficiency. Because of his motivating guilt and anxiety and his relative strength, the person with a neurosis often profits from insight counseling or psychotherapy.

In most cases the minister is dealing with ego malformation and weakness when he counsels with alcoholics, drug addicts, the overtly or borderline psychotic, the chronically depressed or delinquent or dependent, and those with multiple psychosomatic problems. (Many factors in our society contribute to the current proliferation of ego weaknesses—the breakdown of family stability, ethical confusion, extreme mobility, and the depersonalization of technology and urbanization.) In counseling with such persons, a supportive approach is the one which is the most likely to be helpful.

VARIETIES OF SUPPORTIVE COUNSELING

There are at least four types of supportive pastoral counseling: *crisis, stopgap, sustaining,* and *growth.*[11] Supportive crisis counseling constitutes a major pastoral opportunity (see Chapter 9). Stopgap supportive counseling consists of the use of supportive methods with a disturbed person until he can be referred. (See Chapter 10.)

Sustaining counseling is a helping role in which supportive counseling methods are employed periodically, within a long-term pastoral care relationship. The goal is to help the person *continue to function at his own optimal level,* however limited, in spite of his difficult life situation. Many senior citizens,[12] chronically ill persons, and emotionally crippled individuals have remained functional because of the help of a sustaining-counseling relationship with a minister.

The heart of this approach is the ongoing supportive relationship of

[11] In one sense confrontational counseling (see Chapter 13) is also supportive—i.e., it involves supporting a person's inner controls and buttressing his value system to prevent destructive behavior.

[12] The over-sixty-five person may have a relatively strong ego, but one that has become inflexible with age. This is why supportive rather than uncovering methods are usually indicated with older persons.

the person with his church and its minister.[13] Year after year this web of meaningful relationships sustains the person. Within this context, *occasional counseling contacts,* utilizing supportive methods, have a helping effect that far outweighs the limited amount of time invested. In many cases little can be done to change their life situations, but the fact that occasionally they can discuss their problems with their minister gives them strength to bear loads which would otherwise be crushing. Several times a year such persons may "check in" with their pastor, bringing him up to date on their situations and reexperiencing his concern for them on a one-to-one basis. The occasional conference or informal chat can have greater meaning to them than many sessions with another counselor. Because of his symbolic role in their eyes and his continuing pastoral care relationship with them, counseling contacts have a deep, qualitative significance. Every pastor has a network of such sustaining relationships. By being a good parent figure to these persons he helps make their lives bearable, giving them resources for carrying their loads. During periods of particular stress they often turn to him for counseling help in clarifying their problems or finding practical assistance to meet an immediate need.

In supportive counseling it is often important to help the parishioner achieve an attitude of acceptance toward the unchangeable aspects of his problems. When acceptance replaces an attitude of brooding bitterness or self-pity, remarkable changes occur in the person's ability to live constructively within the "givenness" of his situation. The psychic energy which had been invested in resentment becomes available for useful purposes.

Supportive growth counseling is a new and valuable operational concept in pastoral counseling. Many people can utilize a supportive counseling relationship, not merely to continue functioning but as *the psychological environment in which personality growth can occur.* The growth which occurs is in a somewhat different area of personality than is the case in uncovering approaches. It is growth in the person's ability to handle his life situation constructively by making better use of his personality resources and his relationship, rather than a fundamental

[13] Many persons gain inner strength for coping by identifying with their minister as he functions as priest (worship leader), preacher, teacher, and "pastoral director" of their church. A minister's wife observed that many people in a church feel much closer to her husband than he feels to them. They know, from his preaching, how *he* thinks and feels. There is something very sustaining in this identification with a minister and with what he symbolizes.

reorientation of his personality.[14] The two principles which are illustrated in supportive growth counseling are that a person's coping abilities gain strength as they are used, and that a supportive relationship often releases a blocked person so that he *can* use these abilities.

The recovery of an alcoholic in AA is a clear illustration of a supportive growth process. As long as an alcoholic is drinking, his inner resources tend to be immobilized. He is like a car with its motor racing but out of gear. Its wheels do not move. In analogous fashion, the drinking alcoholic's ego resources are "out of gear." They are unavailable for handling adequately adult roles such as marriage, parenthood, and employment. In Bernean terms, his Adult is decommissioned, while his grandiose Child and punitive Parent battle.

AA provides him with a key supportive relationship (his sponsor) which gradually broadens until it becomes a web of supportive relationships (the AA group). *The sponsor functions in a kind of supportive counseling role* which, in relation to the group, is somewhat parallel to the relation between a pastor-counselor and the pastoral care function of an effective congregation. The sponsor, backed by the group, helps the person interrupt the self-perpetuating vicious cycle of addictive compulsive drinking. Then, without bothering about the deep underlying "causes" of alcoholism, the AA approach provides supportive, accepting relationships within which the alcoholic's frightened, floundering ego can regain its strength and its ability to function. It helps him get his personality motor back in gear. He acquires strength by identifying with and seeking advice from his sponsor and other stable AA members. He begins to substitute person-centered activities for alcohol-centered ways of dealing with problems. He discovers that he *can* face his fears, humiliations, and guilt feelings. As he faces and resolves these (in the "moral inventory"), with the help of other AA's, his emotional load lessens and his inner strength grows. The experience of getting and holding a job, making workable plans, and forming deep friendships strengthens his self-esteem and his coping abilities. His previously paralyzed ego gradually recovers the ability to cope with adult responsibilities and relationships. Without depth therapy

[14] The growth which occurs in uncovering counseling and that which results from supportive counseling frequently overlap to a considerable extent. As indicated earlier, genuine personality change may occur gradually in supportive counseling as a result of improved relationships and coping abilities.

his personality and values slowly grow in this supportive growth environment. Throughout the process there is a considerable amount of one-to-one, informal supportive counseling in which more experienced members help the newer, recovering members. The great majority of the thousands of successful AA members have achieved their remarkable recoveries entirely on an ego-adaptive level through the supportive growth approach of AA.[15]

A minister has many opportunities to do supportive growth counseling. Jack is a lonely fourteen-year-old. Shyness, rooted in self-consciousness about his sexual feelings, caused him to withdraw from his peer group. The more he withdrew, the further behind he fell in acquiring the social skills which other teen-agers were learning in their group interaction. The more learning experiences he missed, the more awkward he felt, *and actually was,* in teen-age relationships. If this vicious cycle had been protracted, it would have been virtually impossible for him to have become reintegrated into his peer group without professional therapy.

Fortunately, Jack's underlying fear was not so intense nor the withdrawal from peer relationships so extended as to render a supportive-growth approach ineffective. The original cause of his withdrawal was a common adolescent personality problem. However, the longer the withdrawal continued, the more his fears grew and the more the withdrawal became *a problem in its own right*, requiring direct treatment. This consisted of helping him regain a foothold in a group of his peers, where the interpersonal satisfactions activated his latent gregarious tendencies. This was accomplished by a double strategy. The minister enlisted the help of a more secure boy about Jack's age who was well accepted in the youth group. A friendship developed between them which served as a bridge to group affiliation for Jack. Both boys were also included in a "self-discovery group" for teen-agers—a setting in which Jack had an opportunity to practice relating to his peers and discussing his feelings, under the leadership of an adult trained in group counseling. Through these experiences Jack pulled out of his tailspin of fear and withdrawal and began to grow in his ability to relate. If a

[15] After a period of stable sobriety and of resocialization in the group, some AA's seek psychotherapy because they are uncomfortable or dissatisfied with their growth and want deeper help. Many alcoholics who do not achieve sobriety through AA are persons with underlying psychopathology requiring psychiatric help.

supportive growth approach had not accomplished this, individual or group psychotherapy would have been required to deal with Jack's underlying conflicts.

Supportive-growth counseling often has a permanently beneficial effect because, as in the case cited above, it interrupts what psychiatrist Harry M. Tiebout aptly calls a "runaway symptom." What begins as a symptom of some underlying problem becomes a self-perpetuating pathological process in its own right. Successful interruption of this runaway pathological symptom is essential to the person's well-being. If it is interrupted, it may not be necessary to treat the underlying source of anxiety.[16] The runaway symptom or vicious cycle phenomenon is encountered frequently in pastoral counseling.

DANGERS IN SUPPORTIVE COUNSELING

A supportive counseling relationship is like an orthopedic device which has two valid uses—to provide temporary support while a broken bone heals and as a brace to allow permanently crippled persons to function. There is a danger that supportive relationships may be used as "crutches," in the negative connotations of the word, blocking growth by increasing dependency.[17] This occurs when a minister does things for a counselee which he could do for himself if he had to, thus allowing him to avoid the exercise of his coping "muscles" which alone would produce growth. It is important to be sensitive to the development of unconstructive dependencies in supportive counseling so that the person can be gradually but firmly weaned. The minister should also seek to avoid the prolonged use of supportive methods with persons who need, can afford, and have access to depth therapy. Continued support can keep their pain reduced enough so that they continue to resist and postpone moving into the therapy which could help them at a deeper level.

How can the minister protect his family relationships, mental health, and "creative edge" from the exorbitant demands of a host of depend-

[16] Psychiatrist Lewis R. Wolberg writes: "An individual handicapped by a disturbing symptom often loses self-respect. He withdraws from people. . . . The symptom becomes his chief preoccupation. . . . Here, the removal of a symptom may alter his whole pattern of adjustment" (*The Technique of Psychotherapy*, p. 22).

[17] This is analogous to the case of a person who relies on an orthopedic brace permanently rather than doing the exercises which would render it unnecessary.

ent people as he functions in supportive counseling? Highly dependent people are plentiful in our society. They attach themselves leech-like to available parent figures. The minister can reduce this hazard by: (a) being aware of and resisting any neurotic needs he may have to "collect" dependent relationships,[18] (b) learning how to say "No" when necessary and appropriate,[19] and (c) distributing the dependencies of weak-egoed persons to church groups, pastoral care teams, and community services. Fortunately, the minister is in an ideal position to help dependent people find other supportive relationships.

PASTORAL COUNSELING WITH THE DISADVANTAGED

Pastoral counseling theory, like psychotherapeutic theory generally, has been dominated by middle-class aims and models of healing. Ministers who serve inner-city or working-class churches soon discover that both the *methods* and the *goals* of pastoral counseling, as usually conceived, are ineffective with many persons from lower socio-educational groups. The goals borrowed from psychotherapy—growth through self-awareness, personality integration through resolving inner conflicts, and movement toward self-fulfillment—are alien to the "world" of the majority of these persons. The same is true of the conventional operation model—a series of formal, scheduled, one-to-one interviews in which the person is expected to talk at deeper and deeper levels about his feelings and conflicts. One perceptive student of this problem has observed: "Many of the poor do not express themselves well. They do not see how 'just talking about it' can resolve their problems. . . . Their concerns are immediate, concrete, and pressing. They need to see fast, though limited improvement." [20]

Introspective methods of counseling seem like a waste of time to the person whose particular culture, unlike the middle class, does not condition him to look within to find help. This is particularly true if he feels overwhelmed with multiple practical problems. Goals like in-

[18] The minister's ability to use his authority in growth-stimulating rather than growth-stultifying ways depends on the resolution of his own dependence/independence struggle. To the degree that he has thus made peace with authority (his own and that of others), he will be able to use his authority selectively and in ways that help people mature.

[19] The inability to resist manipulative people is usually an indication of low self-esteem, of which the fear of not being liked is a painful expression.

[20] Dale White, "Mental Health and the Poor," *Concern*, October 15, 1964, p. 6.

sight, self-actualization, and personality growth are foreign to his style of communicating and irrelevant to his understanding of what he needs. A minister from a middle-class background, trained exclusively in client-centered methods, often fails to help such a person because he does not understand his inner world, including his picture of his needs. When such a counselee does not return after the first session, the minister is tempted to believe that he is "unmotivated." Actually, he is powerfully motivated to find help. He terminated because his image of what constitutes help is utterly different from the minister's.

The approach which seems to be more effective with those from the disadvantaged strata of society is essentially *supportive* and *action-oriented*. The focus of counseling is the person's concrete (and often severe) problems. The goal is to help him discover practical ways of improving his job, marriage, or health. Catharsis of feeling is used, not as a pathway to insight but as a way of allowing the minister to put his shoulder under the man's burden. Improvements in his situation need not be dramatic but they must occur fairly soon in the helping process. The counseling should be feeding or nurturing in the sense that the minister actively gives suggestions, advice, useful information (about where to find a job or medical care, for instance), and support. Much of this counseling must be done in informal settings, particularly in homes. The minister who waits for persons from laboring groups to come to his office for scheduled "counseling" will miss most of his potential opportunities to be of help.

Frank Riessman of Columbia University did a survey for the National Institute of Labor Education of new mental health treatment approaches for low-income groups:

> Riessman . . . shows that therapists who play a pastoral type of role are most successful. Those who will leave their offices and relate to their patients informally in their place of work, in the family setting, in informal street visits, etc., soon become trusted members of the patients' community. The poor person welcomes direct intervention during his times of crisis.[21]

This study revealed that informal group therapy, combined with the "helper" approach, is effective with the blue-collar worker. Group members, drawn from similar ethnic and language backgrounds, visit

[21] *Ibid.*, pp. 6-7.

and help each other between sessions. Persons who have recovered from severe problems such as drug addiction or delinquency make excellent group leaders and role models. The similarity of this approach to AA is striking. Of special relevance to pastoral counseling is Riessman's finding that "the psychological difficulties of many low-income patients diminish as they become involved in some meaningful commitment, whether it be religious activity, a hobby, a labor union, or participation in a block committee." [22] In the light of this study, it is obvious that pastoral counseling renders the greatest help to the poor when it is the most *pastoral* in its methods.[23]

Although most counseling opportunities with the disadvantaged consist of crisis situations, there are exceptions as in any heterogeneous group. In this, as in all supportive counseling, it is particularly important to make maximum use of community service resources.

SUMMARY

Psychiatrist Lewis R. Wolberg summarizes the factors which account for the efficacy of supportive counseling:

> 1. A correction or modification of a disturbed environment or other stress source may restore the weakened ego to its former stability. 2. The improved situation that results may permit the individual to exact gratifications essential to his well-being. 3. The patient may fulfill, in the supportive relationship with the therapist, important interpersonal needs, the deprivation of which has created tension. . . . 4. The patient may verbalize freely and gain cathartic release from his fears, guilt feelings, damaging memories and misconceptions which he has suppressed or repressed. . . . 5. The patient may rebuild shattered old defenses, or erect new ones which serve to repress more effectively his offending conflicts. . . . 6. Under the protective aegis of the therapist, the patient is enabled to face and to master life problems that have hitherto baffled him. Greater capacity to deal with these problems not only helps to rectify current sources of stress, but also gives the patient confidence in his ability to adjust to other aspects of his environment. . . . 7. There may be an

[22] *Ibid.*, p. 7.

[23] Revealing studies of the mental health problems of the poor include A. B. Hollingshead and F. C. Redlich, *Social Class and Mental Illness* (New York: John Wiley & Sons, 1958); T. S. Langner and S. T. Michael, *Life Stress and Mental Health* (New York: The Free Press of Glencoe, 1963); B. Overall and H. Aronson, "Expectations of Psychotherapy in Patients of Lower Socio-Economic Class," *American Journal of Orthopsychiatry*, 1963, pp. 421-30.

alleviation of guilt and fear through reassurance, or through prohibitions and restrictions which, imposed by the therapist, are interpreted as necessary disciplines by the patient.[24]

In summary, supportive counseling employs seven procedures—gratifying dependency needs, emotional catharsis, objective review of the problem, aiding the ego's defenses, changing stressful circumstances, action therapy, and religious resources. Various blends of these are utilized in four types of counseling situations calling for supportive methods—crisis, stopgap, sustaining, and growth. The clergyman who develops his skill in supportive counseling opens thereby a wide window of pastoral opportunity.

RECOMMENDED READING

Howard J. Clinebell, Jr., "Ego Psychology and Pastoral Counseling," *Pastoral Psychology,* February, 1963, pp. 26-36.

Howard J. Parad, ed., *Ego Psychology and Dynamic Casework.*

Helen H. Perlman, *Social Casework, A Problem-Solving Process.*

Lewis R. Wolberg, *The Technique of Psychotherapy* "Supportive Psychotherapy," pp. 170-75, 523-47.

REALITY-PRACTICE SESSIONS

PARISHIONER'S ROLE: You are Mrs. V., a widow age eighty-nine, bedfast as a result of a fall which resulted in a fractured wrist and collarbone. You live with your son and his wife. Your faith has been severely tested by your accident. You cannot understand why God seems so far away. Many of your friends have died and you feel extremely lonesome. Several years ago a young man from seminary taught your Sunday school class. He said that Protestants shouldn't pray to Jesus—that it was like Catholics praying to Mary. You have always prayed to Jesus and are still disturbed by the seminarian's statement. You know that you may not live much longer. (Lie down to take this role.)

[24] *The Technique of Psychotherapy,* p. 524.

PASTOR'S ROLE: You are Mrs. V.'s pastor. She is the oldest member of your church. You have a strong pastoral relationship with her but, prior to this visit, she has never discussed her deeper feelings with you. As she talks during this visit, you sense the opportunity to do sustaining supportive counseling as an integral part of your ministry of pastoral care. As you counsel with her make every effort to be aware of her feelings and let her know that you are aware by reflecting what you think she is saying and feeling. Experiment with the various supportive methods described in this chapter. Be sensitive to the possible presence of tension among the family members.

OBSERVER-EVALUATOR: Your function is to help Mrs. V. and the minister increase their awareness of what is occurring between them during the counseling. Pay special attention to the feeling tone of the relationship. Feel free to interrupt the counseling occasionally to call the participants' attention to something they seem to be missing or to make suggestions concerning how the counseling might become more helpful. Be candid in your comments. As an objective observer you will perceive things which they cannot see and of which they need to become aware.

Role-play several subsequent pastoral visits with Mrs. V. Watch the development of the counseling relationship. Experiment with a tape recorder, playing back segments of each reality-practice session. For a verbatim account of how her own pastor actually counseled with Mrs. V., see Cryer and Vayhinger, *Casebook of Pastoral Counseling*, pp. 225-30.

9

Crisis Counseling

He comforts us in all our troubles, so that we in turn may be able to comfort others in any trouble of theirs.—II Cor. 1:4 (NEB)

The pastor moves from one crisis to another with those whom he shepherds. . . . Two thousand years of Christian ministry have conditioned Christians to expect their pastors to be with them at these times of crisis. Therefore, the Christian pastor comes to his task in the strength of a great heritage. Even though he feels a sense of awe in the presence of the mysterious and tremendous crises of life, he also feels a sense of security in the fact that his people both want and expect him to be present at their times of testing.

—Wayne E. Oates[1]

Through the centuries the clergyman has been a helper in personal crises. In our day a minister's effective care and counseling of those struggling in the riptide of crisis constitute a major contribution to the mental health and spiritual growth of his people. The clergyman is a *natural crisis counselor* because of the inherent advantages of his position (discussed in Chapter 3)—his network of ongoing relationships, his many family contacts, his availability, his presence during many of the transition stages and pressure points in the life cycle, and the deeply rooted feeling of trust in ministers which many people possess.

As one who symbolizes the dimension of ultimate meanings and who is the spiritual director of a religious community with a rich tradition, the minister possesses precious resources for fulfilling his crisis ministry.

[1] *The Christian Pastor* (Philadelphia: Westminster Press, 1964), p. 1. This book illuminates the pastor's birth-to-death crisis ministry.

In many cases crises confront people with the emptiness of their lives, the poverty of their relationships. Reflecting on his death camp experience Viktor Frankl declares, "Woe to him who saw no more sense in his life, no aim, no purpose. . . . He was soon lost." [2] In the crisis ministry the clergyman's role as *awakener of meanings* is crucially important. His unique function is to help crisis-stricken people to rediscover the ultimate meaningfulness of life lived in relationship with God, whose steadfast love is real and available even in the midst of tragedy. The minister's role, as defined by society and religious tradition, is somewhere between a good parent and a wise psychiatrist. This is a major asset in supportive counseling. In the eyes of many who seek his help, the minister's image and identity have a profoundly supportive impact. It is in this feeling-context that he administers the rituals and rites with which his religious heritage has surrounded the major crises of birth and growth, living and dying.

THE NATURE AND DYNAMICS OF CRISIS

Psychiatrist Gerald Caplan has provided all the helping professions with valuable new conceptual tools for understanding the psychodynamics of crisis. In his *Principles of Preventive Psychiatry*[3] he points out that everyone is constantly faced with situations demanding problem-solving activity. Ordinarily the disequilibrium (tension) within the person, caused by the problem, is reduced quickly by solving it through the use of familiar skills. A crisis occurs within the person when his usual problem-solving activities are blocked or ineffective, allowing the need tensions to rise unabated. The tension stems from the deprivation of the satisfaction of some fundamental bodily or personality need. Caplan delineates four characteristic phases in the development of a personal crisis:

(1) The problem (stimulus) causes tension in the organism which mobilizes the person's habitual problem-solving responses.

(2) Failure of these responses, and the continuing unmet need, produce inner disturbances including feelings of anxiety, guilt, ineffectuality, and some degree of disorganization of functioning.

[2] *Man's Search for Meaning* (New York: Washington Square Press, 1963), p. 121.

[3] (Basic Books, Inc., Publishers, New York, 1964.) Caplan's basic approach to crisis intervention is outlined on pp. 26-55.

(3) When the tension of the seemingly insoluble problem passes a certain threshold, it becomes a powerful stimulus to the mobilization of additional crisis-meeting resources:

The individual calls on his reserves of strength and of emergency problem-solving mechanisms. He uses novel methods to attack the problem. . . . He may gradually define the problem in a new way, so that it comes within the range of previous experience. Aspects of the problem which were neglected may now be brought into awareness, with the consequent linking with capacities and accessory problem-solving techniques which were previously neglected as irrelevant. . . . There may be active resignation and giving up of certain aspects of goals as unattainable. He may explore by trial and error, either in action or in abstract thought, which avenues are open and which closed.[4]

Thus the problem may be solved or avoided by resignation. Effective crisis counseling aims at helping the person move into this third stage by encouraging him to mobilize his latent coping resources.

(4) If the problem is not resolved the tension of the unmet need mounts until it reaches another threshold—the breaking point where major personality disorganization (mental illness) occurs.

Caplan distinguishes two categories of crises: *developmental* and *accidental*. Human growth is the result of meeting a series of crises successfully.[5] Developmental crises are "normal" in the sense that they happen as an integral part of the growth process. Among these are birth, weaning, toilet training, the oedipal conflict, going to school, adolescence, choosing a vocation, leaving home, leaving school, engagement, the marriage adjustment, pregnancy, parenthood, the middle-age crisis, loss of parents, menopause, retirement, death of spouse, death of friends, and eventually one's own dying. These experiences are the occasions of crises for an individual to the extent that they pose problems for which his previous coping abilities are inadequate.

Accidental crises are precipitated by an "abnormal" and usually un-

[4] *Ibid.*, pp. 40-41.

[5] Personality development takes place through a succession of differentiated phases, each of which has its particular developmental challenge, the ego's task during that phase. Each stage is built on the foundation of the (hopefully) successfully completed previous stages. The transition periods between phases is a time of anxiety and crisis when a person simultaneously feels pushed ahead by maturational forces and pulled back by the security of the familiar. For a discussion of Erik Erikson's "eight stages of man," see *Childhood and Society* (New York: W. W. Norton Co., 1950), pp. 247-74. For a discussion of the implications for pastoral care of the Erikson stages, see Carroll A. Wise, *The Meaning of Pastoral Care*, pp. 86-118.

expected loss of what one believes to be essential sources of need satisfaction. Precipitating experiences include loss of one's job, savings, supporting person, or position of status and respect; an incapacitating accident, illness, or surgical operation; death of a child; marital infidelity and divorce; mental illness or alcoholism; a physical handicap; an unwanted and/or out-of-wedlock pregnancy; moving from a place where one feels secure; a natural disaster or a massive social calamity such as a war or depression. These events produce *emotionally hazardous situations* to which people respond in a variety of ways. In many cases personal crises (in the psychic economies of individuals or families) are the result. So frequent are both developmental and accidental crises that a minister may spend many hours in a single week in crisis-related counseling and pastoral care.[6]

A CRISIS AS A TURNING POINT

A crisis is more than simply a time of pain and stress to be endured. It is important for the counselor to see that it is a turning point toward or away from greater personality wholeness. It is this fact which makes crisis counseling such a strategic helping opportunity. Caplan writes of the person in crisis:

> His new equilibrium may be better or worse than in the past, in that the realignment of forces both inside his personality and in relationships with meaningful people . . . may lead to more or less satisfaction of his needs. He may deal with the crisis problems by developing new socially acceptable, reality-based problem-solving techniques *which add to his capacity to deal in a healthy way with future difficulties.* Alternatively, he may, during the crisis, work out new coping responses which are socially unacceptable and which deal with difficulties by evasion, irrational fantasy manipulations, or regression and alienation—all of which increase the likelihood that he will also deal maladaptively with future difficulties. In other words, *the new pattern of coping that he works out in dealing with the crisis becomes thence forward an integral part of his repertoire of problem-solving responses and increases the chance that he will deal more or less realistically with future hazards.*[7]

[6] In larger urban churches crisis counseling consumes the lion's share of the ministers' pastoral care energies and time.

[7] Caplan, *Principles of Preventive Psychiatry*, p. 43. Italics mine.

Short-term crisis counseling frequently can be of major help to a person simply by steering him away from maladaptive responses and toward a constructive facing of the crisis. Relatively rapid results are possible because forces within the person are teetering in the balance so that a relatively minor influence by the pastor can have a major effect in helping the person cope constructively. If the individual who is coping with a crisis in an unhealthy manner can be helped to face the problem and cope with it in a healthy way, there is usually no need for the counselor to attempt the difficult, time-consuming process of searching for the underlying reasons for the initial maladaptive response.

THE USE OF SUPPORTIVE METHODS IN CRISIS COUNSELING

Mr. P., fifty-five, burdened with tensions, anxiety, and depression, seeks the help of his pastor. He is so distraught that he has been unable to work for several weeks. As he tells about his situation, it becomes evident to the counselor that the onset of his present difficulties followed his job "advancement" to a position of foreman. Up until that time he had functioned well under a strong, paternalistic foreman. Now *he* is the foreman, responsible for the production record of his group, in competition with other groups within the plant. His new position demands leadership and assertiveness.

As counseling sessions continue, the pastor senses the extreme dependency with which Mr. P. relates to him. The pastor-parishioner relationship provides a clue to his general relationships with authority figures. The pastor begins to realize that he is terribly afraid of the very things his new position demands—competitiveness, aggressiveness, and being in a position of having others depend on him. Mr. P. is trapped between his need to remain dependent on a father-like foreman and the demand of the job that *he* become a father figure.

An insight-oriented counseling approach would aim at helping the man become aware of the deeper nature of his paralyzing feelings and to uncover the roots of his feelings, probably in his early relationship with his father. But the counselor senses that these goals are unrealistic because of the man's rigidity and basic weakness as a person. As he has ample opportunity to ventilate and experience the acceptance of his feelings, Mr. P. begins to see that the new position, as he puts it, is "not for me." The limit of the man's self-awareness is that he "needs the satisfaction of working on a lathe" himself, and that it "bugs" him to have to make decisions for those under him. Anything more than superficial insight as to *why* it bothers him seems to be beyond his grasp.

At this point the counselor does not give up because the man is unable to achieve insight. He explores with him other possibilities of employment on the job and encourages him to transfer to another department where he will be able to use his skill at the lathe in the development of new products under the direction of a strong department head.

The pastor continues to see the man in a supportive relationship as he makes his adjustment in the new department. Being in a work environment in which his skill as a lathesman is used and valued, and where his neurotic fear of aggressiveness does not present a problem, his anxiety and depression subside. He can now grow in his ability to handle life.[8]

Crisis counseling utilizes the seven basic methods of supportive counseling described in Chapter 8. In Mr. P.'s case, leaning on the minister *gratified his dependency needs.* This reduced his anxiety, which liberated his reasoning abilities for use in solving his problems. His minimal self-understanding (resulting in his decision to transfer back to lathe work) followed the *emotional catharsis* which reduced the paralyzing pain of his negative feelings. The counseling relationship allowed him to escape far enough from his swirling subjectivity to be able to *review his stressful situation* with some objectivity and to examine the probable consequences of various ways of dealing with his problem. His intense dependency needs and fear of masculine aggressiveness were unacceptable to his self-image and were therefore held out of his awareness by repression. The pastor *aided his ego defenses* by not pushing him (except in a gentle, exploratory way) to become aware of his threatening feelings, and by accepting his conscious level and less threatening reason for not liking his new position. The minister helped *change P.'s life situation* by encouraging him to go back to the lathe, even though he apparently was not capable of becoming fully aware of *why* he needed to do so. *Action therapy* was involved throughout the minister's approach to helping him. During the first interview he encouraged him to *do* something about his situation. When P. talked of the possibility of changing jobs, the minister responded: "Wouldn't it be a good idea to check with the personnel man at the plant to see if a transfer might be possible, in case you decide that that would be the best course of action?" At each stage in the counseling he helped P. prepare to take whatever action seemed possible and wise. At the close of each session the minister said a

[8] Howard J. Clinebell, Jr., "Ego Psychology and Pastoral Counseling," *Pastoral Psychology,* February, 1963, pp. 33-34.

prayer in which he gathered the major feelings of the session and asked for increased awareness of God's sustaining care. This use of *religious resources* gave the helping process a vertical dimension; it reminded P. of his relationship with him who is a "refuge and strength, a very present help in trouble."

The minister's help enabled P. to pull out of his emotional tailspin and to avoid self-perpetuating, maladaptive responses to his inner crisis. If P. had used the defenses of denial and withdrawal when his crisis hit—i.e., if he had not been open to help—it is probable that he would have become trapped in a self-feeding, vicious cycle of anxiety, failure, and withdrawal from interpersonal relationships. His paralyzing anxiety would have caused him to fail as foreman and this failure would have shattered his already shaky self-confidence, making failure on his next job almost certain. Spiraling failure and withdrawal would have increasingly magnified the very anxiety which produced them initially. His maladaptive responses might have become an ongoing part of his faulty equipment for meeting future crises. Turning to the minister was a reality-oriented response which enabled him to avoid this vicious cycle.[9] A major goal in most crisis counseling is to help persons avoid or interrupt emotional tailspins.

More specifically, what are the nonconstructive responses to crises which lead into emotional blind alleys and increase vulnerability to future failure and personality illness?

(1) Denial that a problem exists.
(2) Evasion of the problem (via alcohol, for example).
(3) Refusal to seek or accept help.
(4) Inability to express or master negative feelings.
(5) Failure to explore the nature of the crisis.
(6) Failure to explore alternative solutions.
(7) Projection onto others of total responsibility for causing and/or curing the crisis.
(8) Turning away from friends and family.

The crisis counselor should be alert to the presence of these malignant

[9] One way of ascertaining the prognosis of a person in crisis is to discover the relative adequacy of his pre-crisis functioning. Persons who have a history of some success in coping can usually be helped to recover their normal equilibrium (or better, in some cases) in a relatively short time using supportive, ego-adaptive counseling methods. But even those with limited pre-crisis adequacy may have latent coping resources which can be mobilized.

responses in order to help the person move away from them and toward the following healthy ways of coping:

(1) Facing the problem.
(2) Enlarging one's understanding of it.
(3) Expressing and working through negative feelings such as resentment, anxiety, and guilt.
(4) Accepting responsibility for coping with the problem.
(5) Exploring alternative ways of handling it.
(6) Separating the changeable from the unchangeable in the situation.
(7) Accepting the unchangeable as unchangeable.
(8) Surrendering grandiose, burdensome aspects of one's self-image.
(9) Opening channels of communication with other helping persons among relatives, friends, and professional persons.
(10) Taking steps, however small, to handle the problem constructively.

The growing body of experience in psychiatric crisis clinics is providing valuable insights concerning the methodology of crisis counseling. Here are some of the techniques used at the Benjamin Rush Center for Problems in Living in Los Angeles:

There are several techniques which are utilized here. One is to describe to the consultee the problem as you see it, integrating the present crisis into the perspective of his life pattern, still without losing the here-and-now orientation of the treatment. Another is to help him to gain a cognitive grasp of the issues at hand, at the same time bringing into the open his present feelings to which he may not have access. A third technique is to bring into play previously learned behavior patterns not being employed at present. A fourth is to explore with him the alternative mechanisms of coping with the problem, and different ways in which the problem may be seen and defined. A fifth is to consider re-peopleing his social world and re-distributing the role relationships within the group. A sixth is to clarify and re-emphasize the individual's responsibility for his own behavior, decisions and way of life. . . . As time passes and the hoped-for reduction of anxiety and increased ability to cope occur, a summary is made of the changes which have occurred, thereby reinforcing the adaptive behaviors which are developing. Help is given to the consultee in making realistic plans for the future. . . . Also explored with him are specific ways of warding off future crises with the new coping tools which he has gained during the consultation.[10]

GROWTH THROUGH SURRENDER

One of the keys to understanding successful crisis coping and the personal growth which results is the concept of "surrender" which psychiatrist Harry M. Tiebout has explored with reference to recovery from alcoholism.[11] It is my belief that this concept illuminates what occurs in nonalcoholic as well as alcoholic crises, when a person experiences positive personality changes. At a certain point in the crisis the person "hits bottom," as they say in AA. His denial of his problem collapses and he becomes psychologically open to help from others. Somehow the impact of the trauma has budged loose the mask of self-sufficiency which before fitted so snugly, protectively, and oppressively. His "I-ism" (as one alcoholic aptly labeled it) is surrendered. He relaxes his perfectionism, lets go of his alibis and denials of reality, and his compulsion to "run the show" by manipulating people and circumstances. His isolating wall of defensive pride crumbles and he begins to experience his humanity and "cooperate with life." He becomes open to the growth forces in relationships.

Surrender occurs at a deep, nonvolitional level of the psyche, suddenly or gradually. Somehow, under the impact of the crisis, one's old self-damaging defenses stop functioning. A dramatic shift of intrapsychic forces occurs and is unmistakably evident in the new sense of

[10] W. E. Morley, "Treatment of the Patient in Crisis," Benjamin Rush Center, May 5, 1964 (unpublished manuscript). Patients are seen for a maximum of six visits; crises are typically resolved within four to six weeks. Treatment focuses on specific problems in living. Psychiatrist Louis Paul describes the ways in which counselors unwittingly encourage regression in crisis counseling: "Letting the client wallow in his emotions without requiring that he recognize what specific emotion he is experiencing and toward whom it is directed; focusing on past events to the neglect of present circumstances; and especially the neglect of the precipitating event; . . . refraining from calling upon the patient to use his own resources of self-observation, self-restraint and self-responsibility; . . . encouraging withdrawal from regular work when the client could work in spite of so-called 'symptoms'; filling in the client's inadequacies with unrealistic reassurances and with advice about conduct and about decisions which the client is able to decide for himself; and accepting uncritically the attribution of omniscience and omnipotence directed to the counselor." These are some of the "don'ts!" of crisis counseling. See "Crisis Intervention," in *The Clergy and People in Crisis*, pp. 19-20.

[11] His scientific papers, published in the *Quarterly Journal on Alcohol*, include: "The Act of Surrender in the Therapeutic Process," X (1949), 48-58 "Surrender Vs. Compliance," XIV (1953), 58-68; "Ego Factors in Surrender in Alcoholism," XV (1954), 610-21. David A. Stewart's *Thirst for Freedom* (Toronto: Musson Book Co., 1960) illuminates the dynamics of surrender.

openness, nearness to people, acceptance of the unchangeable in one's situation, and a realistic willingness to "live and let live." The experience of surrender is at the heart of what has been called "conversion" in the Christian tradition. Tiebout states:

A religious or spiritual awakening is the act of giving up one's reliance on one's omnipotence. The defiant individual no longer defies but accepts help, guidance and control from outside. And as the individual relinquishes his negative, aggressive feelings toward himself and toward life, he finds himself overwhelmed by strongly positive ones such as love, friendliness, peacefulness.[12]

It should be emphasized that surrender, as used here, is not the same as "giving up" in a crisis. It is a turning away from a futile, reality-denying stance and toward a positive, reality-accepting way of coping. In accepting his weakness the person finds new strength!

A BERNEAN APPROACH TO CRISIS COUNSELING

Eric Berne's therapeutic approach is very useful in crisis counseling. For instance, with a person in a crisis marked by feelings of panic, it is often helpful to ask (after explaining Berne's Parent-Adult-Child system), "What part of you is afraid?" For him to recognize that it is his inner Child, not his total self, which is frightened releases the person from the dominance of his panic. The effect of this awareness is to help his Adult ego state to gain control. In Bernean counseling the Adult is strengthened by freeing it from the dominance of the Child and by *exercising* the Adult. Berne writes:

Actionism is an essential feature of structural analysis. The Adult is regarded in the same light as a muscle, which increases in strength with exercise. Once the preliminary phases of decontamination and clarification are well under way, the patient is expected to practice Adult control. He must learn to keep the Adult running the show for relatively long periods. . . . What the Adult acquires is not exclusive dominance, but increasing *option*. It is he, and not the Child, who decides more and more effectively when the Child shall take over.[13]

[12] "Alcoholics Anonymous and the Medical Profession" (AA Publishing, Inc., 1955), p. 24. Granger E. Westberg observes that the crisis of illness stops many people in their tracks and forces them to raise basic religious issues, for the first time in many years (*Minister and Doctor Meet,* pp. 8, 10).

[13] *Transactional Analysis in Psychotherapy,* p. 146.

Crisis counseling, in Bernean terms, consists of reducing the fear and guilt of the inner Child by allowing him to draw strength from the counselor's nurturing Parent, and, at the same time, activating and strengthening the Adult by encouraging the person to face reality and move into action. The counselor's Adult allies itself with the counselee's Adult in a joint strategy aimed at bringing his Child under control and releasing his Adult for coping with the problem in a reality-oriented way.

A firm, parental approach helps a counselee control his inner Child. The counselor may remind the person that he doesn't have to let his Child run his life. He may say, in effect, "You have an Adult who can learn to exercise control." A firm stance helps a frightened, disorganized person to "pull himself together" and mobilize his Adult coping abilities. A direct, "I know you feel terrible, *but* . . ." approach is indicated rather than a permissive one.[14]

COUNSELING IN THE CRISIS OF BEREAVEMENT

Caplan's approach to crisis counseling is founded on the work of Eric Lindemann in his 1943 study of bereavement reactions among survivors of those who died in the Coconut Grove fire. In the years since that revealing study the approach has been developed and used by mental health specialists to help persons cope with a wide variety of crises, including the birth of premature babies, urban relocation, entry into kindergarten, difficulties in nurses' training, and surgical operations.

To illustrate the use of crisis methods by the minister, his role in the most universal of human crises—bereavement—will now be examined. It behooves the clergyman to develop a high degree of competence in bereavement counseling. His profession is the one designated by our culture to help the grief-stricken. He is the only person with training in counseling who has automatic entrée to the world of the sorrowing. This gives him a major responsibility and opportunity to be the bereaved person's guide through the valley of the shadow.[15]

The loss of someone who has been a part of one's world of meanings

[14] Ruth Monroe's "intellectualizing technique"—brief sharing of theoretical comments concerning the dynamics of problems such as the person is confronting—can help to mobilize a person's Adult by providing the Adult with conceptual tools for understanding what is happening. See Standal and Corsini, *Critical Incidents in Psychotherapy*, pp. 340 ff.

[15] Oates, *The Christian Pastor*, p. 36.

and satisfactions is a *psychological amputation.* How traumatic it is depends on the importance of the relationship in one's psychic economy. The automatic responses employed in coping with bereavement are the same ones a particular person habitually uses in coping with any severe deprivation, frustration, or loss. They are the coping skills which that person learned from his culture, as it was filtered through the personalities of his parents.

If the individual has learned constructive, reality-oriented coping skills, his psyche will follow a somewhat predictable process of working through the mixture of powerful feelings associated with bereavement and making the adjustments required to live without the deceased. Lindemann called this process, by which the grief wound heals, the "grief work" of the psyche.[16]

The minister's role in normal grief is to cooperate with the psyche's built-in recovery forces. He facilitates the person's "grief work" by using the basic methods of supportive counseling. *Gratifying dependency needs* is essential, inasmuch as the person is experiencing acute deprivation in the loss of a dependency object. Paul E. Johnson declares that a pastor should give "unfaltering companionship in times of crisis . . . to stand by with contagious hope, faith, and love . . . to sustain the anguished soul in hours of distress." [17] Severe loss activates the person's inner Child with its fear of being left to starve. His need to be fed, psychologically and spiritually, is intense. Since he symbolizes the ultimate Source, the minister is a special kind of "feeder." Through acts of ministry, including familiar scripture and rituals, he relates the grieving to him who is the "bread of life." The pastor can encourage the person to turn *toward people* for help and thus allow himself dependency gratification. Turning in upon oneself and refusing to be fed, interpersonally, over a protracted period, is an unhealthy grief response.

When death strikes a loved one the first response is a feeling of numbness (nature's anesthesia), mixed with feelings of unreality—of being in a bad dream. The mind refuses to accept the fact that the person is really gone. The full pain of the loss can be admitted to consciousness only gradually over a period of weeks or months. While respecting the person's *need for his defenses* the pastor can help to offset the feeling-

[16] "Symptomatology and Management of Acute Grief," *American Journal of Psychiatry,* September, 1944.

[17] *Psychology of Pastoral Care* (Nashville: Abingdon Press, 1953), p. 41.

avoiding tendency in our culture by gently using counseling methods to facilitate gradual *catharsis.* During the first and subsequent visits he can help the bereaved talk about the loved one and the circumstances of the death, using reflective listening to encourage emotional catharsis. Throughout the grief counseling process the guiding principle is this: *The experiencing and working through of painful feelings is an indispensable part of the healing!* Blocked feelings = delayed or blocked healing.

An important purpose of the funeral is to facilitate emotional release. The service should emphasize, among other things, the reality of the loss and the appropriateness of mourning. It should use familiar hymns, prayers, and scripture which may help to release dammed-up feelings. A funeral meditation on a text such as "Blessed are those who mourn" may help to facilitate mourning. Nothing should be said which suggests that stoicism in the face of grief is a Christian virtue or that one whose faith is genuine will not experience penetrating grief.

Religious resources have more than a supportive function in bereavement. Death confronts the survivors inescapably with their own mortality and fear of death. Anxiety about nonbeing can be handled constructively only within the context of faith—i.e., within a relationship of trust. Serving in his priestly role the minister uses familiar rituals, scripture, and theological beliefs which renew the bereaved's experience of basic trust. To the extent that these are meaningful or "living" symbols to the individual, they tend to strengthen the trustful quality of his relationships with God and the supportive religious fellowship. The symbols of a religious tradition can touch deep levels of the psyche, renewing feelings of trust which alone enable a person to handle his existential anxiety constructively.[18] (See Chapter 14.) In crisis counseling the original root of the word religion—*religio,* to bind together—has dynamic significance. When a shattering loss fragments one's life, vital religion has the power to bind it together, restoring the sense of inner unity.

In crisis counseling the supportive method of *changing the person's*

[18] Existential anxiety—the threat of nonbeing—is present in all crises—developmental and accidental. Many religious traditions have "rites of passage" in which the hazardous transition phases in human development are recognized by rituals which serve to reduce the anxiety or give the resources to cope with it. Baptism, confirmation, marriage, and funeral rituals are examples of such rites.

life situation often involves helping the person with everyday tasks. Church members should be encouraged and guided in functioning as an extended family to the bereaved, giving whatever help and support is needed and desired. Providing food for a sorrowing family is a symbolic way of communicating the comforting, nurturing concern which has a deeply healing effect rooted in our first experiences of being mothered. The post-funeral meal reaffirms the ongoingness of life, in spite of the tragic depletion of the family organism. Eating together becomes a communion meal, a way of saying, "We can and must go on together!"

In the weeks and months after the funeral the person enters a new stage of "grief work" in which he experiences deeper levels of loss. There is a waxing and waning of grief feelings as they are alternatively held in consciousness and excluded from it. When the strain reaches a certain level, fatigue produces a resting phase during which full awareness is blunted. The supportive, nurturing function of the minister and lay "pastors" remains essential.

In normal grief the person gradually begins to deal with his ambivalent feelings. If, instead, a person continues to overidealize the deceased, he is utilizing the maladaptive defenses of denial and repression. These enable him to avoid the awful pain of dealing with feelings of resentment, anger, and guilt, but they also prevent the grief wound from healing. The wound is infected and cannot heal until the person deals with the repressed negative feelings. When the minister encounters what appears to be blocked "grief work," he should encourage the person to talk about his relationship with the deceased, and continue to do so until the negative elements (which are present in every relationship) are faced and worked through. By responding acceptingly to tentative expressions of mixed or negative feelings, further catharsis is facilitated. Attending the resentment and anger toward the lost one there is usually a load of guilt about these feelings which must also be worked through. The grief wound must heal from the inside. Healing cannot be forced, but the counseling process can help to provide the *conditions for healing* by dealing with the negative feelings which, when repressed, infect the wound.

The grief wound cannot heal fully until one has *accepted the reality* of the loss, has *surrendered*, to some degree, one's *emotional tie to and investment in* the lost person, and has begun to *form other relation-*

ships to provide new sources of emotional food. In working with the bereaved (as with the permanently handicapped), it is crucial to help the person learn to distinguish what can and what cannot be changed in the situation. The familiar "Serenity Prayer" of AA is useful in such counseling:

> Grant me the serenity to accept the things I cannot change,
> The courage to change the things I can,
> And the wisdom to know the difference.[19]

In discussing crisis therapy Gerald Caplan states:

> Not all problems are capable of solution by removal of the threat to need satisfaction; but in these cases, too, a "healthy" type of activity, consisting of *an act of resignation* of this avenue of need satisfaction and *its replacement by alternatives,* can be differentiated from "unhealthy" problem avoidance in which no decision is made and no conflict resolved. Thus, in the crisis of bereavement . . . the sufferer must actively resign himself to the impossibility of ever again satisfying his needs through interaction with the deceased. He must psychologically "bury the dead"; only after this has been done will he be free to seek gratification of these needs from alternative persons. Those who cope maladaptively with bereavement may pretend that the loved one is not dead, or they may magically introject his image by taking his characteristics into their own personality, and they will thus evade the painful act of resignation. This is likely to result in their energies remaining bound up with the deceased, so that they are not free to love others.[20]

Action therapy, in bereavement counseling, consists of encouraging the person to do something about his situation, *whether or not he feels like doing so.* There is genuine healing, for many people, in work.[21] Experience in bereavement counseling confirms the measure of truth which inheres in O. Hobart Mowrer's statement, "It is easier to act your way into a new way of *feeling* than to feel your way into a new way of acting." [22] If a person remains immobilized and cannot resume his normal activities, a pathological grief reaction may be present.

Here are some of the danger signs which may indicate pathological

[19] Reinhold Niebuhr is the author of this prayer.
[20] Caplan, *Principles of Preventive Psychiatry,* pp. 45-46.
[21] This does not apply to those who use hyperactivity to escape from their feelings.
[22] *Critical Incidents in Psychotherapy,* p. 80. (Quoted originally from E. Stanley Jones.)

grief, particularly if they persist: increased withdrawal from relationships and normal activities; the absence of grieving; undiminished mourning; severe depression which does not lift; psychosomatic problems; disorientation; personality changes; severe, undiminishing guilt or anger; loss of interest in life; continuing escape by means of drugs or alcohol. By skillful bereavement counseling, in the early phases of maladaptive responses, the pastor can diminish the frequency of such pathological, self-damaging responses. But when these symptoms appear and persist, in spite of the minister's efforts, a psychiatric referral is imperative. The longer a person's grief work is delayed, the more painful and costly to his mental and spiritual health it will be.

CRISIS COUNSELING WITH FAMILIES

The principles of crisis counseling are applicable in family as well as individual crises. For example, in the family crisis produced by addictive drinking, a supportive counseling approach is indicated. The wife (or husband) of the alcoholic is too disturbed by the tornado-like chaos in which the family is existing to allow insight-counseling to be helpful. The only realistic goal is to help her deal more constructively with the *runaway family crisis* in which she is emotionally submerged:

> Just as alcoholism is best approached as a "runaway symptom" (Tiebout), the family's problem is approached most effectively when seen as a *runaway adaptation to the crisis of alcoholism*. . . . The very mechanisms which came into being in response to the crisis, tend to intensify the crisis. For example, the family increasingly isolates itself, as alcoholism develops, in an effort to protect itself from social disapproval. But this very isolation produces . . . even greater fears of "what others will think." [23]

Supportive-adaptive pastoral counseling seeks to reverse this maladaptive, out-of-control mechanism by encouraging the family to reenter social relationships. By involving them in Al-Anon and the church fellowship, their fear can be diminished and their supply of interpersonal satisfactions enhanced.

In family crises there are often pressing practical problems which must be faced. Helping the alcoholic's spouse handle these constructively

[23] Howard J. Clinebell, Jr., "Pastoral Care of the Alcoholic's Family Before Sobriety," p. 23. This article describes in more detail the use of "release" as a working concept in family crisis counseling.

will enable her to begin to reassemble her shattered self-confidence. As the external pressures of the situation are reduced, she may be able to mobilize her inner resources. Knowledge about the nature of alcoholism will strengthen her ego-adaptive abilities and steer her away from futile responses such as nagging. Early in the counseling the minister should urge the spouse to join the local Al-Anon group. She will receive massive emotional support from the group and the special empathy of persons who have "lived in the same squirrel cage."

The spouse of a drinking alcoholic can be helped to protect herself and her children from many of the destructive effects of his illness by "releasing" him emotionally. This concept, derived from Al-Anon principles, involves four things:

(1) *Surrendering her obsessive and futile attempt to control her husband's drinking.*

(2) *Giving up the many ways in which she has stood between him and the natural consequences of his irresponsible behavior.* As long as she makes excuses for him, covers his bad checks, and generally mothers him, she prevents him from experiencing the painful consequences which may be precisely what he needs to become open to help.

(3) *Abandoning her assumption that all improvement in her situation depends entirely on whether or not he stops drinking.*

(4) *Developing a more fulfilling life for herself and her children, regardless of what the alcoholic decides to do.* "Release" serves to interrupt the self-perpetuating neurotic interaction in which the wife's attempts to "help" the alcoholic are interpreted by him as an interference in his life, which he uses to justify his continued excessive drinking.[24] If the wife surrenders her need to control, by releasing him, it often hastens his surrender to his need for help. Whether or not this occurs the wife's "release" of the alcoholic predictably reduces the destructive impact of his illness on the family. The concept of release is useful in most marriage counseling, particularly in cases where one party is not open to help. Encouraging the other party to release the one who is rejecting help frequently has a constructive effect on the situation.

[24] After joining Al-Anon, an alcoholic's wife described her pre-release situation by this quote from Leo Tolstoy: "I sit on a man's back choking him, making him carry me, and yet assure myself and others that I am very sorry for him and wish to ease his lot by all possible means—except by getting off his back." *What Then Must We Do?* (London: Oxford University Press, 1935), revised ed., Chapter 16. Perhaps she was too hard on herself, but there is a considerable amount of this kind of interaction in many neurotic marriages.

In summary, the significance of crisis counseling cannot be overemphasized. The late Anton T. Boisen put it well: "The great opportunity of the pastor is, I think, with the distressed, with those who are in jeopardy, with those who are passing through periods of acute crisis and mutation." [25] To guide and support these persons through times of stress is a high privilege of the minister.

RECOMMENDED READING

The Clergy and People in Crisis, Proceedings of an Institute for the Clergy (Los Angeles: Mental Health Development Program), May 18, 1965.

Ernest Bruder, *Ministering to Deeply Troubled People* (Englewood Cliffs, N.J.: Prentice-Hall 1964).

Gerald Caplan, *Principles of Preventive Psychiatry* (New York: Basic Books, 1964), pp. 26-55.

Howard J. Clinebell, Jr., "Ministering to the Mentally Ill and Their Families," in *Mental Health Through Christian Community,* Chapter 11.

——— "Pastoral Care of the Alcoholic's Family Before Sobriety," *Pastoral Psychology,* April, 1962, pp. 19-29.

——— *Understanding and Counseling the Alcoholic* (Nashville: Abingdon Press, 1956).

Edgar N. Jackson, *Understanding Grief* (Nashville: Abingdon Press, 1957).

Howard J. Parad, ed., *Crisis Intervention: Selected Papers* (New York: Family Service Association of America, 1965).

REALITY-PRACTICE SESSIONS

1. PARISHIONER'S ROLE: You are Mr. P. (described in this chapter). Come to your pastor for help with your problem.

PASTOR'S ROLE: You are Mr. P.'s pastor. As you counsel with him, utilize as many of the seven methods of supportive counseling as seem appropriate to the developing situation.

[25] *The Exploration of the Inner World,* p. 271.

2. PARISHIONER'S ROLE: You are a middle-aged woman whose husband died four months ago. You are feeling the loss very intensely and find it almost impossible to go to meetings, especially to church. Your husband knew of his illness only six weeks before his death.[26]

PASTOR'S ROLE: You have called on Mrs. J. several times since the funeral, but were reluctant to ask her about her grief because of the presence of company. This time she is alone. After brief initial comments about the weather, you ask, "How has it been with you since John's death?"

An observer-evaluator should be used as in the previous reality-practice sessions. In addition, use a tape recorder, playing back a part of the session.

[26] For a verbatim account of how her pastor counseled with Mrs. J., see Cryer and Vayhinger, *Casebook in Pastoral Counseling*, Case No. 10, pp. 67-70. Compare your approach with his.

10

Referral Counseling

Referral is not a pastoral failure. It is a subtle and important helping art. . . . I propose that we think about it as illustrative of the more generally useful skill of helping people to focus their needs and clarify their feelings.

—Thomas W. Klink[1]

Skill in the art of referral is indispensable in parish-centered counseling. The pastor is a general practitioner with many significant functions and innumerable demands on his time. As Wayne E. Oates says pointedly:

> One of the reasons that pastors do not have time to do their pastoral ministry is that they insist on doing it all themselves. . . . They have failed to build a detailed knowledge of their community as to the agencies, professional and private practitioners, etc., who could help them in their task.[2]

By default, the lone pastoral counselor often deprives some troubled people of needed specialized help which is available in the community. In discussing ministering to a teen-age unwed mother, C. W. Brister hits the heart of the matter: "The minister calls upon community resources, not in order to pass the buck, but because he wishes the best for all persons concerned." [3]

[1] "The Referral: Helping People Focus Their Needs," *Pastoral Psychology,* December, 1962, p. 11.

[2] *Protestant Pastoral Counseling,* pp. 112-13.

[3] *Pastoral Care in the Church* (New York: Harper & Row, 1964), p. 162.

Since many people trust his judgment and turn to him spontaneously when trouble strikes, a minister is in a strategic position to assist them in finding competent, specialized help. A wise referral is one of the most significant services he can render a suffering parishioner. A family who, in the midst of a traumatic problem, is guided by its minister to effective help, is usually eternally grateful to him. A minister can multiply his service to the troubled manyfold by using all the helping resources of his community to the hilt.[4]

Unfortunately some ministers feel that to refer is to admit inadequacy or failure. In one study of Family Service Agencies, it was found that only 3 percent of referrals came from churches.[5] A nationwide study of where people take their problems revealed: "The helping process seems to stop with the clergyman and physician in the majority of cases, and far more so with the clergyman than with the physician."[6] In fact, physicians referred eight times as many persons to mental health facilities and practitioners as did clergymen.[7] Obviously some ministers have a great deal to learn concerning the importance of "pastoral care by referral," as Klink has phrased it. At the other extreme, there are a few ministers for whom referral is as automatic and as mechanical as the salivation of Pavlov's dogs. Because of this too-rapid referral reflex their unique helping potentialities as ministers are not discovered. They miss some of the deepest satisfactions of their profession by not attempting to establish therapeutic relationships with those who may need precisely what they have to give. Troubled parishioners sometimes get the feeling that their minister is "passing the buck." They may get this feeling because he is.

Properly conceived, referral is a means of using a team effort to help a troubled person. It is a *broadening* and *sharing*, not total *transfer* of responsibility. It employs the division-of-labor principle that is the basis of interprofessional cooperation. John L. Mixon and Seward Hiltner put it well:

> In some areas the pastor recognizes that expert knowledge, which he does not have, cannot have, does not need to have, is required if all possible help is

[4] Howard J. Clinebell, Jr., *Mental Health Through Christian Community*, p. 228.
[5] John L. Mixon, *The Church and Community Agencies*, p. 6.
[6] *Action for Mental Health* (New York: Basic Books, 1961), p. 104.
[7] Quoted by Klink in "The Referral: Helping People Focus Their Needs," p. 10.

to be given. And at the same time he realizes that *there is still an important job for him in the situation.*[8]

Only by drawing on the specialized skills of others can he have time and energy to fulfill his unique *pastoral* function.

WHOM TO REFER

With what persons should a minister utilize referral to broaden the base of help?

(1) Those who can be helped more effectively by someone else.[9]

(2) Those who do not respond to his help after five or so sessions.

(3) Those whose needs obviously surpass his time and/or training.

(4) Those with problems for which effective specialized agencies are available in his community. In larger communities this usually includes alcoholics, the blind, unwed parents, the crippled, the mentally retarded, adoptive parents, those needing legal aid, the aged, transients, the emotionally disturbed, the mentally ill.

(5) Those with severe chronic financial needs. Public welfare agencies with trained social workers are appropriate referrals.

(6) Those who need medical care and/or institutionalization.

(7) Those who need intensive psychotherapy.

(8) Those about the nature of whose problem one is in doubt.

(9) Those who are severely depressed and/or suicidal.

(10) Those toward whom the minister has a strong negative reaction. The anxiety which usually underlies such antipathy will tend to vitiate one's counseling effectiveness with such a person. If the pastor can discover *why* he reacts as he does and work through his negative feelings, he may do effective counseling and grow as a result of the experience.

It is important for a pastor to build working relationships with the physicians of his community. A counselee who has not had a physical

[8] *Community Help on Pastoral Problems* (New York: Federal Council of Churches, 1948), p. 9.

[9] I am indebted to Paul Hersh's list of seven reasons for referral: Obvious psychopathology, limitations of time and training, doubts as to the nature of the problem, the need for long-term psychotherapy, transference problems, countertransference problems, when the pastor feels that someone else can help better than he. "A Study of Criteria for Guiding the Clergyman in his Care and Referral of Parishioners Who Are in Need of Special Counseling or Psychotherapy," unpublished Ph.D. dissertation, University of Southern California, 1958.

check-up recently should be strongly encouraged to do so. The parishioner's permission to consult with his physician should be obtained by the pastoral counselor. If the pastoral counselor has the slightest suspicion that neurological, endocrine, or other medical problems may be lurking behind or complicating interpersonal conflict, he should *insist* that the person consult his doctor. A collaborative relationship with a physician is also vital in counseling with those who have psychosomatic problems, depressions, suicidal tendencies, alcoholism, other addictions (including food and work addiction), menopausal problems, physical handicaps, chronic or terminal illness, sexual problems, geriatric problems, pronounced mood swings, severe anxiety, weak egos. In most communities there is at least one physician who will welcome a collaborative relationship with a competent counseling pastor. In such mutually helpful relationships referral becomes a two-way street, as it should be.

Here are some of the signs of severe mental illness, indicating a need for a psychiatric referral:

(a) The person believes that others are attempting to harm him, assault him sexually, or influence him in strange ways. (b) He has delusions of grandeur about himself. (c) He shows abrupt changes in his typical pattern of behavior. (d) He hears voices, sees visions, or smells odors which do not exist. (e) He has rigid, bizarre ideas and fears which cannot be influenced by logic. (f) He engages in a repetitious pattern of compulsive actions or obsessive thoughts. (g) He is disoriented (unaware of time, place, or personal identity). (h) He is depressed to the point of near-stupor or is strangely elated and/or aggressive. (i) He withdraws into his inner world, losing interest in normal activities.[10]

When these signs appear the minister should help the person's family get him to psychiatric treatment without delay. The recovery rate from mental illness is higher if intensive treatment is instituted at an early stage. The family physician is the minister's and family's logical ally in such situations. He can administer sedation or other emergency medical care and can make arrangements for hospitalization. Often he is an effective link with a psychiatric facility or individual psychiatrist.

The basic question of *ego strength,* as discussed in Chapter 8, has an

[10] Clinebell, *Mental Health Through Christian Community,* p. 244. See pp. 242-60 for a discussion of "Helping the Mentally Ill and Their Families."

important bearing on what type of referral to make.[11] Persons with weak egos generally respond best to help which is primarily supportive rather than uncovering. The goals of such therapy are to help the person gain strength by blocking regression, limiting his impulsive "acting-out," helping him handle his adult responsibilities and use his personality strengths (rather than trying to erase his liabilities). Social casework agencies are most apt to provide this form of ego-adaptive therapy. Persons with psychoneurotic problems and a reasonable degree of ego strength often are able to respond to the various forms of uncovering psychotherapy, including psychoanalysis.

CONSULTATION OR REFERRAL

A clergyman can counsel safely and productively with many people he otherwise should refer, if he has regular access to a psychiatric consultant. There is growing awareness among the mental health professions that providing consultation to the "care-giving professions," including clergymen, is essential if the yawning gap between the supply of, and the need for, trained counselors is to be even partially bridged.[12] Regular case conferences with a competent psychotherapist or specialist in pastoral counseling extends the range of a minister's helping abilities, gives him expert assistance in handling counseling crises, and alerts him to subtle dangers in certain counseling relationships. Because of his medical training a psychiatrist is particularly valuable as a consultant, *provided* he is also well trained in psychodynamic theory and psychotherapy. The use of pastoral case conferences and consultation groups will be discussed in Chapter 17.

WHERE TO REFER

John L. Mixon, an experienced social worker, declares:

The two most important aspects of a good referral are: (1) a knowledge of the resource, its program, functions, intake policy, etc., and (2) the use

[11] For an insightful article on this issue by psychiatric social worker Minnie L. Waterman, see "Pastoral Decision: To Counsel or Refer," *Journal of Pastoral Care* (Spring, 1960), pp. 34-38.

[12] See Caplan, *Principles of Preventive Psychiatry*, pp. 212-65 for an excellent discussion of types and methods of mental health consultation.

of sound counseling procedures in interpreting the resources and the possible help the individual might expect to receive.[13]

A clergyman should begin to prepare himself for an effective referral ministry immediately after arriving in a new parish. This involves two things—assembling a growing "referral file" of community resources and building relationships with the social agencies and other helping professionals. A referral file becomes increasingly useful as the minister accumulates information about social agencies; directories of psychiatrists, clinical psychologists, marriage counselors, and AA groups; phone numbers of emergency psychiatric facilities, mental health clinics, and suicide prevention centers.

A minister should check to see if his community has a welfare planning council or other community chest agency which provides a directory (and perhaps a phone information service) of community services. Copies of such directories should be in the pastor's study and the church library. In rural and small communities, where nearby referral resources are scarce, the pastor's knowledge of the *closest* facilities is doubly important. In any community competent professionals (particularly doctors and ministers) who have been in the area for a while are sources of reliable referral information. In isolated regions correspondence with state mental health departments or with the national voluntary organization in a particular problem area will bring information concerning the most accessible help.

What are the major problem areas in which the minister needs to draw on community resources in his counseling? A referral manual by Charles F. Kemp includes a "Handbook of Agencies and Resources," listing help in these areas: adoption and child placement, alcoholism, business problems, child guidance, child welfare, community welfare services, correctional institutions, education, employment, family life, financial assistance, the handicapped, health, housing, industrial problems, legal assistance, mental health facilities, minority groups, older persons, retardation, transients, unmarried mothers, veterans, vocational guidance, youth services. This manual, entitled *The Pastor and Community Resources,* also includes a directory of national resources—church related, governmental, and voluntary; and a section in which the pastor may enter his own working list of local phone numbers and

[13] Personal communication, May, 1965.

addresses. The parish pastor would do well to keep Kemp's manual at his fingertips as a valuable tool in his referral file.

Accurate evaluations of the competence of the various counselors and psychotherapists in one's community often are difficult to acquire. The reputation which a therapist has among physicians and ministers provides a rough guide. Beyond this it is helpful for a minister to become personally acquainted with as many as possible of his community's therapists and social agency personnel. By having lunch with such persons, visiting the local child guidance or mental health clinic, and attending the "open meetings" of AA and Al-Anon, he builds relationship bridges which can prove immensely useful when he needs to make a referral. As he works with these persons in helping a troubled parishioner, the relationship grows stronger. The most trustworthy estimates of a therapist's personal authenticity and competence can come from direct contacts with him and from observing the overall results of referrals to him.

A cooperative team spirit among the helping professions of a community does not happen by accident. Someone must take the initiative. In order to do his own pastoral work optimally, a minister needs such an informal team. What is more, he is in an ideal position to take the initiative in this, perhaps starting with a weekly breakfast meeting of a small group of his laymen who are in the helping professions. Such meetings enhance communication on problems of mutual concern and build working relationships. This dialogue can help the participants view their several professions as lay ministries. C. W. Brister writes: "The 'priesthood of believers' must operate in community service, or this great Christian principle remains only an ideal instead of a reality." [14]

HOW TO REFER

The minister of a rural church recognized that a man who came to him "for help against a conspiracy" was suffering from paranoid delusions. A psychiatric referral, though obviously essential, was difficult since this particular illness, by its very nature, made the man unaware of his need for help. Only by patient counseling with his family over a period of weeks could an appointment with a psychiatrist and subse-

[14] Brister, *Pastoral Care in the Church*, p. 160.

quent involuntary hospitalization be effected. In the interim the pastor maintained a supportive role with the man. He listened and did not attempt to dissuade him from his delusions. He did raise some gentle questions concerning whether all the threatening aspects of his situation were objectively real or within his feelings, but he did not push the man. He stayed close to the burdened family while they were arranging, with their doctor's help, for hospitalization.

This is an example of *stopgap supportive counseling*, the emotional first aid which a minister gives while persons are being motivated to accept more basic help or waiting until such help is available. This is an invaluable form of help, employing the principles of supportive counseling described in Chapter 8. Because of resistances to psychiatric help and the length of waiting lists, the gap which must be "stopped" often extends over many weeks or even months.

Here are some guidelines for effective referral counseling: First, *create this expectation*. The minister's function of assisting persons in finding specialized help should always be mentioned when his availability for counseling is presented in the church bulletin or newsletter. If the seed of this expectation has been planted in the counselee's mind, the shock or threat of being referred may be reduced.

Second, *mention the possibility of referral early in any relationship in which it is likely to occur*, explaining why specialized help may be needed. Persons who have mustered their courage to come to the pastor, expecting help from him, usually feel some degree of rejection if it becomes necessary to refer them. This is true even if they understand intellectually the necessity of the referral. The longer the pastor waits to mention referral, the more it will tend to arouse rejection feelings.

A third guideline is one that is most often neglected. *Start where the person is in his perception of the problem and the kind of help that is needed*. Until a minister understands this picture and accepts the feelings attached to it he is in no position to make a referral. On the one side, there is the counselee's inner picture of his problem and its solution. On the other, often far away psychologically, is the counselor's perception of the nature of the problem and the help needed.

The fourth referral guideline is *to work to bring the counselee's perception of the problem, and its solution, close enough to the counselor's perception to permit the referral to "take."* This often requires several sessions or even months of patient work in counseling. Many pastoral referral attempts fail because the counselee's perception of his situation is fundamentally different from that of the pastor. The person therefore "resists" the pastor's referral either by not going to the suggested source of help or by not continuing long enough to receive therapeutic benefits.

Thomas W. Klink emphasizes the linking of two vital helping processes—*acceptance of feelings* and *support for reality testing*—in enabling a person to work through to an effective referral. The pastor must stay close to the individual's feelings while he helps him move toward accepting the reality of his need for specialized help. If he tries to push the person, without clarifying and accepting his feelings, and focusing his sense of need in a realistic direction, the referral will usually fail.

The fifth guideline is really one aspect of the fourth. *Help the person resolve emotional blocks with reference to the particular helping agency recommended*. Before suggesting that a person with alcoholism go to AA, it is important to find out how he sees his problem (guideline 3). Does *he* feel that his drinking is a cause or an effect of his other problems? Does *he* have any desire for help in stopping his drinking? If so, AA is for him. In suggesting AA it is important to ask the person what he has heard and how he feels about that group. This query, about any agency to which one is making a referral, is a valuable means of discovering the fears, misinformation, and emotional resistances which otherwise will sabotage the referral. Dealing with these inner blocks is often a lengthy process, but it is an essential part of *motivating* a person to accept help from that source.

The sixth guideline is *to interpret the general nature of the help which the person may expect to receive, relating it to the person's own sense of need*. This should be done without making the mistake of overselling the potential values of the help—a mistake which makes the helping agency's work more difficult—or committing the agency or therapist to a specific treatment approach. (See footnote 16.)

The seventh guideline is *to establish strong enough rapport with the person so that his relationship with the minister may serve as a bridge over which he may walk into another helping relationship*. The use of this bridge of trust is facilitated if he knows that the minister is personally acquainted with the person to whom he is referred. The minister is fortunate if he can say, "The person I want you to see at the mental health clinic is a friend of mine." In any case, he should say, "If you would like, I will talk with him about your situation so that he will know something about it before you go." This is a way of breaking the ice for the person and establishing a bridge for him with the therapist. Here is how the bridge principle is used in referring alcoholics to AA. The pastor says: "Mac, if I understand you, you are beginning to suspect that you have a problem with alcohol. I'd like for you to chat with a friend of mine who has been through the mill himself on this problem, and found an answer that works for him. Let's see if he's free to drink a cup of coffee with us, O.K.?" At the three-cornered coffee klatch which follows, the AA member (who, hopefully, is also in the minister's church) will probably make arrangements to take Mac to an AA meeting.

In making referrals to therapists and social agencies, it is generally wise *to let the person make his own appointment.* This keeps the initiative with him and, in addition, allows the relationship with the new helping source to begin on the phone. As Mixon and Hiltner state:

> It is important not only that they find the best possible solution, but that *they have the feeling that they are participating in finding it*—not just sitting helplessly by waiting for someone to find it for them. Even so simple a thing as calling the agency for an appointment is a great allayer of anxiety.[15]

It is wise for the minister to check with a therapist or agency before suggesting that a person contact them, to make sure that he can be seen, and to brief the intake worker on the case.[16] It is also wise to ask the person to phone the pastor after making his appointment and after being seen for the first time. If he does not do so, the minister should

[15] *Community Help on Pastoral Problems,* p. 25.

[16] John L. Mixon suggests these principles for making good referrals to social agencies: "(a) Secure basic information regarding the agency. This should include an understanding of the purpose, function, and intake policy. To guess at possible services to be rendered by an agency resulting in indiscriminate referrals is a waste of everybody's time and frustrating to the person to be served. (b) Do not commit an agency to a specific service or solution. The agency must be free to assist within the limits of its resources and in relation to the real needs of the applicant. (c) Provide such information as you may have to the agency called upon, either by letter or by phone. (d) Follow up all referrals. This will enable you to evaluate the services for the future. Your understanding of what took place will assist you in further consultation if the person returns to you." (Personal communication, May, 1965.)

phone him "to see how things went." This procedure expresses the pastor's continuing concern and allows him to follow through with those who resist obtaining the specialized help he recommended.

The eighth guideline is *to attempt to motivate a person to try a given therapist or agency, even if he is only mildly "willing."* A skilled psychotherapist may be able to remove resistances to help which have not yielded to previous efforts. With resistant alcoholics I first do all I can to reduce their resistance to AA and then urge them to expose themselves to an AA group regularly for a month, whether or not they particularly like it. In some cases this exposure allows the informal group therapy and philosophy of AA to make an "end run around their defenses." Their resistances gradually dissolve as they experience the satisfactions of sobriety and the warm acceptance of the AA fellowship. If one waits until an alcoholic is "completely ready" for help, he may be in the mental hospital or cemetery first. The same applies to many other problems. Of course, it is not wise to push a person beyond a certain point—the point at which the backlash phenomenon makes him more resistant to help.

The ninth guideline, *to let the person know that one's pastoral concern and care will continue undiminished after the referral,* helps to lessen the sense of rejection. A "Pastor's Guide to Community Services" makes this wise recommendation:

> After you refer continue to show Christian concern and friendliness. Keep in touch with the agency . . . so that you can work together effectively to help the client. No community agency can take the place of a pastor or the fellowship of the church. In a healthy, collaborative working relationship, both the agency and the church should feel free to express any question or criticism of the other so that there can be better mutual understanding and appreciation.[17]

Frequently such a collaborative relationship is not easy to maintain, but it *is* the relationship which is in the best interests of the party being helped. In referrals for psychotherapy it may be necessary for the pastor to gradually diminish his supportive counseling in order to motivate the person to move into another relationship. A person who is in psychotherapy should not be allowed to drain off his problems by continuing

[17] Produced by Protestant Community Services of the Los Angeles Council of Churches, 1965. The paragraph quoted is from the Introduction.

to counsel with the pastor. In most cases the relationship should be one of *pastoral care* but not pastoral counseling. Otherwise the person may attempt to use one parent figure against the other in a self-defeating manner.[18]

WHEN REFERRAL SOURCES ARE LACKING

Lack of essential referral resources should do more than frustrate a minister. It should touch his prophetic nerve and motivate him to help create the most needed resources. With the availability of the federal "community mental health center" program, and other state and national programs, there is less and less excuse for a community to be without essential services. If enough people of goodwill are informed of the unmet needs and if some individual or group takes the initiative, referral resources can be created. A minister or a dedicated layman who is in a helping profession occupies a strategic position to spark and lead such a community project.

The lack of mental health referral resources on an ability-to-pay basis constitutes an acute need in many communities, both for middle and lower income groups. A study of five socioeconomic classes in New Haven[19] revealed that the bottom group—the "poor"—had a rate of psychiatric illness almost three times that of any other class. Ninety percent of these illnesses were diagnosed as *psychoses*, as compared to the upper two classes where only 35 percent of psychiatric problems were psychoses. Both the rate and intensity of mental illness is much greater for the poor, the group which almost never can afford private psychiatric help. The high cost of private therapy makes it unavailable, on any extended basis, to most middle income groups.

RECOMMENDED READING

Charles F. Kemp, *The Pastor and Community Resources* (St. Louis: The Bethany Press, 1960). Published for the Department of Social Welfare, National Council of Churches.

[18] If a pastor and a psychotherapist do counseling with the same person, during the same period of time, it is essential that they keep in communication regarding what is occurring in each relationship. If this is done, the help of the minister and the therapist can be complementary.

[19] Hollingshead and Redlick, *Social Class and Mental Illness*.

Thomas W. Klink, "The Referral: Helping People Focus Their Needs," *Pastoral Psychology*, December, 1962, pp. 10-15.

John L. Mixon, *The Church and Community Agencies* (Philadelphia: Board of Missions of The Methodist Church, 1961).

Wayne E. Oates, *Where to Go for Help* (Philadelphia: Westminster Press, 1957).

Minnie L. Waterman, "Pastoral Decision: To Counsel or to Refer," *Journal of Pastoral Care*, Spring, 1960, pp. 34-38.

REALITY-PRACTICE SESSIONS

PARISHIONER'S ROLE: You are Mrs. B., the mother of a seventeen-year-old son, Jim, who has taken money from the cash register at the store where he worked after school. Your husband, Ed, is a carpenter. You have two teen-age daughters who are younger than Jim. Your husband and you are deeply disturbed by Jim's delinquency and willing to do whatever is necessary to obtain help for him.[20]

PASTOR'S ROLE: You sense that Jim's behavior is probably one aspect of a complex family disturbance and that the parents should be referred with Jim to the local family service agency. Attempt to make this referral following the guidelines set forth in this chapter.

OBSERVER-EVALUATOR: Try to empathize with both Mrs. B. and the pastor, being aware of the extent to which the latter helps Mrs. B. clarify her feelings and focus her needs.

In another session practice referring an alcoholic to AA and an emotionally distraught man to a psychiatrist.

[20] For a verbatim account of how a minister handled this case, see Cryer and Vayhinger, *Casebook in Pastoral Counseling*, pp. 162-66. Other case material for use in practicing referral counseling: Case No. 35, "Mental Illness Masquerading in Religious Terms," pp. 196-99; Case No. 36, a disturbed, incoherent woman is referred to a psychiatrist, pp. 199-203; Case No. 20, a three-generation family problem involving a referral of grandfather to a home for the aged, pp. 117-22.

11

Educative Pastoral Counseling

> Get wisdom; get insight.
> Do not forsake her, and she will keep you;
> love her, and she will guard you.
> —Prov. 4:5-6

He taught them as one who had authority.—Mark 1:22

In our "race between education and catastrophe" we need the ministry of creative education. Every local church and every hard-pressed family becomes a center for creative learning in the midst of the realities and concrete dilemmas we face. On the scale of urgency to survive we must grow or perish. Learning is the first and last business of every growing-dying, time-bound finite person. . . . Wherever persons meet from moment to moment before the necessities of nature and the free grace of God, we must be learning the great lessons of our existence, in the sharp focus and revealing truths of life and death.

—Paul E. Johnson[1]

A high school youth talks with his pastor about an emotionally charged vocational choice. A Protestant girl seeks guidance in her dilemma concerning her romance with a Catholic lad. A couple comes for prebaptismal preparatory conferences. A young adult seeks clarification on a perplexing theological issue. A social action committee asks

[1] "Where We Are Now in Pastoral Care," *Christian Advocate*, September 23, 1965, p. 8. Dynamic education should "bring us alive to the new possibilities of humanness" (Joseph Matthews, address, School of Theology at Claremont, November 15, 1965).

for the minister's help in planning its approach to a prejudice-laden issue. All these situations have one thing in common—to meet the needs of the persons involved, the minister must be able to function simultaneously as teacher and counselor. He must be a *teacher-counselor.*

Many of the minister's finest counseling opportunities require a blending of the skills of creative education and dynamic counseling. And so he engages in *educative counseling,* a helping process which integrates the insights and methods of two pastoral functions with the single objective of fostering the growth of persons. This involves the personalized communication of certain knowledge or beliefs, methods or skills, within the context of a counseling relationship and as a part of the process of counseling. Educative counseling goes far beyond merely imparting information. By utilizing counseling skills and sensitivities, it helps the person understand, evaluate, and then apply the information that is relevant to constructive coping with his particular life situation.

There are, of course, educative ingredients in almost all pastoral counseling. In types such as supportive, decision-oriented, and marriage counseling, educative aspects play a significant part. In referral, vocational, theological, premarital, prebaptismal, predivorce, and preretirement counseling, educative counseling looms so large as to be indispensable to the helpfulness of the process. It is appropriate, therefore, to label these types "educative pastoral counseling." [2]

This is a natural and inescapable form of counseling for the pastor because, as his role is defined, he is both a counselor and an educator with a certain tradition, message, and *Weltanschauung*. Educative counseling methods are among his most valuable tools for helping people. They are particularly useful in *preventive group counseling*—small group experiences designed to prevent future problems by preparing people to meet some particularly demanding situation constructively (e.g., childbirth, retirement, going to college). The concept of "educative counseling" helps to resolve the unnecessary conflict, in some ministers' minds, between their roles as counselors and as proclaimers of the gospel. This conflict is the result of the client-centered image of the counselor as relatively passive, and of the false dichotomy between knowledge and

[2] Counseling-oriented education and education-oriented counseling actually form a continuum. Awareness of this allows the minister to move freely toward a greater emphasis on the educative or the counseling dimensions as the needs of a particular person, couple, or family require. A synonym for educative counseling is "pastoral guidance."

feelings in the Rogerian approach. The conflict is resolved when transmitting knowledge and dealing with feelings are seen as complementary, interacting factors in the counseling process, and when the image of the minister as educative counselor is understood and accepted as an appropriate image.

THE GOALS OF EDUCATIVE COUNSELING

Educative counseling shares the common elements of pastoral counseling described in Chapter 4—establishing rapport, disciplined listening, responding to feelings. It becomes "educative" as it moves toward three goals: (1) *Discovering what facts, concepts, values, beliefs, skills, guidance, or advice are needed by the person or likely to be helpful in coping with his problems;* (2) *communicating these directly or helping the person discover them* (e.g., through reading); (3) *helping the person utilize this information to enhance his understanding, facilitate a wise decision, or handle a difficult situation constructively.*

To discover what may be relevant to a person's needs requires listening and interacting with a person. It requires becoming aware of his internal and external (interpersonal) frames of reference. To distribute information and advice in counseling, prior to understanding the person's situation, weakens the counselee's trust in the counselor. Ideally, the teaching aspects of counseling should be focused as sharply on the person's particular needs as is the medicine which a competent physician gives for a specific malady. In discussing "guiding" as one of the four historic dimensions of ministry, William A. Clebsch and Charles R. Jaekle state:

> Fundamentally, the guiding ministry assumes that useful wisdom, which edifies and illuminates the meaning and direction of a person's life, can be made available within the framework of the helping act. . . . The wisdom *must be fashioned or shaped to the immediate circumstances of the troubled person* in order that it may be appropriated and used in the context of the particular trouble at hand. Guiding as a pastoral function does not develop ethical principles . . . for general application to the process of living, but rather forges decision-guiding wisdom in the heat of specific troubles and strives to facilitate its use in particular situations.[3]

[3] *Pastoral Care in Historical Perspective,* p. 50. Italics mine.

The minister shares those aspects of his experience, insight, and knowledge which he senses, from his awareness of the person's problems, will be helpful to him as *tools* or *building materials* in constructing a workable approach to his situation. He does not try to "sell" the individual on a certain approach to his problems. Instead, he encourages him to wrestle with the material communicated, to use that which "speaks to his condition," and to reject the rest. The "subject matter" of educative counseling, as in all counseling, is *the person* and not the ideas, however valid. The content of educative counseling provides a kind of launching pad for the person's own thought processes, by which he searches for constructive approaches to current problems or demanding future experiences—confirmation, marriage, parenthood, divorce, retirement.

> Guidance commonly employs two identifiable modes. *Eductive*[4] *guidance* tends to draw out of the individual's own experiences and values the criteria and resources for such decisions, while *inductive guidance* tends to lead the individual to adopt an *a priori* set of values and criteria by which to make his decision.[5]

Educative pastoral counseling blends *inductive* and *eductive* methods of guidance in varying proportions. The minister communicates information in this spirit: "Here are some facts (concepts or methods) which, from my experience and understanding, appear to be valid. I believe they will be useful to you in meeting your needs. I share them for you to consider and will help you evaluate their relevance to your situation." The method is inductive in that it draws on the minister's store of knowledge and insight from his religious tradition, study, and experience. It is eductive in that it seeks to draw out the person's inner problems *and resources*, effecting encounter between these and the ideas presented. Counseling methods are used to help the person diminish his emotional blind spots and inner conflicts which otherwise would prevent him from understanding, evaluating, and then utilizing the relevant ideas. The minister-counselor should not be timid about sharing his knowledge acquired from study and training and whatever wis-

[4] From *educere,* "to lead forth" (Latin).

[5] Clebsch and Jaekle, *Pastoral Care in Historical Perspective,* p. 9. Client-centered therapy is a relatively pure eductive approach. The inductive approach, in the church, has traditionally appealed to codes of ethics and moral theology.

dom about life he has derived from counseling others and from his own struggles. The difficult but crucial goal is to find, in Granger E. Westberg's words, "a healthy balance between real authority based on expert knowledge, and the person's right to work through human problems in a free and empathetic relationship." [6]

The educative counselor is a kind of coach whose function is to assist the person in acquiring skills in deciding and coping. A coach ordinarily doesn't play the game, but it is his job to share whatever expert knowledge he possesses about it.

A devout Protestant young adult consults her pastor for help with a difficult decision—whether to terminate a romantic relationship obviously moving toward engagement with a Catholic man. Such a person needs accurate information on such matters as the Catholic position on birth control and the requirement that all children of mixed marriages be reared as Catholics. She needs to know the basic views of the two traditions on the Bible, the church, religious authority and freedom, the nature of salvation. She needs to face the particular tensions and conflicts which characterize many mixed marriages. From his training and experience the minister has at least some of the knowledge she needs. Without it she lacks a sound basis for making an informed decision. Complete objectivity is impossible in such emotionally laden decisions, but possessing reliable facts can increase the degree of objectivity present.

The sharing of information, however accurate, is seldom, if ever, enough. Almost invariably, powerful drives, affections, fears, conflicts, and prejudices are present. These must be dealt with if the person is to make a wise decision. Information becomes useful only as it is related to *that* person's inner world of meanings. Skilled counseling facilitates the integration of need-satisfying knowledge with the person's feelings, attitudes, and convictions. Only such integrated knowledge is functional in decision making and problem solving.

THE DYNAMICS OF EDUCATIVE COUNSELING

The fundamental question in discovering the possibilities and limitations of educative counseling is this—*What is the function of knowledge in causing and "curing" human problems?* As Rogers states, "Most

[6] *Minister and Doctor Meet,* p. 18.

maladjustments are not failures in *knowing*"[7] but root in emotional blocks. It does not follow, however, that the communication of information is unimportant in counseling.

The lack of valid information is often one significant dimension of a troubled person's problems in coping. Seldom, if ever, is it the *only* significant factor. Lack of accurate knowledge is sometimes a *cause* and frequently a *complicator* of interpersonal problems. Mrs. E.'s realistic fear of an unwanted pregnancy formed a vicious cycle with her relatively mild neurotic sexual conflicts. This produced diminishing returns in the couple's sex life, which strained their interpersonal relationship. Their pastor referred Mrs. E. to a competent gynecologist who recommended a more effective contraceptive method. This diminished the fear of pregnancy and improved their relationship.

The extent to which a person is able to use knowledge depends on his degree of mental health. No amount of information about "reality" will, in itself, transform a psychotic's deep need to distort his perceptions. And yet, as "remotivation therapy" has shown, even a regressed schizophrenic has some conflict-free areas of his psyche. The further one moves from psychoses, on the mental health continuum, the larger the healthy parts of the psyche and the more knowledge and skills become useful as ego tools.

Five assumptions constitute the theoretical foundation of educative counseling:

(1) Intellectual knowledge constitutes one important ego resource for most people, to some degree.

(2) Most counselees have sufficient conflict-free personality areas to allow them to make some use of information derived from educative counseling and elsewhere.

(3) A minister possesses knowledge which can be useful to many counselees.

(4) Counseling can help a person *utilize* relevant information.

(5) Insights, facts, and skills serve a person by enabling him to cope more efficiently with the challenges he confronts. This strengthens his sense of identity and worth.

[7] *Counseling and Psychotherapy*, p. 29. Rogers was reacting to an older approach to counseling consisting of exhorting, advising, and persuading. He retained the either-or, feeling-knowing dichotomy of that approach, but opted for feelings instead of knowing. Educative counseling seeks to move beyond the either-or to a both-and position.

In her study of how normal children cope with stressful situations, Lois Barclay Murphy made this discovery:

> Over and over again we saw how the impact of a new challenge intensified the child's awareness of himself; his capacity to meet such a challenge enhances his pleasure, his sense of adequacy, and his pride. . . . Through his coping experiences the child discovers and measures himself. . . . We can say that the child creates his identity through his efforts in coming to terms with the environment in his own personal way.[8]

THE DANGERS OF EDUCATIVE COUNSELING

In his educative counseling the minister faces certain pitfalls. The most ominous is *manipulating the counselee*. It requires considerable emotional maturity to present ideas about which one feels intense conviction (in theology, for example) without subtle pressure on the counselee to conform. Such pressure communicates disrespect for his precious human right to choose his own meaningful philosophy of life. A Siamese twin danger of this is slipping from *rational authority*, the healthy authority of competence (Erich Fromm), into authoritarianism, the authority of superior force which stunts personality. Still another pitfall is that of regarding information *per se* as adequate to help troubled persons. This leads to what could be called "salvation by words," a shallow, ineffective approach to counseling. It is important to listen for the hidden cries for help which often come disguised in innocuous-appearing requests for information.

As noted in discussing supportive counseling, giving advice and sharing information are useful ways of nurturing persons under stress by gratifying dependency needs. The danger is that in markedly dependent people such approaches may *foster even greater dependency*. When a minister senses that this is happening, his task becomes that of weaning the person by being gradually less advising and guiding. This is difficult because the dependent person's emptiness makes him long to be led and fed.

A final danger is that the pastor will *equate* his *transmitting* of information *with genuine learning* on his counselee's part. As Nathaniel Cantor makes clear: "Significant learning stems from the self-directed

[8] *The Widening World of Childhood, Paths Toward Mastery* (New York: Basic Books, 1962), p. 374.

motivation of the learner who wants something positive and creative for an unexpressed or unfulfilled need." [9] In educative counseling *the person's sense of need is always the place to begin.* Through counseling his awareness of the nature of his needs may expand. But genuine learning will occur only when his sense of need and certain ideas collide head on.

It is well to remember that authoritarian educative counseling can stifle the sacred spark of human creativity. Cantor declares:

> Most of us learn how *not* to learn. That is, we learn very early how to avoid tangling with the authority of adults who are significant in our lives. . . . We learn to curb self-expression a good deal of the time. We learn how to submit, run away, cut corners, rationalize, defend ourselves, and to distort. . . . In brief, we are driven "to adjust" to threats, anxieties, and fears.
>
> *Behavior which lessens anxiety is adjustive not integrative.* The essence of integrative behavior is the capacity to exercise one's curiosity, to derive positive satisfaction from the *spontaneous* expression of one's skills and powers. Motivation which leads to the spontaneous expressions of one's self is different from the kind of learning which seeks to lessen anxiety and avoid threat.[10]

Educative counseling should aim at stimulating integrative learning—the kind that releases a person's God-given potentialities.

THE METHODOLOGY OF EDUCATIVE COUNSELING

Because premarital guidance is the parish minister's most frequent (and, in some cases, most frustrating) educative counseling opportunity, I will use it to illustrate the methodology of this type.

There are two categories of educative counseling: (a) *those in which people come at the minister's request*—premarital, prebaptismal, church membership preparation, and (b) *those in which the counselee takes the initiative,* seeking guidance on vocational, theological, and other problems. The counselor's rule of thumb is that minister-initiated types ordinarily require a greater proportion of direct *instruction* than do the counselee-initiated types. Many premarital sessions are actually *individualized education* rather than counseling, in that the couples are not motivated by a desire for help with particular problems. But

[9] *Dynamics of Learning,* pp. xiv-xv.
[10] *Ibid.,* pp. xiii-xiv.

individualized education can be highly valuable in its own right, particularly if counseling skills and sensitivities are integral to the process. The pastor who learns to do counseling-oriented education will find increasing opportunities to do actual counseling with some of his premarital couples. Here are some of the methods which are useful:

(1) *As in other counseling, relate warmly, acceptingly, and feelingly so that a sturdy relationship will grow.* Establishing a trustful relationship with the couple is the overarching goal of the premarital sessions. Such a relationship bridge helps make the minister and the church emotionally accessible to them. They can use this bridge if they want help with a problem, now or in the future.

(2) *Provide structure by asking low-threat, open-ended questions, beginning with general informational queries about positive aspects of their relationship.* Structuring tends to reduce the new-experience anxiety which most couples bring to the first session.

PASTOR: Since I'm going to share this important milestone in your lives, it seemed right that we should get better acquainted. Tell me, how did you meet?

By continuing to ask gently leading questions he helps the couple talk about how their relationship began and developed. In the process he gets a tentative picture of their current interaction and of the parental families which shaped it. A modification of Virginia M. Satir's method of taking a "family life chronology" can be very useful in premarital counseling.[11] Threatening or embarrassing questions should be avoided, because they block the growth of genuine dialogue in the counseling.[12]

Some ministers have found *background information forms* helpful in providing anxiety reducing structures and in "priming the pump" of interaction on significant levels. These instruments are easily used and much less threatening than personality inventories.[13] They provide an

[11] See *Conjoint Family Therapy*, pp. 112-35.

[12] Reuel L. Howe's *The Miracle of Dialogue* is valuable as preparatory reading for informal and educative counseling.

[13] The Marriage Council of Philadelphia, 3828 Locust Street, has developed a "Background Schedule." *In Holy Matrimony* (Nashville: The Methodist Publishing House, 1958), the marriage manual of The Methodist Church, has tear-out information forms to be filled out by the bride and groom. For a discussion of the use of personality tests in premarital counseling see Charles W. Stewart, *The Minister as Marriage Counselor*, pp. 55-58.

abundance of information quickly. To the pastor's perceptive eyes the information invariably includes clues which point to fruitful areas for discussion.

Structure can be provided by mentioning purposes and possible topics of the sessions together. A tentative, informal "outline" reduces a couple's fear of the unknown. The outline should be used only to provide flexible points of departure in the sessions. With highly verbal couples an unstructured, open-ended approach is usually effective:

PASTOR: Naturally you want to build the best possible relationship through the years of your marriage. To help you get launched in this direction is one reason we're meeting. As you have been thinking about your marriage, what thoughts or questions have come to your minds?

If a couple does not respond by opening up an issue in which they are interested, it is well for the pastor to provide structure by asking leading questions or by mentioning some of the topics on his "agenda":

PASTOR: As we meet for these three sessions there'll be some topics I'll suggest, but we'll save as much time as you want for the questions that come to your minds. We'll go through the ceremony step by step, to discuss its meaning as well as the mechanics. At some point I'd like to share some thoughts about how a couple can keep their love growing over the years. How does all this sound to you?

(3) *Do everything possible to remove the sense of threat, so they will feel free to reveal needs and worries.* In addition to building rapport and providing structure, threat reduction involves communicating to the couple that they are not "on trial." At the outset the minister may say, "I consider it a privilege to share in the launching of your marriage." This initial reassurance cannot be given of course until the minister is certain that there are no insurmountable obstacles to the marriage or to his participation.[14]

(4) *Gradually become aware of the couple's learning readiness*—i.e., *their degree of awareness of needs related to their marriage.* This is done by responding to their positive and negative feelings as these emerge in the flow of conversation, and by gradually asking more feeling-

[14] I am thinking of severe emotional disturbance on the part of one or both, and of the ecclesiastical strictures in some denominations against remarriage of divorced persons.

centered and relationship-probing questions; for example, "How do you feel when he is quite late for a date?" Couples who answer in surface-level clichés, revealing only positive feelings, are either unaware of their multifaceted relationship or they feel they *must* put their best foot forward with the minister. The latter type will bring their less socially acceptable feelings out of hiding only when they feel safe in the relationship.

A useful method of need discovery, adapted from marriage counseling, is to scrutinize specific vignettes of interaction involving conflict.

PASTOR: (after rapport is well established) What happens when you disagree over something you both feel strongly about? Could you think of an example that we could look at together?

(5) Learning readiness varies greatly in different areas. It is helpful, therefore, *to open up various key topics briefly, watching for interested responses which may indicate awareness of need.* Obviously this should not be done in "lecturettes" but informally and, if possible, in a personalized way.

PASTOR: Most of us have some trouble with communication in marriage. John and Mary, our hypothetical couple, have been married about a year. Mary gets her feelings hurt when John is pre-occupied with business. She has trouble letting him know what is really "bugging" her. Does this happen to ring any bells with you?

Mentioning areas of possible discussion is a pump-priming or bait-casting operation. The minister follows the couple's responses, depending on which bait they take. Here are some areas which often produce fruitful dialogue: money, budgets, in-laws, housing plans, family planning, parenthood, wife's outside employment, mutual need satisfaction, values in marriage, special needs of men and women, conceptions of roles, improving communication, dealing with differences, influences of family backgrounds, first year adjustments, mutual sexual satisfaction, meeting crises, the reciprocity of sexual and ego needs, the role of religion in enriching family life.

(6) When even a flicker of interest appears in a couple's responses, *concentrate discussion on that area for a while, encouraging them to examine it and seek to communicate needed information.* The pastor

begins with what *they* are interested in and builds on that. He shares certain ideas, experiences, and beliefs which seem relevant to the couple's needs. Then he invites dialogue around the axis of their needs. After brief, informal sharing he immediately encourages feedback by asking, "Does this happen to strike a responsive chord in your experience?" or "How do *you* feel about this?" He focuses on a given topic long enough to give the couple an ample opportunity to understand what he has said and to discuss it, if they wish. If a topic proves fruitless, he moves on to another. The process is one of "seed sowing." The minister knows that if he keeps on sowing, some of the seeds will fall on the fertile soil of the couple's interests and needs. In the give-and-take of this dialogic method of premarital counseling, the couple gradually acquires a more creative perspective on their relationship. As Nathaniel Cantor observes, "Learning probably takes place in small increments which accumulate into insights." [15]

Some topics are so vital, from the minister's viewpoint, that he feels he should give a general orientation in those areas, even if the couple shows no sense of need with reference to them. In moderation such presentations will not harm the quality of the relationship with the couple. Occasionally some of the seeds he sows in this way may fall on receptive soil. One of my "must" topics is *mutual need satisfaction*—i.e., how a couple can feed each other's heart hungers. Eric Berne's PAC approach may be used to arouse a couple's interest in the nature of their interaction, including their need satisfaction patterns.

(7) *Discussion should focus on present feelings and current problems, in addition to anticipated future problems.* In Peace Corps training "anticipatory guidance" was found to be most effective when it dealt with current experiences of trainees in handling the minor crises of the training program—e.g., their feelings of deprivation resulting from leaving their families and their resentments arising from constantly being tested and observed during training. These feelings were similar to those which were anticipated overseas. Concentrating on them allowed the small training groups to work with *live feelings*.[16] A similar approach to premarital guidance gives attention to how the couple copes with tensions, feelings, and problems arising during the prewedding period, including the anxieties of premarital counseling.

[15] *Dynamics of Learning*, p. 281.
[16] Caplan, *Principles of Preventive Psychiatry*, pp. 84-85.

A couple's worries about the future are, of course, *present* feelings and should be examined thoroughly. When needs, problems, or worries are revealed, the premarital sessions become counseling in the full sense of the word. It is usually unproductive to dwell on possible future conflict areas of which they have no awareness. To do so seems, from their view, to be either irrelevant or a prophecy of gloom. With reference to the future it is much better to concentrate on a positive topic such as "the care and feeding of a growing marriage."

(8) *Several sessions (a minimum of three) should be spent with each couple to allow rapport to become consolidated between sessions.* Discovering in the first session that the minister is human and cares about them often permits a couple to open up in subsequent sessions. Between sessions carefully selected book chapters should be assigned as "homework." [17] This primes the interaction pump and exposes the couple to awareness-stimulating material. The pastor may say during the second session: "What particular ideas appealed to you as you read this chapter?"

(9) *A line-by-line discussion of the wedding ceremony* allays anxieties about their parts in it and provides an ideal entrée to a discussion of its profound meaning. This leads naturally into an exploration of the spiritual dimension of their relationship.

Throughout premarital counseling, the minister should bear the *goals of the process* in mind: (a) reducing their anxieties about the mechanics of the wedding; (b) giving them some guidelines for the early adjustment stages of marriage; (c) strengthening their sense of adventure, rapture, and joy; (d) undergirding or strengthening their sense of adequacy and helping to make it at least slightly more realistic; (e) setting an example for them of openness of communication on such taboo topics as sex and anger; (f) introducing them to the "language of relationships" (Reuel Howe); (g) supplying them with whatever information they may desire relative to achieving a satisfying, growing relationship; (h) giving them a "juicy taste" of a somewhat deeper level of communication than they have hitherto experienced; (i) helping them sense the wonder of the presence of the God of love in their love; (j) helping them experience the difference between "holy matrimony" and just getting married; (k) making oneself emotionally available so

[17] Chapters from a book such as Dorothy W. Baruch and Hyman Miller's *Sex in Marriage, New Understandings* are excellent for this purpose.

that they may use the relationship for more extended counseling, before or after the ceremony. The minister should hold to these goals with a very light grip, remembering that if only the *master goal* is achieved—the establishment of a robust relationship with the couple—the premarital sessions have been eminently worthwhile.

HIGH MOTIVATION EDUCATIVE COUNSELING

Those forms of educative counseling in which the parishioner, impelled by the pain of his problem, takes the initiative can be described as "high motivation" counseling. Maintaining a significant level of dialogue in such counseling is much less difficult than in forms of educative counseling in which the parishioner comes because the minister or the customs of the church require it. To illustrate the role of positive guidance and sound knowledge in high motivation educative counseling, one aspect of divorce counseling will now be discussed briefly. Persons in both pre- and post-divorce counseling are typically highly motivated by a sense of failure and interpersonal pain, particularly if children are involved.[18] With some 400,000 divorces per year in this country, involving 200,000 children, clergymen should be much more active than they are in helping minimize the personality damage and maximize the potentialities for learning in these crises. Since only one fourth of divorced persons remain single longer than five years, most divorce counseling is also preparation for remarriage.

A closer look now at the *content* of one facet of divorce counseling—that of minimizing emotional damage to children. Here are some of the recommendations which the pastor should help the parents consider and, if possible, implement:

(1) Avoid senseless rancor which will expose the child to added trauma.

(2) Obtain counseling to deal with their own resentments, guilt feelings, rage, hurt, and grief, so that they will not attempt to use the child as a "therapist."

(3) Obtain psychotherapy, after the acute crisis has passed, to discover and resolve the inner conflicts which contributed to the disintegration of the marriage.

[18] In spite of their pain, divorcing couples often avoid the clergyman because of their guilt. A special pastoral effort is necessary even to maintain contact with such couples. The minister should take the initiative in offering them the opportunity for counseling.

(4) Help the child avoid blaming himself for the parents' problems.

(5) Be honest with the child about what is happening.

These additional recommendations are offered by a psychiatrist on the staff of a children's hospital: Don't inform young children about an impending divorce until definite plans for their future have been agreed upon. Don't allow children under twelve to make the choice concerning which parent they will live with. Don't separate siblings. Other things being equal, the child should be placed with whichever parent remarries. One household should be established as "home" for the child, with the other as a place to visit. Parents should not use the child as a confidant or to spy on each other. "Every effort should be made to help them retain whatever feelings of love or respect they may have for each parent." [19] For full psychological growth a child needs a close relationship with two parents (or parent substitutes), whether or not they are living together.

Because of the intensity of their negative and hurt feelings, many divorcing couples are unable to implement sound recommendations such as these unless they have extensive counseling. Some will respond to the offer of help, because the welfare of their children is involved. Educative counseling with such persons includes communicating to them the best of what is known concerning minimizing the damage to children in the process of divorce. Equally important is helping them work through the emotional blocks and interpersonal hostility which otherwise interfere with their taking constructive action in the situation.

COUNSELING ON SOCIAL PROBLEMS

Educative counseling skills are invaluable assets in dealing constructively with social problems and challenges such as the brotherhood revolution. Paul E. Johnson declares: "The pastor in our world is called to a ministry of reconciliation within the tight walls of the small family or wherever there is conflict in the larger family of man." [20] Small study-action groups[21] offer an ideal setting within which accurate information can be presented on a given social conflict, and an opportunity provided for emotionally charged attitudes to be examined in the light of

[19] Graham B. Blain, Jr., "The Children of Divorce," *Atlantic Monthly*, March, 1963, pp. 98-101. (For references on divorce counseling, see footnote 26, Chapter 6.)

[20] "Where We Are Now in Pastoral Care," p. 8.

[21] Educative *group* counseling will be discussed in Chapter 12.

the religious view of man. There is, of course, no easy way to change prejudicial attitudes or effect reconciliation between estranged groups—racial, religious, political, ethnic, or national. But precisely because of the psychological complexities and difficulties involved, it is imperative that whatever is valid from the fields of counseling, group dynamics, and social psychology be applied to such problems. An intense (and appropriate) concern for suffering individuals should not deter counselors from investing a part of their energies in widespread experimentation in applying counseling skills to intergroup conflicts. Otherwise, counselors rightly can be charged with a kind of psychological pietism which ignores the relevance of their art to the towering social issues of our world in revolution. The efforts of Rogers and his followers to apply client-centered approaches to family life, teaching, leadership, and intergroup problems are hopeful examples of what may prove to be a key contribution by counselors (including pastoral counselors) to the resolution of those gigantic social problems which threaten human progress, if not the very survival of mankind.[22]

Pastoral work which combines the skills of the creative educator and the effective counselor can be an invaluable instrument in the church's prophetic ministry. Educative counseling methods, especially when used in small groups focusing on particular social problems, can help reduce the misinformation, fear, and prejudice which block the learning of constructive attitudes and the forming of new relationships. Insights from pastoral psychology can help guide the planning of effective social action strategy and its implementation.

RECOMMENDED READING

Nathaniel Cantor, *Dynamics of Learning* (East Aurora, N.Y.: Henry Stewart, 1946).

Charles F. Kemp, *The Pastor and Vocational Guidance* (St. Louis: Bethany Press, 1961).

J. Kenneth Morris, *Premarital Counseling, A Manual for Ministers* (Englewood Cliffs, N.J.: Prentice-Hall, 1960).

[22] *Client-Centered Therapy*, pp. 320-83; *On Becoming a Person*, pp. 273-359. The following papers apply psychiatric insights to international problems: G. B. Chisholm, "The Psychiatry of Enduring Peace and Social Progress," *Psychiatry*, Vol. IX (February, 1946); "Psychiatric Aspects of Prevention of Nuclear War," Group for the Advancement of Psychiatry, *International Journal of Psychiatry*, Vol. I (July, 1965).

Lewis J. Sherrill, *The Gift of Power* (New York: The Macmillan Company, 1955).

Ross Snyder, "A Ministry of Meanings and Relationships," *Pastoral Psychology*, December, 1960, pp. 18-24.

Granger Westberg, *Premarital Counseling, A Manual for Ministers* (New York: National Council of Churches, 1958).

REALITY-PRACTICE SESSIONS

1. PARISHIONERS' ROLES: Invite a team member's wife to take the role of a prospective bride. The first counseling situation is that of a young couple who have grown up in the same church, are well known to the minister, and are previously unmarried. Then take the roles of a young couple who met at a cafe near an army base. She is nineteen and divorced. He is a twenty-one-year-old G.I.

   PASTOR'S ROLES: Give premarital guidance to each of these couples.[23]

2. PARISHIONERS' ROLES: You are two members of a youth group in an inner-city church. There has been major conflict with the group because of the prejudices of the two ethnic groups from which you come and of which you are the unofficial, but recognized, leaders. You are unhappy about the way in which this conflict has split the youth group. The prejudices are based, in part, on mutual ignorance of the customs of the two ethnic groups.

   PASTOR'S ROLE: Call the two young people in for a talk. Use the principles of educative and role-relationship counseling to attempt to effect reconciliation.

An observer-evaluator should be used in all these sessions.

[23] For a verbatim account of the way in which a minister handled the second couple, see Cryer and Vayhinger, *Casebook in Pastoral Counseling*, Case No. 12, pp. 77-85.

12

Group Pastoral Counseling

When the day of Pentecost had come, they were all together in one place. . . . And they were all filled with the Holy Spirit.—Acts 2:1, 4

Intimate sharing of feelings, ideas and experiences in an atmosphere of mutual respect and understanding enhances self-respect, deepens self-understanding, and helps a person live with others. Such an experience can be helpful to persons at any level of illness or health.

—Jerome D. Frank[1]

Group counseling methods constitute the most promising resource for major creative advances in pastoral counseling! Group counseling approaches, applied to a wide spectrum of problems in living, can release a Mississippi-like stream of help in a congregation's life together. They can allow a church to become an increasing force for preventing personality problems by stimulating growth toward wholeness. Although exciting developments are occurring in the use of group pastoral counseling in many different places, most churches have scratched only the surface of the rich possibilities in this direction. There can be no doubt that whatever a clergyman or seminarian does to increase his mastery of the group counseling art will strengthen his ministry to persons at many points.

THE ADVANTAGES AND VALUES OF GROUP COUNSELING

Group counseling has several significant advantages, as compared with individual counseling methods. First, much of the pastoral coun-

[1] "Group Methods in Therapy," Public Affairs Pamphlet 284, pp. 3-4.

seling now done individually could be done *more effectively* in small groups. Generally speaking, the various counseling methods described in this book can be employed in group counseling, often with more effectiveness than in individual counseling. For example, married couples using the Bernean approach quickly identify the games other couples in a group are playing. This brings the games into the open where they can be dealt with.

A second advantage is that it is obviously better stewardship of his time to help five to fifteen people simultaneously than to spend the same period in helping one individual. This is crucial in the light of a minister's desire to help lift as many loads as possible in the time he has available. Group counseling is the key to broadening a church's caring ministry. It allows scores of people to drink the nourishing milk of meaningful small group relationships. The pastor who masters this method has a way of supporting, challenging, nurturing, and helping many times the number he could serve by individual counseling.

Third, group counseling methods can be used to stimulate the growth of many who will not come for formal "counseling." A man who describes himself as "not the type who would go to a minister for counseling" reports that two years of participation in a "depth Bible study" group has influenced his life profoundly. Group counseling methods, though not formally labeled, are used as a part of the process by the pastor who leads the group.

A fourth advantage is that group approaches allow counselees *to help each other*. One of the vital new elements in group therapy is the presence of mutually "giving" relationships, as distinguished from the largely "taking" relationships of individual therapy. The counseling group participant is often *helper* and *helped* in the same session. This is a major advantage for persons who fear dependency and cannot accept a one-way counselor—counselee helping relation. Group counseling is closer to the reciprocity of everyday life. As a way of releasing the helping potentialities that are dormant in most people, group counseling is a contemporary implementation of the ancient injunction, "Bear one another's burdens" (Gal. 6:2). In an effective therapy group the group as a whole becomes an instrument of healing and growth.

Fifth, the small group is a natural milieu for *short-term educative counseling*. Three sessions of prebaptismal counseling with a group of four to six couples invariably stimulate learning which far exceeds that of a couple-by-couple approach. The couples learn from each other and are nurtured by the group's *esprit de corps*. By example, the less inhibited couples encourage the others to open up.

Group counseling is a natural methodology in the church, since groups of all sizes constitute the fabric from which the church's program is made. It is a natural form of counseling for a minister who is essentially a group worker, the leader of a social organism composed of many subgroups. His knowledge of group dynamics (the forces which make groups "tick") and his skill in group counseling can be invaluable aids in working with a church's many noncounseling groups. The presence of even a few vital counseling groups can have a positive leavening effect on the spiritual climate of an entire church. As a means by which *koinonia* becomes a reality in the church on main street, group counseling is "integral to the ministry of the church." [2]

TYPES OF CHURCH GROUPS

Five types of groups constitute an optimal church program: (a) *work and service*, (b) *study*, (c) *supportive-inspirational*, (d) *counseling*, and (e) *psychotherapy*. Each type can play a role in a church's ministry to persons. The vast majority of church groups combine the first three functions—service, study, and fellowship—in varying proportions. Church-sponsored psychotherapy groups are relatively rare. The major frontier in the church's group life is the fourth type—*group counseling* or modified group therapy. Here the possibilities are almost unlimited.

Elsewhere I have discussed the essential roles of service, study, and fellowship groups in a dynamic church.[3] Suffice it to say that the major contribution of group counseling insights to such groups is to help make membership in them a need-satisfying experience. Leadership training, using group counseling methods, is the key to rejuvenating existing groups and organizations.

Here are some of the functions of a creative group-centered leader (and of a group counselor):

(1) He seeks the maximum distribution of leadership among the group members. (2) He sees that all members of the group have an opportunity to par-

[2] Joseph W. Knowles, *Group Counseling*, p. 7.

[3] *Mental Health Through Christian Community*, pp. 157-61.

ticipate in group decisions. (3) He encourages freedom of communication. (4) He seeks to increase opportunities for participation. (5) He attempts to create a nonthreatening group climate in which feelings and ideas are accepted. (6) He conveys feelings of warmth and empathy, thus encouraging others to do likewise. (7) He sets the tone by paying attention to the contributions of others, perhaps reflecting what they say with, "Let's see if I understand what you mean . . ." (8) He helps build group-centered (as contrasted with individual-centered) contributions by his "linking function," pointing to the relationships among various individuals' contributions to the discussion.[4]

A leader of this type is a communication catalyst who facilitates the group process, enabling the group's potentialities to be released. As meaningful relationships deepen through communication, personality needs are satisfied.

What experiences are most effective in training creative leaders so that the church school, youth fellowship, men's club, woman's club, couple's club, senior citizens' fellowship, and all other groups can maximize their capacities to stimulate the growth of persons? The answer is *group counseling* and *sensitivity training groups*. (See Chapter 17.) These can occur in a leadership workshop series, an intensive weekend "leader renewal retreat," or an ongoing growth group for leaders. Psychiatrist Gerald Caplan describes a well-functioning group as one "in which the system of authority is clear and acceptable, the communication network open, and the roles of members meshed in a complementary way."[5] Church group leaders who use their authority appropriately, keep communication lines open, and help members relate in mutually satisfying ways actually possess some of the basic skills and sensitivities required in group counseling. The most efficient way of increasing one's ability as a creative leader or a group counselor is participation in a sensitivity training or therapy group. Leadership *techniques* are important, but their usefulness often is constricted by the leader's personality problems and insensitivities. *To vitalize his church's groups a minister should establish a "leadership enrichment group" using sensitivity training and modified group therapy methods.* It will pay rich dividends.

[4] Paraphrased from Thomas Gordon, *Group Centered Leadership and Administration* (Boston: Houghton Mifflin, 1956) in *Client-Centered Therapy* by Carl R. Rogers, Chapter 8.

[5] *Principles of Preventive Psychiatry*, p. 45.

GROUP PSYCHOTHERAPY IN THE CHURCH

Paralleling its conventional groups every church should have one or more groups with specific counseling goals—dealing openly with feelings and attitudes; giving support during personal crises; seeking solutions to problems of living; increasing marital and parental effectiveness; growing in spiritual strength, interpersonal awareness, and self-acceptance. Some of these goals can be achieved as by-products in creatively led noncounseling groups. But a need-oriented church also should have certain groups in which these goals are the groups' explicit *raison d'être.*

"Group psychotherapy" (often abbreviated "group therapy") describes a cluster of group approaches[6] to therapy, having these common characteristics:

(1) The group has an avowed therapeutic purpose which the members know in advance. (2) Its activities are limited to those which are directly psychotherapeutic (although there may be post-sessions for informal socializing). There are no projects, agendas, programs or instruction in the formal sense. (3) The dominant concern of the group is its members' growth in self-awareness, self-acceptance, and in their ability to form creative relationships. (4) Complete freedom of expression is encouraged and expected, including negative feelings about other members and the leader. (5) There is a continual and intensive focus on interaction *within the group,* on the premise that this reflects the members' general interpersonal patterns of relating. (6) Such groups are usually small, six to eight being a common size. Many such groups continue over several years.[7]

Jerome D. Frank summarizes the ways in which group psychotherapy can be helpful:

Therapy groups differ from individual therapy chiefly in their greater nearness to everyday life. They differ from ordinary social groups in their encouragement of honest expression of feeling and in granting status for reasons other than achievement.[8] This combination of factors helps patients to discover unsuspected similarities, which counteracts their sense of isolation and

[6] More than twenty-five methods are described in the group therapy literature. See Raymond J. Corsini's *Methods of Group Psychotherapy,* p. 4.

[7] Adapted from George R. Bach's *Intensive Group Psychotherapy.*

[8] The "ticket of admission," instead of success, is admitting that one has failed in certain relationships.

> facilitates production of attitude change. Therapy groups arouse patients emotionally through their pressure to self-revelation, through differences in outlook, and through rivalries arising from differences in life experiences and from stimuli in the group situation itself. They increase members' hopes and heighten their self-respect through fostering a sense of group-belongingness, affording examples of progress to each other, and giving them opportunities to help each other. They promote cognitive and behavioral change through the provision of multiple models, encouragement to express and examine feelings toward fellow group members and the therapist, and pressure to maintain communication despite conflict. Changes produced in the group are stabilized by the members' internalization of group standards, which usually are healthier in some respects than those of the individuals composing the group.[9]

People tend unconsciously to try to re-create their original family relationships in the groups to which they belong. In a therapy group this natural "transference" tendency is used as a vital part of the therapy. The person, in effect, has a "new family" and a new opportunity to mature emotionally.

A West Coast church sponsored a psychotherapy group, led by a member who is a social worker. The associate minister, who had had extensive training in pastoral counseling, was co-therapist. The group was limited to ten and was "open-ended"—new members being added as others terminated. The group met weekly for one and a half hours (the usual group therapy pattern) in the church's education building. It was open both to church members and non-members. The therapists contributed their services. Participants made a nominal weekly contribution which covered expenses such as psychiatric consultation. As a service to troubled families the group was highly effective. During a two and a half year period over seventy people participated, many of them with severe problems in living. This project demonstrated the therapeutic possibilities of using a clergyman as a co-therapist. Instead of inhibiting the open expression of raw feelings, the minister's presence seemed to be a catalyst. During the second half of the group's existence a theological student was brought in as a trainee in group therapy methods.

This group, and others like it, shows that unmodified group psychotherapy can be a valuable part of a church's counseling ministry, *pro-*

[9] *Persuasion and Healing* (Baltimore: Johns Hopkins Press, 1961), pp. 189-90.

vided well-trained therapists are available. Group psychotherapy is a complex art—more so than individual psychotherapy. It involves enabling the group to become the instrument of healing so that therapy is *by* the group and not just *in* it. Persons with only limited counseling training should avoid attempting group psychotherapy unless they are under the supervision of a trained group therapist. The intimate sharing of feelings over extended periods produces strong bonds among the group members which sometimes leads to sexual pairing. Powerful transference reactions occur. There may be hostile "acting out." Only skilled leadership can reduce the risks in group therapy. The element of unavoidable risk should not cause a church to veto having a therapy group. The only way to avoid all risks is to avoid all counseling and all relationships with the very people who most need the church.

If a church has a minister of counseling or a mental health professional with group therapy training, it is perfectly appropriate to provide this form of depth help to relatively disturbed persons. If such leadership is not available a church should focus on *group counseling* (modified group therapy) for relatively healthy persons. Whether or not a church has a psychotherapy group, the mainstream of its efforts in this area should be group counseling for the host of people who are not "sick" psychologically but who can profit greatly from a group sharing experience. In any church there are many persons in this category—those facing some period of heavy stress, those with garden-variety problems and unhappiness, and those who simply desire to grow spiritually, improve their relationships, or enhance their creativity.

VARIETIES OF GROUP PASTORAL COUNSELING

A minister's understanding of group dynamics and his general training in counseling can be applied with great profit to *group counseling.* The more training (particularly clinical) he has had, the better able he will be to discover the counseling potentialities which exist in many small groups, and the less he will need to modify the straight group therapy approach to stay within the limits of his competence.

Group pastoral counseling differs from group psychotherapy in one or more of these ways:

(1) The group may be larger, usually a maximum of fifteen. The intensity of interaction tends to vary *inversely* with size.

(2) The group's purposes are broader, including such goals as education, service, and inspiration.

(3) The leader may function as teacher providing content and structure.

(4) The group's life-span may be shorter and agreed upon in advance.

(5) The frequency of meeting may be reduced.

(6) The process is directed at specific problems or topics rather than at general personality change.

(7) The leader may intentionally limit the depth of interaction by not encouraging the expression of highly personal feelings,[10] including group members' feelings about each other.

(8) Group counseling is more likely than group therapy to attract and to meet the felt needs of relatively "normal" people, although unmodified group therapy also may be highly beneficial to such persons.

Modifying the group therapy approach in one or more of these ways *tends to make the therapeutic process less intense* and therefore easier for less highly trained leaders to use constructively. Group counseling retains these characteristics of group psychotherapy. It deals with personal problems in a small group setting. Openness regarding feelings and topics which are tabooed in most social situations is encouraged and expected. Communication on a deeper level is fostered and valued. This, plus the elimination of interpersonal barriers, produces profoundly meaningful relationships. Both group counseling and group psychotherapy aim at significant personal growth, but on different levels.

Within a church program the applicability of group counseling methods is limited only by the leaders' vision, training, and willingness to experiment. Vital churches in many places are using all sorts of new group patterns. The flowering of small, intimate sharing groups is one of the exciting developments in contemporary religious life. Many different labels are used—"discovery group," "personal group," "encounter group," "prayer group," "*koinonia* group," "growth group," "sharing group," "Yokefellow group," "Bible exploration group," "fellowship group," and just plain "group." I agree with Robert C. Leslie's view that

[10] Robert L. Brizee distinguishes private vs. public feelings, pointing out that a pastor can judge the depth of a group by the extent to which private feelings are expressed. Further, he can help a counseling group avoid becoming a psychotherapy group by not focusing on highly personal (private) feelings should they be expressed.

one of the healthiest signs of church renewal is the number of these groups which are springing up on all sides.[11]

As indicated previously small groups constitute the optimum setting for *educative counseling* (utilizing the basic principles described in Chapter 11). Ideally, *a church should create a network of educative counseling groups so that persons in all ages and stages, with many different needs, can find personal help.* To show the wide range of usefulness of this approach, here are examples of educative counseling groups designed to meet the needs of persons in each of the "eight stages of man." [12]

Stage 1—Infancy (birth to fifteen months). *Developmental goal:* Basic trust. *Relevant counseling group:* "preparation for parenthood" group. An Ohio church conducted educative counseling groups for expectant parents at regular intervals. Such groups help couples deal with anticipatory anxiety and work through conflicted feelings about parenthood. They also communicate valuable information to this strongly motivated (by a sense of need) group. Margaretha A. Ribble's *The Rights of Infants* is a useful resource book for expectant or new parents, as is *Your Child Is a Person, A Psychological Approach to Parenthood Without Guilt,* by Stella Chess, *et al.*[13] Gerald Caplan calls the work of such groups "anticipatory guidance" or "emotional innoculation":

> In small-group or individual discussions, the specialist then draws their attention to the details of the impending hazard and attempts to evoke ahead of time a vivid anticipation of the experience, with its associated feelings. . . . He then helps them begin to envisage possible ways of solving the problems, including mastery of their negative feelings. When the experience itself arrives, the hazards will be attenuated because they have been made familiar by being anticipated, and the individuals will already have been set on the path of healthy coping responses.[14]

[11] "The Uniqueness of Small Groups in the Church," *Pastoral Psychology,* June, 1964, p. 33.

[12] Erik H. Erikson, *Identity and the Life Cycle.* A local church should have groups designed to meet the needs of persons in each of these stages of life. Groups of all five types may be needed to accomplish this.

[13] The Ribble book was published by Columbia University Press, 1943, and the Chess book by Viking Press, 1965.

[14] *Principles of Preventive Psychiatry,* p. 84.

Stage 2—Early Childhood (fifteen months to two and a half years). *Goal:* autonomy. *Relevant counseling group:* a parent study and fellowship group. Churches which are aware of the crucial importance of constructive parent-child relationship during the preschool years often provide a study group for such parents. In one church a young couples' Sunday school class had a child study focus for several years, under the leadership of a competent child psychologist. The sharing in this class became deep and satisfying. Anxieties about parenthood were reduced and valuable information communicated. A more typical pattern is the study-fellowship group for mothers of young children. Whatever a church can do to strengthen, inform, and inspire parents of preschool children will pay rich dividends, both spiritually and psychologically, far into the future.

Stage 3—Play Age (three to six). *Goal:* initiative. *Relevant counseling group:* child-study nursery group. A Long Island church used an educative counseling approach in an ongoing child-study program for mothers of preschoolers. The group met one morning a week throughout the school year. A steering committee, elected by the group, planned the child-study programs, in consultation with the minister. A typical meeting began with informal sharing over coffee, followed by a brief program geared to the interests and needs of the mothers—e.g., a review of a chapter from Dorothy W. Baruch's *New Ways in Discipline*[15] or a talk on "Handling a Child's Fear of Death." The lively discussion which followed invariably focused in part on the feelings of the participants. While the mothers met in the church parlor, the children took part in a nursery school in the basement, under the direction of trained volunteers. The mothers' group experience helped reduce the loneliness that is the lot of many young mothers, bolstered their self-confidence, and provided useful information on many topics. The nursery school experience helped the children to master skills and learn to relate to other children and adults outside their homes.

Stage 4—school age (six to twelve). *Goal:* industry. *Relevant counseling group:* parents' study group. In the course of his pastoral work, Edgar N. Jackson frequently encountered a sense of need among parents of pre-adolescents. So he invited five or six couples to meet for eight sessions to discuss mutual concerns. He began each session with a brief statement on such subjects as the psychology of parent-child

[15] New York: McGraw-Hill, 1949.

relationships. This precipitated discussion which moved to the group counseling level—i.e., the parents' feelings and problems. This approach can be applied to a variety of "parent enrichment groups," beamed at different age groups and beginning with the particular needs and problems expressed by them.

Stage 5—adolescence (puberty to twenty). *Goal:* identity. *Relevant counseling groups:* "sex and the whole person" groups. A number of West Coast churches have used a group educative counseling approach to sex education with high school youths. In addition to presenting accurate facts within the context of the Christian perspective, the series provided an opportunity for the young people to explore their attitudes, expectations, and apprehensions in the area of sex. The parents met concurrently in a separate group, using a similar approach.

Teen-age self-discovery groups are often very effective. A number of churches have experimented with both short-term and long-term groups. Such small group experiences help young people discuss their feelings and problems openly, relate more effectively, and discover their own personal faith. In some cases the educative counseling approach has been used with confirmation classes and depth Bible study groups for youth. Donald R. Rhoades has written: "More than any other institution . . . the church provides the child and adolescent with a second family type of association, assisting the process of growing free from family localisms." [16] Discovery and growth groups for adolescents can facilitate the maturation process in this way.

Stage 6—young adulthood. *Goal:* intimacy. *Relevant counseling groups:* "group premarital counseling." Psychiatrist Lena Levine and social worker Jeanne Brodsky have demonstrated the effectiveness of premarital counseling in groups of two to six couples. Their series consisted of three sessions of three hours each, devoted respectively to love, sex, and parenthood. They report:

> The basic factual information that is given can help correct misinformation and thus clear the way for healthier attitudes. . . . The group session acts as a stimulus for them to talk to each other about problems and helps them in their interpersonal communication. The group also stresses the basic needs of all people, and so helps to develop an awareness of the sameness of all. This makes possible a lessened feeling of isolation and at the same time increases

[16] *A Faith for Fellowship* (Philadelphia: Westminster Press, 1965), p. 112.

awareness of the uniqueness of each individual as a result of his heritage and life experiences. The group process makes possible the more rapid release of fears, anxieties, and guilt, and helps bring out specific conflicts, some of which can be resolved immediately through the group. Other more deeply rooted difficulties are at times revealed, and the need for additional help is more readily accepted because of the group support.[17]

"Growing Together," a marital enrichment group for young adults in the first years of marriage, was offered by a West Coast church. Role playing of typical adjustment problems of new marriages was used to open up the group quickly. This was an excellent example of preventive pastoral care. With one exception the couples came to the group, not because their marriages were failing but because they desired to make good marriages better. Marital enrichment groups are useful with couples of various ages. A book such as Eric Berne's *Games People Play* makes an excellent interaction stimulator in such groups.

Stage 7—middle adulthood. *Goal:* generativity. *Relevant counseling group:* "creative years group." The middle years are stressful ones for many people in our culture. An East Coast church formed a marital enrichment group for couples thirty-five to fifty. It was led by the minister using Reuel Howe's *The Creative Years*[18] as a resource. At each session a couple gave a synopsis of one chapter's key ideas. Then they role-played a marital scene high-lighting a particular problem. Much of the discussion centered on problems of deepening marriage relationships and finding inner meanings to cope with the value crisis of the middle years.

Stage 8—the mature years. *Goal:* ego integrity. *Relevant counseling group:* "preparation for retirement." A New York church has experimented with anticipatory guidance groups for men on the verge of retirement or recently retired. The minister drew the groups together by simply inviting six to ten men to meet with him for a series of six times to share ideas on "Making the Most of Retirement."

Educative counseling approaches have been used effectively with small groups of senior citizens.[19] With this age group it is particularly important to avoid the label "counseling."

[17] "Group Premarital Counseling" (Planned Parenthood Federation, 1953).

[18] (New York: Seabury Press, 1959).

[19] For a discussion of the use of group methods with older adults, see Helen I. Driver, *Counseling and Learning through Small-Group Discussion*, pp. 420-29.

In addition to counseling groups set up along age lines, a church should have interest-centered groups which cut across age lines. In most churches spiritual-growth-oriented approaches, such as the Yokefellow groups, or depth Bible study group such as Robert A. Raines *koinonia* groups, are the most effective types for involving sizable numbers of adults, across age lines, in educative-counseling groups. These will be discussed in the chapter on existential counseling.

SOME PRINCIPLES OF EDUCATIVE GROUP COUNSELING

(1) These factors seem to be involved in attracting members to a group: (a) The approach is designed to meet the *felt* needs of a particular group of persons in the congregation.[20] (b) A nonthreatening label and soft-sell publicity are used. (c) A personal invitation is extended by the minister or group leader to selected individuals. (d) The group's purpose is stated clearly in advance and repeated at the first meeting.

(2) An effective educative counseling group must be small enough to permit frequent participation by all its members.

(3) The initial presentation in a session should be brief and immediately relevant to the felt needs of the group. At the outset the leader should ask each member to say what he hopes to get from the experience. This gives him a tentative impression of the group's needs and learning readiness. Long lectures are *verboten* because they kill dialogue. After a maximum of ten minutes of "seed planting" the leader should invite feedback and keep raising pertinent questions until he involves the group. He may increase feeling-level involvement on the part of group members by personalizing an issue with a hypothetical but true-to-life case, or by sharing from his own experience. The bulk of the session is spent in group wrestling with the issues as they relate to each person's situation.

(4) Having a resource book, a topic, or a flexible outline of how the various sessions may be used tends to reduce group (and leader)

[20] The schedules of many churches are already surfeited with meetings. A careful evaluation of existing groups may indicate that the congregation's energies are deployed in many ways which do not meet the needs of persons in the *present* situation. The decision concerning which types of counseling groups should be developed ought to be based on the unmet needs of a particular congregation. Some churches follow the practice of developing a number of counseling groups which *parallel* the regular structure of groups in the church. This has much to commend it.

anxiety, as does the brief functioning of the leader as an "instructor." The less structure a group has, the higher the anxiety level. Too much structure curtails group spontaneity and reduces personal involvement. An excess of instruction or direction traps a group in leader-centered dependence, which defeats the purpose of group counseling. Group-centeredness is generated by throwing the group on its own resources, gently refusing to "carry" them, and involving the maximum number in decisions, planning, and program participation.

(5) The leader functions in the "group centered" manner described earlier in this chapter. He attempts to create a warm, accepting climate. He listens closely to what each person says and reflects both content and feeling. He encourages openness of communication. He draws less aggressive members into the interaction by asking, "How do you feel about this matter, Carl?" He builds group-centeredness by linking what various people say, pointing to the connections or contrasts in their positions. He may occasionally summarize what has been said, giving the group an overview of its interaction and progress. He encourages feeling-level communication by *responding* to statements of feelings as they emerge. When someone opens a door to a deeper level of interaction by mentioning a personal problem, he helps the group walk through that door by focusing on the problem.

(6) The leader may suggest tools which the group can use to enhance interaction. For example, each person can be asked to "draw your childhood family," using different-sized circles to represent the relative influence of each and the distance between persons. Each group member then comments on what he has drawn. The same can be done with current family constellations. Both stimulate rapid involvement. Another useful tool is role playing. To illustrate, a young man who consistently failed to obtain jobs for which he was interviewed brought up this problem during a young adult encounter group. The minister-leader suggested that the man reenact the interview of the day before, a group member taking the company personnel director's part. It was apparent immediately, to the group, that the young man unwittingly was sabotaging his chances by his behavior during the interview. Another group member then played the young man's role allowing him to stand off and see himself in action, making a negative impression. In this case the person did not need to discover the underlying causes of his self-

defeating behavior in order to change his approach enough to obtain the next job for which he applied. Thus his failure cycle was interrupted. This use of role playing is called sociodrama.

(7) The leader attempts to be aware of the group as a whole, as well as of each individual. He may occasionally comment on the overall group process as he perceives it. He may suggest that an observer-recorder be selected to help the group become aware of its own interaction. This is rewarding but threatening at first. It should be suggested only after a group gains some sense of its own identity.

The Christian movement began as a small sharing group.[21] The contemporary rediscovery of the power of small groups is an exciting development in the churches. The imaginative use of such groups is one of the major frontiers in pastoral counseling.

RECOMMENDED READING

George R. Bach, *Intensive Group Psychotherapy* (New York: Ronald Press, 1954).

John L. Casteel, ed., *Spiritual Renewal Through Personal Groups* (New York: Association Press, 1957).

Howard J. Clinebell, Jr., *Mental Health Through Christian Community,* "Mental Health and the Group Life of the Church," pp. 149-70.

Raymond J. Corsini, *Methods of Group Psychotherapy* (New York: McGraw-Hill, 1957).

Paul F. Douglass, *The Group Workshop Way in the Church* (New York: Association Press, 1956).

Helen I. Driver, *Counseling and Learning Through Small-Group Discussion* (Madison, Wis.: Monona-Driver Book Co., 1958).

Helen E. Durkin, *The Group in Depth* (New York: International Universities Press, 1965).

Joseph W. Knowles, *Group Counseling*[22] (Englewood Cliffs, N.J.: Prentice-Hall, 1964).

Robert C. Leslie, "Small Groups in the Church," *Pastoral Psychology,* June, 1964.

[21] Small groups have played a crucial role in most of the spiritual renaissance periods through the centuries. It is noteworthy that the eighteenth-century Methodist class meetings were described by Thomas Coke and Francis Asbury as "spiritual hospitals." Samuel Emerick, "The Role of the Church Renewal Center," *Religion in Life* (Winter, 1961-62), p. 27.

[22] This book deals with group *therapy* in the church.

REALITY-PRACTICE SESSIONS

If possible, combine two reality-practice teams or augment one team to form a six-member "parents group." The leader's role is to do educative group counseling, employing the functions of the group-centered leader. One person should be designated as observer-recorder to maintain awareness of the dynamics of interaction within the group process. This will not be an easy session, but it should be one of the most rewarding.

13

Confrontational Counseling

Mercy and truth are met together.—Ps. 85:10 (KJV)

Confrontation as a counseling technique offers the teacher and pastor endless opportunities for creative encounter. When there is awareness, sensitivity, and knowledge, the face-to-face struggle opens new pathways to relatedness between persons and possibilities for growth.

—James A. Knight[1]

Blessed is he whose transgression is forgiven. . . .
When I declared not my sin, my
body wasted away through my groaning all
day long.
For day and night thy hand was
heavy upon me;
my strength was dried up as by
the heat of summer.
I acknowledged my sin to thee,
and I did not hide my iniquity . . .
then thou didst forgive the guilt
of my sin.—Ps. 32:1-5

William A. Clebsch and Charles R. Jaekle have pointed to the most egregious lack in contemporary pastoral care:

There are many indications that the function of reconciling as a creative and meaningful part of Christian pastoral care has fallen upon evil days. Per-

[1] "Confrontation in Counseling with Special Emphasis on the Student Setting," *Pastoral Psychology*, December, 1965, p. 48.

haps more than the other three functions of the cure of souls, reconciling has suffered from misunderstanding and erosion.[2]

In the Christian heritage the ministry of reconciling has enabled persons to renew a right relationship with God and with neighbor by utilizing two interdependent modes—*discipline* (a fraternal word of correction, a pastoral admonition, or sterner church discipline) and *forgiveness* (confession, penance, and absolution). Within Protestantism this ministry has fallen into neglect, as a result of an overreaction to sterile moralism. This neglect has been reinforced by permissive counseling theories. As a result a considerable segment of Christendom has been virtually deprived of this ministry of pastoral reconciliation "at a time when alienation is at the root of much human woe and anxiety." It is sad but true that "there is no place in the structure and rhythm of the life of a modern congregation where a serious discussion concerning the state of one's soul is expected." [3]

A revival of pastoral effectiveness in reconciling is a paramount need in contemporary pastoral counseling. Clebsch and Jaekle declare:

> The reconciling function enjoys an extraordinarily rich heritage in the church and remains a manner of helping for which there is, as yet, no prominent non-pastoral substitute. The burden of guilt under which moderns live—guilt engendered by alienation from fellow man that interprets itself as also alienation from God—is a form of human trouble with which the pastoral ministry has had longer and deeper familiarity than has any other helping profession. Partly by virtue of insisting that broken human relationships involve a breach of man's ultimate relationship with his Creator, pastoral care takes the human need for reconciliation with a seriousness unsurpassed by that of other healing arts.
>
> We foresee in the resuscitation of the reconciling function, synthesized with that of healing, the best hope for a transformed pastoral care that is at once continuous with the history of pastoring, integrated with the churches' theological formulations, open to new psychological insights, and able to meet creatively the aspirations and needs of modern men and women.[4]

These authors see a renewal of this dimension of pastoring as offering a sound basis for interprofessional dialogue:

[2] *Pastoral Care in Historical Perspective,* p. 63.
[3] *Ibid.,* p. 66.
[4] *Ibid.,* p. 81.

From the vantage point of a renewed emphasis upon reconciling, the practitioner of the pastoral art may enter more fully into conversations with representatives of the other healing arts, not only as a listener but as an artist able to make significant contributions from accumulated wisdom gained through two millennia of hearing confessions, pronouncing forgiveness, and exercising discipline in an effort to bring to reconciliation countless numbers of men and women in every area of the Western world. Such a renewed emphasis upon reconciling could precipitate the ministry of the cure of souls into a new realization of its therapeutic power for our time.[5]

Protestant pastoral counselors have tended not to take guilt as seriously as its destructive effects warrant. Having rejected legalistic moralism as sub-Christian, we have failed to discover acceptable methods of resolving guilt. It is imperative that we do so. Psychiatrist Edmund Bergler has observed, "A feeling of guilt follows every person like his shadow, whether or not he knows it." [6] Certainly guilt is the crucial factor in the problems of many of those who seek pastoral help.

THE THREE FACES OF CONSCIENCE

A pastor encounters three types of conscience problems—*appropriate* guilt feelings, *neurotic* guilt feelings, and the *relative absence* of guilt feelings. Guilt and its Siamese twin, alienation,[7] are complex and varied phenomena. To effect reconciliation the pastor's counseling methods must take cognizance of this complexity and variety.

How guilt is handled depends, to some extent, on whether it is appropriate or neurotic. All guilt has its objective and subjective aspects. Objectively, appropriate guilt is the result of actual damage to persons; subjectively, it stems from the misuse of that degree of inner freedom one possesses. It is the consequence of violating the values which the mature side of one's conscience regards as authentic and significant. In contrast, neurotic guilt feelings are produced by the immature side of conscience—i.e., values which were rewarded or punished by one's parents. This side is motivated by fear of punishment and rejection, rather than a positive striving for what one wholeheartedly affirms as good. Neurotic guilt results from breaking internalized parental prohibition.

[5] *Ibid.*, p. 82.

[6] *The Battle of the Conscience* (Westport, Conn.: Associated Booksellers, 1948), p. vii.

[7] Guilt is both the cause and the effect of alienation from God, others, and vital aspects of oneself.

Objectively, it often focuses on ethical trivia (which teen-agers call "Mickey Mouse morals") or on negative feelings and sexual impulses. Such moralism lacks inner freedom. It is driven or compulsive and therefore devoid of genuine ethical choice.

In many counselees appropriate and neurotic guilt feelings are intricately intertwined. The neurotic elements can be identified by these characteristics: (a) They do not respond to the forgiveness process. (b) They seldom motivate constructive amends or changes in the guilt-producing behavior. (c) They seem to produce masochistic satisfactions. As a counselee put it, "I get my kicks from wallowing in guilt."

The genuine and appropriate elements in a counselee's guilt feelings can be resolved via a five-stage process: *confrontation*, *confession*, *forgiveness*, *restitution*, and *reconciliation*. Confrontation is an indispensable skill in pastoral counseling involving the careful use of the minister's authority. Its essence is "speaking the truth in love" (Eph. 4:15) thus helping a person confront the realities of his situation and discover his responsibility in it. The creativity-damaging guilt in some counselees is like an open wound. Confrontation is obviously not needed. But in others the guilt is hidden from themselves and from other people. If it is to be resolved, it must enter their awareness and the openness of the counseling relationship. Hidden guilt is easy to overlook. In vicious marital conflict, for example, the guilt which a couple feels appropriately (because they *are* damaging each other) is often hidden behind their mutual personality assassination.[8] Unless the counselor recognizes their guilt and intervenes (e.g., "I should think it would make you feel very badly to be hurting each other so much"), the guilt will grind on, continuing to feed their blind attack and blocking reconciliation.

A middle-aged man discussed with his pastor the affair he was having with his secretary. Instead of exploring the inner conflicts which undoubtedly contributed to the man's behavior, the minister firmly helped him face the destructive consequences of his irresponsible behavior for himself, his children, and his wife. This mobilized his appropriate guilt. The pastor then supported the side of the man which wanted to break off the exotic but damaging relationship. He encouraged him to do so

[8] As Lawrence S. Kubie points out, men and women seem to be infinitely ingenious in their ability to find new ways of being unhappy together (*Neurotic Interaction in Marriage*, Victor W. Eisenstein, ed., p. 15).

at once and arranged for the man and his wife to enter marriage counseling.

In couple and group marriage counseling, one confrontation technique is for the minister to take the place of one spouse and role-play what he sees occurring between them. This confronts them with the absurd, self-defeating games they are playing.[9] Tape recording a couple's interaction (with their permission) during a counseling session and then playing it back to them has a powerful confrontational effect. In marriage enrichment groups, healthy confrontation is stimulated by reading and reflecting on the wedding vows, or by discussing the implications for one's marriage of a statement such as this: "To love a person productively implies to care and to feel responsible for his life, not only for his physical existence but for the growth and development of all his human powers."[10] Such discussion brings latent guilt feelings to the surface, where they can be faced and appropriate action taken. The same is true of the confrontational aspect of preaching on personal or social problems.[11]

The counselor who is always accepting and permissive, and never acceptingly confronting, is unwittingly guilty of "cruel kindness."[12] A counselee's awareness of his guilt and alienation is his doorway to help. An omnipermissive counselor's behavior is something like the cruel kindness of the alcoholic's spouse who prevents him from becoming open to help (i.e., "hitting bottom") by overprotecting him. People do not change until they experience pain in their present adjustment. Confrontation exposes them to the pain which is resulting from their irresponsible behavior.

Inescapably, the minister is a symbol of the values of his community and tradition. Many people come to *him* for help precisely because they feel guilty, often without being consciously aware of it. If his acceptance of their feelings is mistakenly seen by them as condoning their person-

[9] This approach was suggested to me by Edward Turner.

[10] Erich Fromm, *Man for Himself* (New York: Holt, Rinehart & Winston, 1947), p. 100.

[11] It is completely appropriate that we experience guilt concerning our sins of both commission and omission in such gigantic social problems as racial injustice, the squandering of our planet's resources on genocidal weapons, the destructive population explosion, and the fact that over half the earth's people are still malnourished. We should feel guilty enough to take decisive action to end these terrible wrongs. The absence of guilt about such matters is a sign of the underdevelopment or atrophying of conscience and indicates the need for prophetic confrontation in both preaching and counseling.

[12] John C. Ford's term for the effects of overprotecting alcoholics.

hurting behavior, they will be confused and let down by him. The minister should never be timid in counseling about what he regards as right. The question, of course, is *why* and *how* he stands for what he does. If he is reasonably aware of his own sin and weakness, and if he has experienced forgiveness in his own life, it will be easier for him to stand firm without being moralistic or self-righteous, or rejecting his fellow-sinners. If he is judgmental—usually the result of his own unresolved guilt—he will deepen the person's painful guilt and alienation.

Acceptance is the key to effective confrontation. A person will be more apt to experience *self-confrontation* (the most effective kind) if he knows that the truth is spoken *in love*. Otherwise, he will usually become defensive. William Glasser makes it plain that the prerequisite for confronting a patient with reality is establishing a relationship with him.[13] Only then can the therapist help him learn to fulfill his needs by living responsibly within reality. Honest confrontation within the context of acceptance will usually strengthen a relationship, not weaken it.

Hearing confessions and serving as a channel of God's forgiveness (as a representative of the church and its heritage) are *priestly* as well as *pastoral* functions. The implications of this are often overlooked in pastoral counseling. After extended counseling with a man crippled by guilt from the irreparable damage he had done another, a minister suggested that they go together to the church sanctuary. Wearing his pulpit robe to symbolize his priestly or representative function, he invited the man to pray for an awareness of God's forgiveness as he knelt at the Communion railing. Then the minister gave a prayer of absolution and the two joined in the Lord's Prayer.[14] The priestly acts were, in this case, bearers of the "reconciling symbols" of Christianity by which guilt can be transformed and transcended (Tillich). They were channels of grace by which forgiveness came alive for that man. It should be noted that the effectiveness of the priestly acts was built on the foundation of a meaningful counseling experience.

If confession and absolution are to facilitate reconciliation, they must never be detached from *restitution* and a strenuous effort to live respon-

[13] *Reality Therapy*, pp. 21 ff.

[14] Holy Communion is often meaningful in such situations.

sibly. A person's inner channel of forgiveness stays blocked until he has done everything possible to repair his harm to others. "Cheap grace" (Bonhoeffer) is really no grace at all. AA's Twelve Step recovery program shows the importance of ethical self-confrontation. Seven of the twelve steps are devoted to "a searching and fearless moral inventory," including admitting "to God, to ourselves, and to another human being the exact nature of our wrongs," making "a list of all the persons we have harmed," and making "direct amends to such persons whenever possible, except when to do so would injure them or others." [15] It is no accident that such a process often leads to a "spiritual awakening." The pastor should help his nonalcoholic counselees to be just as searching and specific in clearing their lives of moral debris. This is the price of forgiveness, inner peace, and restored relations.

Philip A. Anderson describes his counseling with a recovered alcoholic who said he was "just plain not happy":

> My response to this was to say that when I was not happy about myself it usually involved a rather simple mechanism, namely, I had done something which I was not very proud of or happy about or I had not done something I should have done. I went on to illustrate my point by citing a personal experience. . . . When I had not adequately prepared a sermon, I was most unhappy on Sunday morning. So I was prompted to ask Bill what he had been doing lately.[16]

The counselee replied, "Funny you should ask that. The truth is that I have given up drinking but I still waste too much time." They talked about how his irresponsible behavior had allowed his business to deteriorate. Then Anderson asked him about his marriage. He began to verbalize his irritation toward his wife.

COUNSELOR: But what are *you* doing, not what is your wife doing, about your marriage?

COUNSELEE: Funny you should ask that. I've been having an affair with another woman for about six months, and I'm sick of it.

[15] For a discussion of the twelve steps, see *Alcoholics Anonymous* (New York: AA Publishing Co., 1955), pp. 58 ff.; and *Twelve Steps and Twelve Traditions*, by a co-founder of AA (New York: Harper and Row, 1952).

[16] "A Ministry to Troubled People," *The Chicago Theological Seminary Register*, February, 1965, p. 5.

COUNSELOR: Bill, I'm not surprised that you aren't happy. You are living an irresponsible life which you are hiding from your wife and associates. You don't have any right to be happy.

Bill agreed. Counseling focused on Bill's responsibilities. His wife soon joined the counseling, the marriage problems came under scrutiny, and a reconciliation was achieved in that relationship. As Bill began to act more responsibly he reported that he was beginning to be happy again.

Anderson's approach is an illuminating example of the confrontational thrust in contemporary counseling, which is also represented by Glasser's "reality therapy" and, in more extreme form, Mowrer's "integrity therapy." It concentrates on current rather than past relationships and on responsible behavior rather than on feelings. Acting more responsible in the here and now, rather than waiting until new feelings produce constructive behavior, is the central emphasis.

Pastoral counseling should learn from this thrust. Most people have greater capacity than they suspect to live responsibly *now*. In most cases they will be much happier with themselves if they do so. They will tend to activate this potentiality for responsible living if the counselor firmly expects them to move in this direction. A direct, confrontational, action-oriented counseling approach enables the person to break out of his guilt paralysis and begin to function more responsibly. When a person is behaving in irresponsible ways which produce spiraling guilt, fear of discovery, lack of openness and honesty in relationships, he is trapped in a vicious cycle. The guiltier he feels, the more he hides; and the more he hides, the greater the buildup of guilt and fear. An approach which deals directly with the guilt and irresponsible behavior, by emphasizing honest confession and constructive action, can help a person to break out of this self-perpetuating cycle.[17] The tremendous sense of relief and release experienced by many AA members when they take their "moral inventory" and make constructive amends is an example of this.

An illuminating insight concerning the existential impact of confrontation is presented by H. H. Garner and R. F. Jeans:

> Confrontation makes the patient unmistakably aware of the presence of the therapist as a person who has interfered with the blind acting out of his escape

[17] These are prominent emphases in "integrity therapy"; see the books by Mowrer and Drakeford under Recommended Reading.

from freedom of choice, who has challenged the patient's solution to his conflicts in a decisive way, and made him think about it.[18]

Repressed guilt—appropriate and/or neurotic—is hidden behind a wide variety of problems encountered in counseling.[19] This guilt, of which the persons often are only vaguely aware or completely unaware, feeds, complicates, deepens, and perpetuates their problems in living. The confrontational-confessional approach may serve to de-repress this guilt, bringing it into the open where it can be resolved by counseling methods and by responsible action on the person's part.

One of the keys to effective pastoral counseling is what Paul Tillich called the *principle of mutuality:*

> The basic principle for the attitude of pastoral counseling is mutuality. The counselor must participate in the situation of the person needing care. This participation expresses itself not only in words of acceptance, but also in ways of communicating to the counselee the fact that the counselor was and is in the same situation. This can be done by telling a concrete story in which the counselor experienced the same negativities for which the counselee needs care. It can be in words which make it clear to the counselee that the counselor understands well on the basis of his own experience. If such a thing happens, the subject-object situation—the great danger for all pastoral care—is overcome.[20]

This principle is at no point more crucial than in confrontational counseling. Somehow the minister must "depedestalize" himself in the eyes of the counselee. He must let the person know that, in a fundamental sense, he is "in the same boat"; he too is under judgment and in need of grace. If he confronts the person from a pedestal of ethical "one-upmanship," or seems to be doing so, the guilt-burdened person

[18] Quoted by James A. Knight, "Confrontation in Counseling with Special Emphasis on the Student Setting," p. 52, from their paper "Confrontational Techniques in Psychotherapy: Some Existential Implications," *Journal of Existential Psychiatry*, Spring, 1962, pp. 397-98. Garner and Jeans contrast the effects of confrontation with those of counselor passivity: "The concept of a state of helplessness and of being in the clutches of forces of past experiences is too frequently fortified by the interpretation of the therapist's passivity as a confirmation of his feeling that he is incapable of taking any action to alter the situation" (p. 404).

[19] In commenting on Mowrer's position, Rollo May writes: "The repression of guilt feelings with its concomitant generation of neurotic anxiety . . . in some ways is pervasive of our culture as a whole" (*The Meaning of Anxiety* [New York: Ronald Press, 1950], p. 109).

[20] "The Theology of Pastoral Care," *Clinical Education for the Pastoral Ministry*, Proceedings of the Fifth National Conference on Clinical Pastoral Education, November 9-11, 1956, ed. by Ernest E. Bruder and Marian L. Barb (published by the Advisory Committee on Clinical Pastoral Education, 1958), p. 5.

is forced to respond defensively. In contrast, the implementation of the principle of mutuality has an automatic de-repressing effect on hidden guilt feelings. In "integrity therapy" this is done by the counselor serving as a model of openness. "As early as possible in the interview the therapist 'opens his life' to the troubled person. . . . Only after his own gesture of trust does the therapist look for a response from the subject."[21] This self-disclosure removes the helping person from any pedestal he may have been on in the counselee's mind and serves as a dynamic "invitation to openness" (Drakeford). By describing (briefly) his own struggles with guilt, depression and fear the pastor practices the principle of mutuality. Whatever answers he has found now have more convincing meaning to the troubled person.[22] To be therapeutic, self-disclosure must be more than a gimmick to elicit confession. It must be derived from the pastor's deep feeling of mutuality with other sinners and an awareness of the healing power of grace in his own life and relationships.

It should be emphasized that some guilt feelings are so deeply repressed that only intensive and skilled psychotherapy can reach them. If guilt is flowing from deep, unconscious neurotic conflicts, confession and action therapy will not suffice. But it is possible and constructive to help a person bring into full awareness guilt feelings of which he is only dimly aware. This may allow deeper guilt to become accessible. Focusing in counseling on why a person has difficulty acting more responsibly is sometimes an efficient way of reaching the "key log" in the inner logjam of guilt.

As a person begins to relate more responsibly, new sources of need satisfaction open to him. Glasser states: "As important as confronting reality is, it is only part of the therapy. The patient must learn to fulfill his needs in the real world . . . and we must teach him how whenever we can."[23] The heart of confrontational counseling is facilitating a counselee's encounter with the reality which he has been avoiding (which produces his guilt) and helping him learn to live with that reality.[24]

[21] John W. Drakeford, *Integrity Therapy*, p. 79.

[22] The AA member, when talking to an alcoholic still trapped in his addiction, tells of his own struggles with alcoholism.

[23] Glasser, *Reality Therapy*, p. 60.

[24] Living in harmony with reality is expressed in religious terms as "doing the will of God."

NEUROTIC GUILT AND PASTORAL COUNSELING

Many counselees are crippled, spiritually and interpersonally, by neurotic, hairshirted consciences. They feel chronic, inappropriate guilt derived from a faulty, immature, or rigid value system. Their self-evaluation includes no element of *live grace*. They tend to squander their ethical energies in compulsive self-castigation over minor moral matters or over their "bad" feelings. Consequently, there is a little energy left for the important "core moralities" (Ross Snyder), and a relative lack of sensitivity to the needs of others. The goal of counseling with such "puritanized" persons is to help them achieve less cruel, more Christian consciences, and reconciliation in those relationships previously alienated by neurotic guilt.

Neurotic guilt feelings are reduced temporarily if a person is "spanked" psychologically. Punishment temporarily lessens guilt. (This explains why guilt-ridden people are attracted to moralistic preachers and counselors.) Regular verbal pummeling serves as a form of neurotic atonement, thus lessening guilt feelings. In most cases the results do not last, however; nor do they produce constructive change in behavior. In Bernean terms this is a Parent-Child path to forgiveness.

The ideal goal of counseling with the neurotically guilt oppressed is *self-forgiveness*. This occurs in two stages. First, the self-castigating person identifies with and internalizes the less rigid and more self-accepting value structure and conscience of the counselor.

COUNSELEE: You shook me up when you said, after I had gone over and over how guilty I felt about my sexual feelings, "I wonder why it's so difficult for you to treat your own feelings with Christian charity."

The pastor becomes a new and more accepting parent figure from whom the person learns something of what Alfred Adler called "the courage of one's own imperfections." By internalizing aspects of the minister's more positive and life-affirming value system, the person's inner Parent becomes less punishing of his inner Child.[25] The punitive Parent is decommissioned, to some extent, and the person achieves increasing inner freedom from the compulsive moralism which had crippled his mature ethical (choice-making) capacities. Reconciliation of conflicted aspects

[25] Neurotic guilt consists of the punishment of the inner Child by the inner Parent, because the prohibitions of the Parent have been broken.

of himself enables him to become reconciled in his relationships with others.

The second stage of self-forgiveness is self-acceptance based on the affirming of one's unique personhood, including the affirmation of those values which one comes to regard as genuinely good. The counselor helps the person exercise his inner Adult's ability to examine competing values and to choose those which are consistent with his growing awareness of the good life. This process of letting go of dependence on the value structure of one's parents and of finding one's own meanings and values occurs in normal development during adolescence.[26] If this ethical maturing is blocked, long-term counseling may be required to release the person to become an adult ethically. Neurotic guilt feeling are often linked with deep unconscious conflicts requiring psychotherapy to produce constructive resolution.

Both neurotic and appropriate guilt are often present on different levels of a person's psyche. Neurotic guilt, particularly about trivia, frequently hides genuine guilt about superficial values, unlived life, and person-hurting irresponsible behavior. The neurotic guilt is superimposed on the deeper guilt as a camouflage.[27] On the other hand, what appears to be genuine guilt may hide deeper guilt-producing conflicts based on unresolved problems in psychosexual development, e.g., oedipal attachments.[28]

[26] Freud regarded the detachment from dependence on parental authority as "one of the most significant but also one of the most painful psychical achievements" *Three Essays on Sexuality, Collected Works* (New York: The Macmillan Company, VII, 227, 1953.)

[27] O. Hobart Mowrer appears to dismiss all neurotic guilt on this basis. In my view this is an error resulting from an oversimplified model of the nature of guilt and of the relation between neurotic and appropriate guilt. Much neurotic guilt is *just that* and must be so treated in counseling. Mowrer tends to make the person's value system an absolute and to interpret all personality problems as repressed guilt resulting from disobeying his conscience—i.e., violating his value system. (See *The New Group Therapy,* pp. 181-214.) This view ignores the crucial factor in many personality problems—distorted, immature, or internally conflicted value systems which give persons sick or immature consciences. Such consciences produce guilt in response to behavior that is *constructive,* when evaluated by the criterion of personality growth and wholeness (e.g., middle-aged, unmarried man who has spent his life meeting the whims of a dominating, demanding mother experiences severe guilt when he begins to move toward autonomy—i.e., maturity). Such persons are disturbed because the value systems by which they are attempting to live are internally inconsistent, or are contradictory to the principles of mental growth and health which are integral to the psyche. To bring their behavior into conformity (by confession and making amends) with their distorted consciences, as "integrity therapy" seeks to do, violates their real integrity as persons.

[28] For example, what appears to be appropriate guilt in unwed adolescent girls who become pregnant is often only a surface cover-up of an intense, unconscious sense of neurotic guilt stemming from their oedipal acting out involved in becoming pregnant.

In pastoral counseling with the guilt-laden it is wise to begin by dealing with the obvious guilt problem. This may prove to be only a surface-level manifestation of deeper guilt or conflict. If, after extended confessional catharsis and serious efforts at reconstruction of relationships (restitution), self-forgiveness does not begin to emerge, a deeper conflict is probably present. This will have to be dealt with through depth counseling in order to help the person. If a counselee resists making amends, it is important to focus on why he continues to neglect a crucial prerequisite to a sense of forgiveness. In effect, the counselor confronts the person with his need to act and to do so in a responsible way. If neurotic guilt is blocking the forgiveness process, this confrontation may be effective, providing the counselor helps him work through the inner conflicts which are keeping him from relationship-repairing action. Confrontation is not effective, however, if the person receives it in masochistic fashion, using the counselor's confronting words as a form of neurotic punishment (which reduces the pressure of the guilt, but only briefly). Other neurotically guilt-ridden people defeat confrontation by responding with seemingly endless, compulsive atonement behavior, which allows them to avoid their deeper conflict.

The suspected or obvious presence of neurotic guilt should not rule out the use of confrontation, even if the underlying conflict is not accessible through the counseling that is available. Where the conflict is relatively mild, confrontation may succeed in interrupting a vicious cycle of behavior and feelings, so that the person's constructiveness in living is enhanced without the necessity of resolving the conflict. This is often the case in counseling with adolescents and young adults, in whom the élan toward maturation tends to be very strong.

A teen-age girl, disturbed about her steadily worsening relationship with her mother, sought the minister's help. A number of sessions were devoted to exploring her ambivalent feelings toward her mother. She expressed her anger and also her positive feelings toward her mother, but there was no improvement in their relationship. Finally, the minister recommended that she try putting her positive feelings into action during the following week. At the next counseling session, she reported: "I was just furious at you for suggesting that I do something to show that I loved my mother. . . . But I found myself setting the table without being asked, and enjoying it. I have no idea why. It just happened. We're getting along fine—the best we have in five years."

What apparently occurred was that the counselor's confronting "push" interrupted the momentum of long-standing negative interaction between the girl and her mother. By doing something helpful the girl reduced her guilt load and reestablished communication with her mother. The minister continued to counsel with the girl for a while, regarding her relationships. But his action had rescued her from spiraling guilt and reestablished a relationship which could then be helped further by counseling. Normal teen-age-daughter–mother conflicts occurred frequently, but communication was not broken. From his knowledge of the girl's family situation, the minister was aware of the presence of neurotic problems sufficient to trigger the negative spiral in the mother-daughter relationship. His short-term counseling with her certainly did not resolve any deep inner conflicts in the girl. Fortunately, this was not essential in order to help her reestablish the relationship. If her inner conflicts regarding the mother had been severe at the time of the counseling, it is unlikely that the minister's recommendation would have been followed or, if followed, would have produced lasting benefits.[29]

THOSE WITH UNDERDEVELOPED CONSCIENCES

Confrontational methods are essential in counseling with those having weak, underdeveloped consciences. Such persons are characterized by one or more of the following: (a) lack of appropriate guilt, anxiety, and sense of responsibility; (b) ineffective self-control; (c) chronic irresponsible behavior; (d) shallowness of feelings and relationships; (e) a manipulative *modus operandi.* Freud once observed, in writing to his friend Pastor Oskar Pfister, "Ethics are a kind of highway code for traffic among mankind." [30] Many people have not learned to respect this code. They have not internalized the culture's guiding values and therefore have not learned to control their asocial impulses. Such "char-

[29] The "learning-theory therapists" would interpret what occurred in this case as simply the extinction of a maladaptive stimulus-response pattern and the substitution of a more productive set of stimulus-response patterns in the mother-daughter interaction. The latter was begun because of the implicit reward (approval) in the minister's recommendation. The new pattern was reinforced (i.e., learned) by the satisfactions which resulted from it. In their view it is unnecessary to discover the initial stimulus which began the negative interaction. Once a stimulus-response avoidance pattern is learned, it becomes self-reinforcing; the person avoids the very experiences which would modify it.

[30] *Psychoanalysis and Faith, The Letters of Sigmund Freud to Oskar Pfister* (New York: Basic Books, 1963), p. 123.

acter problems" result from various backgrounds—cold, loveless homes; those with a weak or absent father; or homes where parents mistook overpermissiveness for love and did not maintain dependable discipline. As Erik Erikson has shown, virtues such as hope, purpose, competence, fidelity, love, care, and wisdom are vital elements in the ego's strength.[31] Persons who lack these are seriously handicapped. In its extreme form this disorder is called "sociopathic personality." Our culture, with its manipulative "marketing orientation" (Fromm), spawns character problems in all degrees and with great frequency.

The permissive, insight-oriented counseling approach may be effective with guilt- and anxiety-loaded psychoneurotics but it usually fails miserably with those who have character problems.

A girl of seventeen came to her pastor to discuss her sexual activities. Her father was an emotionally nonresident commuter. Although she consciously felt little or no guilt about her activities, she was fearful of "getting caught." If the minister had responded to her reports of promiscuity in a passive or permissive way, she would have interpreted this as more of the weak, detached permissiveness of her father. She needed more acceptance than she was getting at home, but not more permissiveness! On the contrary, what she needed was for the minister to be both an accepting and a firm father-figure from whom she could gain strength in controlling her own behavior and in relation to whom she could establish her own constructive limits. After rapport was well developed, the minister made it clear that from his point of view, certain behavior is harmful to persons and therefore morally wrong. Using accepting confrontation he helped her face rather than avoid the probable consequences of her behavior. Most important, he helped her become aware of and work through her confused, lonely, rebellious feelings which provided the fuel for the behavior. In reflecting on this experience, the minister realized that the girl was, by her behavior, pleading for some adult to set limits. In fact, this is probably why she had come to a minister.[32]

Sociologist David Riesman suggests that permissive therapies are useful with counselees who have been exposed to arbitrary power and for

[31] *Insight and Responsibility* (New York: W. W. Norton, 1964).

[32] Clinebell, *Mental Health Through Christian Community*, pp. 232-33. I described the process of counseling those with weak or defective consciences as "superego counseling," in that volume. This is a form of supportive counseling in that the counselee draws on the inner controls of the pastor to support his inadequate value and control structures. Thomas W. Klink puts it well: "The modern pastor must represent transcendent values to persons who live in settings untouched by traditional controls" (*Depth Perspectives in Pastoral Work*, p. 65).

whom a permissive, accepting situation is a new experience: "But many of the college-educated have been brought up permissively both at home and at school and find little that is liberating in a therapist who accepts them." [33]

A therapist who works mainly with disturbed adolescents reports that character problems predominate among his counselees, that psychoneuroses are rare, and that Rogerian and psychoanalytic methods have proved to be strikingly ineffective with most of them. *Learning-theory therapy* has provided the most successful method. The therapist's emphasis is on setting and enforcing limits on the deviant behavior so that constructive patterns may be learned and reinforced through the rewards and punishments of the structure. For example, instead of being lenient and permissive with school truancy, he recommends that the school authorities take immediate disciplinary action. It is essential that the youth involved know that this was his recommendation.[34]

Here are some principles of counseling with weak-conscienced persons:

(1) *Establish a relationship*. This is the most difficult and crucial step with this type of counselee.

(2) *Confront the person with the self-defeating nature of his reality-denying behavior*. As Glasser puts it, "The therapist must reject the behavior which is unrealistic but still accept the patient and maintain his involvement with him." [35]

(3) *Block the irresponsible, acting-out behavior.*

(4) *Reward responsible behavior with approval.*

(5) *Help the person learn to satisfy his needs in socially constructive, reality-oriented ways.*

(6) *Explore his aspirations and help him make and implement realistic but satisfying plans for the future.*

Jerome D. Frank states that persons who have difficulty controlling their impulses need to feel that the therapist has concern for them based on their potentialities.

[33] Standal and Corsini, *Critical Incidents in Psychotherapy*, p. 84.

[34] From a communication with Bill Sharp. Robert A. Blees, in *Counseling with Teen-Agers*, describes his method of limit setting in counseling with persons in "the middle teens," pp. 65-80).

[35] *Reality Therapy*, p. 21.

This concern is best conveyed by a strong attack on the deviant behavior as unworthy of the patient. This type of attack, paradoxically, heightens the patient's self-esteem rather than damages it, because it is obviously based on real concern and respect.[36]

Permissiveness, on the other hand, makes such a person feel that the therapist is indifferent or does not expect much of him. This hurts his already shaky self-esteem further. Consistent firmness is the *sine qua non* of helping him.

William Glasser's "reality therapy" assumes that it is impossible to maintain self-esteem if one is living irresponsibly. He declares: "Morals, standards, values, or right and wrong behavior are all intimately related to the fulfillment of our need for self-worth." [37] Thus he aims at teaching patients to maintain "a satisfactory standard of behavior," to credit themselves when they are right and correct themselves when wrong. Self-respect comes through self-discipline and loving closeness to others.

Persons with severe character disorders are difficult to help, even in the hands of a highly trained psychiatrist. But many people with milder character problems can benefit from skilled pastoral counseling following confrontational principles. This is particularly true of adolescents whose difficulty is simply a retardation of conscience maturation. By identifying with the pastor's (hopefully) more mature conscience, a counselee can gradually unlearn destructive patterns and internalize more dependable inner controls.[38]

A future orientation is essential in much pastoral counseling, including confrontational counseling. A favorite question in reality therapy is, "What is your plan?" This stimulates a person's constructive thinking and his hope about the future. Glasser writes: "We must open up his life, talk about new horizons, expand his range of interests, make him aware of life beyond his difficulties." [39] Many troubled people do not feel there really is a future for them. Awakening such a person's con-

[36] *Critical Incidents in Psychotherapy*, p. 249

[37] Glasser, *Reality Therapy*, p. 11.

[38] With weak-egoed, chronically disorganized persons, it is essential to help them begin to do something constructive. This will tend to strengthen their coping abilities. See "The Case of Mrs. H." by Herbert Mardis in *The Chicago Theological Seminary Register*, 1965, pp. 11-15.

[39] *Reality Therapy*, p. 31.

structive dreams for the future can be decisive in helping him break from the unconstructive patterns of the past.

In counseling with persons who have weak inner controls, it is essential to help the person discover something about which he can really care. A chaplain who leads group therapy with young adults having a history of behavior problems reports: "I try to find one thing the individual gives a damn about, and then build on that!"

THE USE OF CONFRONTATION IN OTHER COUNSELING

Confrontational methods are valuable in a variety of counseling situations not centering on problems of conscience. A minister met a teen-age parishioner (Sam) loafing at a filling station during school hours.

PASTOR: I see you decided not to go back to school.

SAM: Yeh, I couldn't seem to cut the mustard.

PASTOR: What are your plans? Maybe there's something else you should be preparing for.

SAM: Don't really know what I want to do. I suppose something will come along.

They talked about the future. The minister stressed the desirability of Sam's choosing a route now that would lead to some work he would find satisfying. Subsequently, as counseling continued in the pastor's study, the county psychologist, the county coordinator of special education, and the state employment agency representative were involved to help the youth make and implement realistic plans.[40] Eventually he entered job corps training to become a refrigeration technician. By confrontative and educative counseling methods the pastor had interrupted what could have become a chronic failure cycle.

Psychiatrist James A. Knight has found confrontation to be particularly useful in helping young adults move toward maturity. He states:

> The young person is in need of face-to-face relationships with authorities who demonstrate their concern for the individual both by support and by judgment. During the tumultuous periods of psychological growth, confrontation at appropriate times will serve to open pathways for growth and to set necessary limits to behavior.[41]

[40] This is an excellent example of the pastoral counselor's use of community resources.
[41] "Confrontation in Counseling," p. 49.

He cites R. J. Lifton's delineation of the three steps involved in personal change—*confrontation, reordering,* and *renewal.*[42] Following a confrontation experience a person begins the process of reeducation and change which Lifton calls "reordering." This may include a personal "emptying" through confession and exploring past emotional patterns. This emptying is accompanied by the absorption of new feelings and ideas, the validity of which is tested in new relationships. This leads to the stage of open renewal:

> Renewal depends upon a new interplay between identity and ideology. The person views his relationships to old authorities as steps along his personal path toward greater independence. Renewal can be consolidated only by an awareness of genuine self-knowledge and a readiness to accept its consequences.[43]

Confrontational methods often are important in referral counseling. A young man reported intense fear that he would harm his girl friend. Knowing of his poorly controlled rage and his previous impulsive behavior toward women, the minister insisted that he commit himself for psychiatric treatment. He confronted the man with the real danger that he might do something irreparably destructive. Rather than resenting the pastor's firm stance the man was obviously relieved and willing to comply. The minister had used the strength of his position to protect the man and his girl friend from the man's destructive impulses.

In crisis situations confrontation is often essential. Hospital chaplains sometimes use a kind of confrontational shock therapy in an attempt to revive the will to live in patients who have given up. As Thomas Klink indicates, this is a "keen-edged method" which can do much harm, unless it is used with great care. However, it is sometimes necessary to use it as a last resort in an effort to rescue the person from his tailspin of slow suicide.[44]

Viktor Frankl's therapeutic approach relies heavily on confrontation. He confronts his patients with the necessity of finding values which

[42] *Ibid.*, p. 54. Lifton's book is *Thought Reform and the Psychology of Totalism* (New York: W. W. Norton, 1961), pp. 463-64.

[43] "Confrontation in Counseling," p. 54.

[44] For a verbatim example of extreme "shock therapy" counseling see Cryer and Vayhinger, *Casebook in Pastoral Counseling,* Case No. 31, pp. 171-73. Another illustration is the case of the young mother who wanted to die, in *Spiritual Therapy* by Richard K. Young and Albert L. Meiburg (New York: Harper & Row, 1960), p. 15.

will give their existence meaning. He blocks attempts to play what Berne calls "wooden leg" by the conviction, communicated with authority, that however dismal a person's situation he is free to choose his attitude toward it and is responsible for so doing. He then helps his patients discover the personal meanings which will mobilize their coping abilities.

Confronting a counselee with the way he is relating to the counselor in that session or moment can restore openness in a counseling relationship and provide the counselee with an opportunity to achieve significant insights. It can interrupt futile counselee-counselor "games." After two sessions of maneuvering in couple counseling the wife said, "Do you understand what I mean? I'm probably confusing you." The pastor replied: "I think I understand what you're saying right now, but I'm wondering what's going on in our relationship as a whole. I have the feeling we're sort of playing verbal games here—trying to find out what the problem is and, at the same time, trying to keep it hidden. We seem to have talked around it for two sessions." The startled couple soon centered down on what was really troubling them.

When the counselor makes a major error or misses the counselee's wavelength completely, it is well to discuss it openly, as soon as possible.

PASTOR: As I thought about our last talk, I realized that I had probably missed what you were trying to tell me at the end. I noticed that you got very quiet. How did you feel when I said . . .?"

The minister's nonapologetic self-confrontation usually helps repair damaged rapport in such situations. By admitting his fallibility he strengthens the relationships.

NEO-MORALISM—THE DANGER

Confrontational methods are analogous to a powerful medicine. Used properly they can be a potent means of healing. Yet the dangers of misuse are increased by their potency. James A. Knight observes: "Pastors and teachers have not always understood the meaning of confrontation in counseling. It is often confused with a vertical type of authoritarianism, moralistic preachments, or hostile attacks indulged in under the guise of 'righteous indignation.'"[45] These principles can provide some protection against the danger of moralism: (a) Confrontation should be used with great care and restraint. (b) The emphasis should be on helping the person face reality (self-confrontation) as *he* comes to understand it, and discover his own responsibility within it. In the final analysis the minister's level of personal maturity will determine whether he misuses confrontational methods to manipulate others or discovers their tremendous potentialities as instruments of reconciliation in relationship-centered counseling.

RECOMMENDED READING

Philip A. Anderson, "A Ministry to Troubled People," *The Chicago Theological Register*, February, 1965, pp. 5-11.

James B. Ashbrook, "Judgment and Pastoral Counseling," *Journal of Pastoral Care*, March, 1966, pp. 1-9.

Robert A. Blees, *Counseling with Teen-Agers*, pp. 65-80.

John W. Drakeford, *Integrity Therapy, A New Direction in Psychotherapy* (Fort Worth, Tex.: Southwestern Baptist Theological Seminary, 1965).

William Glasser, *Reality Therapy, A New Approach to Psychiatry* (New York: Harper & Row, 1965).

James A. Knight, "Confrontation in Counseling with Special Emphasis on the Student Setting," *Pastoral Psychology*, December, 1965, pp. 48-55.

O. Hobart Mowrer, *The New Group Therapy* (Princeton, N.J.: D. Van Nostrand, 1964), "Psychotherapy as Social Re-Integration," pp. 104-16.

REALITY-PRACTICE SESSIONS

PARISHIONER'S ROLES: 1. You are a man who killed several enemy soldiers during the Korean war. You come to the minister for help with your relentless agony of guilt.[46]

2. You are a young adult, age twenty-five. As a teen-ager you rebelled against the rigid code

[45] Knight, "Confrontation in Counseling," p. 49.

[46] For an account of the handling of this case see Cryer and Vayhinger, *Casebook in Pastoral Counseling*, Case No. 49, pp. 267-72. Other cases of guilt counseling include Case No. 48, pp. 262-66 and Case No. 8, pp. 59-63.

of your fundamentalist background; you still feel intense guilt about activities such as dancing and smoking in which you engage regularly.

3. You are the sexually promiscuous girl described in this chapter.

PASTOR'S ROLES: These cases represent the three major types of problems of conscience. Use the counseling approaches described in this chapter.

It is recommended that a tape recorder be used to enhance awareness of the interaction during these sessions.

14

Counseling on Religious-Existential Problems

As you ought not to attempt to cure the eyes without the head, or the head without the body, so neither ought you to attempt to cure the body without the soul . . . for the part can never be well unless the whole is well. . . . And therefore, if the head and body are to be well, you must begin by curing the soul.

—Plato[1]

Anxiety is the awareness of finitude. Man . . . always lives in the conscious or unconscious anxiety of having to die. Non-being is present in every moment of his being. The vicissitudes of existence threaten him from all sides. Suffering, accidents, disease, loss of relations to nature and man, loneliness, insecurity, weakness, and error are always with him. Finally, the threat of having to die will become the reality of death. All this he must bear, and all this he can bear only in the power of that in which nonbeing is eternally conquered—the power of the divine. It is the function of pastoral care to communicate this power and to mediate the courage to accept finitude.

—Paul Tillich[2]

Explicit theological problems—problems of doctrine, doubt, creedal confusion, the nature of prayer, and so forth—are the primary motivating force for only a small minority of those seeking pastoral help.[3]

[1] "Charmides," *The Dialogues of Plato,* Benjamin Jowett, trans. (New York: Random House, 1937), I, 6.

[2] "The Theology of Pastoral Care," p. 3.

[3] The fact that this is true is indicative of the thought climate of our times. Our prevalent spiritual problems tend not to be understood or described in theological terms.

When a minister does encounter such problems, he spontaneously draws on his theological training, tradition, and personal convictions. In so doing he should utilize the basic methods of sound pastoral counseling (Chapter 4) and of educative counseling in particular (Chapter 11). In functioning as *pastoral theologian* he combines counseling skills with theological insights. The counselor-theologian serves a valuable function—that of helping people fathom and appropriate their traditions' wisdom about life's meaning. He assists them in filling traditional symbols with personal meaning. As a theological counselor his function is to help remove the blocks which inhibit a person's growth toward a more mature (i.e., in harmony with reality) faith and more need-satisfying relationship with God.

When explicit theological issues are "presenting problems" in counseling, the minister should be aware that they *may* be surface manifestations of deeper psychological problems. It is usually appropriate to deal with theological problems as problems in their own right, but to be alert to other problems which may lurk in the shadows. A middle-aged man came for help with a distressing loss of vitality in his prayer life. As he put it, "Prayer has gone *dead* for me." He asked for the title of a book on prayer. The minister suggested several but encouraged him to continue talking about his problems by asking: "What has been happening lately? Has anything been heavy on your mind?" This opened the sluice gates. The man poured out his guilt feelings regarding the suicide of a near relative, for whose death he felt some unreasonable but painful responsibility. Subsequently, this problem was worked through in a series of counseling sessions and the man's prayer experience "came *alive*." The inner mountain of guilt which had blocked him from God had been removed.

The onset of a psychotic break is sometimes attended by a sudden, obsessive interest in religion—e.g., in "getting right with God" or in "finding the secret of the universe." This interest may have a paranoid coloration—delusions of grandeur (a messiah complex) or persecution. In one study of mental hospital patients 20 percent merely clothed their psychoses in religious ideas. Ten percent seemed to use religion as a "last straw." Another 17 percent gave evidence of basic religious problems, interwoven with unresolved conflicts with parent figures.[4]

[4] Wayne E. Oates, *Religious Factors in Mental Illness* (New York: Association Press, 1955), pp. 6-7.

Although religious problems may hide psychological problems, the reverse is also true. Spiritual emptiness is a significant factor in many neurotic problems. Hiltner writes: "People may get sick emotionally not only because of immediate frustrations but also because they are troubled about their own meaning and destiny." [5] Viktor Frankl's phrase, "value vacuum," describes the emptiness which renders many people vulnerable to anxiety and interpersonal conflict. In his review of Peter Vierech's *The Unadjusted Man: A New Hero for Americans,* Geoffrey Brunn writes: "Ours is an orphan age, severed from its historic past by the transforming impact of dynamic technology. Today every individual in the 'lonely crowd' is haunted by a sense of desolation and incommunicable singularity." [6] In this "age of longing" (Arthur Koestler) countless millions have found no resources for coping with that common human experience described in Melville's classic line, "a damp, drizzly November in my soul." [7] Like the characters in the play *Waiting for Godot,* they are bored and nauseated by the empty meaninglessness of their existence. The purposelessness of our "mislaid generation" [8] provides fertile soil for the seeds of marital mediocrity, interpersonal conflict, and mental illness.

Strong currents in the contemporary psychotherapeutic world challenge the view of some therapists that all religious problems are merely symptoms of deeper psychological problems. Carl G. Jung, Erich Fromm, Viktor Frankl, Gordon Allport, Rollo May, and other "existentialists" in psychotherapy have held this view to be reductionistic and unsupported by the hard clinical evidence which suggests that psychological problems often root in spiritual pathology. Jung regarded "the religious problems which the patient brings . . . as relevant to the neurosis and as possible causes of it." [9] Fromm views neurosis as a secret, private religion. The therapist needs to know what the patient's answer to the question of existence is; most of what are considered "psychological problems" are only secondary consequences of this "answer"—his secret religion to which all his efforts and passions are devoted.[10]

[5] *Pastoral Counseling,* p. 17.
[6] *Saturday Review of Literature,* January 5, 1957, p. 20.
[7] Herman Melville, *Moby Dick* (New York: The Modern Library, 1950), p. 1.
[8] Gerald Sykes, *The Hidden Remnant* (New York: Harper & Row, 1962), p. 72.
[9] *Modern Man in Search of a Soul* (New York: Harcourt, Brace, 1933), p. 269.
[10] *Zen Buddhism and Psychoanalysis* (New York: Harper & Row, 1960), p. 91.

It is easy to miss the spiritual-existential facets of the problems a pastor encounters in counseling. Often they are hidden. If, for whatever reason, a counselor is tuned mainly to the wavelength of psychosocial aspects of human problems, he will not hear the spiritual longing which is present. Conversely, lopsided attention to the "religious" dimension precludes awareness of the complex psychosocial factors which interweave with the spiritual-existential factors. To be effective as a *pastoral* counselor one must be tuned simultaneously to the horizontal and the vertical dimensions of *every human problem.*[11]

A guilt-ridden, bedfast woman, age seventy-eight, said to her minister: "I'd almost rather die—much as I dread that—than to have to lie here much longer." [12] Instead of encouraging her to discuss her feelings of uselessness and her fear of dying, the minister told her he was sorry she felt as she did—an almost certain way to turn off her expression of feeling. In the next interview, she again discussed dying.

PASTOR: "You aren't afraid, are you?" (A blocking question.)

WOMAN: Not exactly. No—I wouldn't say that. Maybe. But there are so many things I ought to do that I haven't done. I wonder if I'm ready to go. Do you think God punishes us for the things we do that are wrong?

The pastor answered that "the Bible teaches that there is a judgment." He went on to reassure her glibly that she had been a good woman and had nothing to worry about. The woman's obvious guilt and fear of death were not taken seriously. Her profound existential problem—facing death—was missed almost completely by the pastor, probably because of his own existential anxiety.

THE EXISTENTIAL DIMENSION IN ALL HUMAN PROBLEMS

In certain types of problems the religious-existential aspects tend to be obvious and pressing. According to Erik Erikson, the later adolescent is highly exposed to problems of existential identity and, therefore, anxiety.[13] It is no accident that schizophrenia frequently begins at this

[11] American pastoral care has properly stressed the dangers of religious reductionism in viewing human problems, but in so doing has sometimes fallen into psychological reductionism.

[12] For a verbatim account of this pastoral visit, see Cryer and Vayhinger, *Casebook in Pastoral Counseling*, Case No. 44, pp. 240-45.

[13] *Young Man Luther* (New York: W. W. Norton, 1958), p. 113. This book is an illuminating study of the psychology of late adolescence and young adulthood.

time. Existential factors also play major roles in the crisis of the middle years, when one's youthful illusions of physical immortality crumble before the realities of aging. Psychologist Herman Feifel has discovered that "a primary subconscious concern of the person over fifty, as revealed through projective testing, is preoccupation with his own death." [14] Existential-religious factors are often near the surface in crisis counseling, particularly in counseling with the sick, the dying, and the bereaved. These are experiences which crack the fragile shell of pseudo-omnipotence which most of us wear, confronting us with the brevity and vulnerability of our lives, and forcing us to be aware of the clock that relentlessly is ticking away, bringing us moment by moment closer to the grave.

Though often not so obvious and in some cases completely hidden, there is an existential-spiritual dimension in *every problem* with which pastor and parishioner struggle in counseling. This is true because existential anxiety is inherent in every human experience.

> Anxiety in general is the response of the human organism to anything that is perceived as a threat to what one regards as essential to one's welfare or safety. Pathological (neurotic) anxiety arises when contradictory impulses, desires or needs clamor simultaneously for expression or satisfaction. It is the result of inner conflict. It serves the function of keeping material that is unacceptable to the self-image repressed. In contrast, existential anxiety is nonpathological or normal anxiety. It arises from the very nature of human existence. Man is the animal who knows he will die. He is trapped by his rootage in nature. He is subject to its forces of sickness, pain, and death, and he lacks what Big Daddy, in Tennessee Williams' *Cat on a Hot Tin Roof,* calls the "pig's advantage"—viz. ignorance of his mortality.[15]

As Martin Heidegger observes, our knowledge that we must die is the background music that plays faintly in the distance all during our lives. "At times we may blot it out, but there are other times when it swells in volume and tempo, and we cannot be unaware of it." [16]

As Paul Tillich made clear, the threat of nonbeing, which produces

[14] Margaretta K. Bowers, *et al., Counseling the Dying,* p. 2.

[15] Howard J. Clinebell, Jr., "Philosophical-Religious Factors in the Etiology and Treatment of Alcoholism," *Quarterly Journal of Studies on Alcohol,* September, 1963, p. 477.

[16] Bowers, *et al., Counseling the Dying,* p. 21. The source is Martin Heidegger's *Being and Time* (New York: Harper & Row, 1962).

existential anxiety, has three forms—the threat of fate and death, emptiness and loss of meaning, guilt and condemnation.[17] He writes: "This anxiety is potentially present in every moment. It permeates the whole of man's being." [18] It is a part of his "heritage of finitude." It is the shadow which touches all other anxieties and gives them their power.

Existential anxiety is the raw material from which all anxiety is formed. Anxiety about death is both the prototype and wellspring of all other anxiety. A woman who knew she was born out of wedlock, unwanted, the result of an accident, lamented, "I feel I have no right to be." She was expressing the haunting sense of rejection and existential anxiety resulting from the precarious circumstances of her coming into being.

There are no psychological or psychotherapeutic answers to existential anxiety. It is "existential" in that it is inherent in man's very existence as a self-aware creature. But *its impact on the individual can be either creative or destructive,* depending on how it is handled. That which one uses to cope with existential anxiety is, psychologically speaking, one's "religion." This may be one of many forms of idolatry—the deification of possessions, health, "success," alcohol, the state, a church, one's family, making these matters of "ultimate concern" (Tillich). Neurotic problems can also be understood as attempts to avoid existential anxiety. Ironically, the use of these defenses against nonbeing inevitably produces precisely what is feared—nonbeing.[19] That is, the neurosis lessens a person's aliveness. Tillich viewed neurotic anxiety as a way of avoiding the threat of nonbeing by avoiding being (i.e., defending oneself against the fear of death by not being fully alive).

There seems to be a reciprocal relationship between neurotic and existential anxiety. Tillich observed that a high degree of neurotic anxiety renders one vulnerable to the threat of nonbeing[20] and, conversely, "those who are empty of meaning are easy victims of neurotic anxiety." [21] Each form of anxiety tends to reinforce the other.

If one attempts to cope with existential anxiety by pseudo-religious

[17] *The Courage To Be* (New Haven: Yale University Press, 1952), Chapter 2.
[18] Paul Tillich, *Systematic Theology* (Chicago: University of Chicago Press, 1951), I, 193.
[19] See J. F. T. Bugental, *The Search for Authenticity,* p. 15.
[20] *The Courage to Be,* p. 67.
[21] *Ibid.,* p. 151.

(i.e., idolatrous) or by neurotic means, the inevitable results are the diminishing of the creativity, awareness, and authenticity of one's life. J. F. T. Bugental writes:

> Neurotic anxiety is the distress occasioned by our yielding up of our authentic being-in-the-world to illusory hopes of being secure, of avoiding tragedy. It is always accompanied by some reduction of our total being, and for that reason is inevitably a cancerous growth in our lives. . . . We are less real in our living and so our anxiety is renewed, thus requiring greater defensive efforts. Neurotic anxiety tends, thus, to be ever-increasing anxiety.[22]

The only constructive means of handling existential anxiety is an authentic religious life which includes the actualization of the image of God within the person. In what has become the most quoted passage from *Modern Man in Search of a Soul,* Jung reported: "Among all my patients in the second half of life—that is to say, over thirty-five—there has not been one whose problem in the last resort was not that of finding a religious outlook on life." [23] This is consistent with Tillich's observation that the "power of the divine" is that within which "nonbeing is eternally conquered." Life-enhancing religion enables a person to confront rather than evade his existential anxiety. As Tillich made clear, only as this normal anxiety is confronted and taken into one's self-affirmation can it enhance instead of cripple one's life. Within the context of meaning or trust, it becomes, in Kierkegaard's word, a "school." In the very experience of facing anxiety, an individual develops the inner certitude of faith.[24] Anxiety is the teacher who searches one's life thoroughly and roots out the trivial.[25] Thus, existential anxiety becomes the "mother of the drive to know." [26]

THE GOAL OF EXISTENTIAL-RELIGIOUS COUNSELING

The goal of this dimension of pastoral counseling is to help people grow in the vitality and depth of their spiritual lives. This growth

[22] *The Search for Authenticity,* p. 25.

[23] P. 264.

[24] Sören Kierkegaard, *The Concept of Dread* (Princeton: Princeton University Press, 1944), p. 104.

[25] *Ibid.,* p. 142

[26] See Fred Berthold, Jr., "Anxious Longing," in *Constructive Aspects of Anxiety,* Seward Hiltner and Karl Menninger, eds. (Nashville: Abingdon Press, 1963), p. 71.

occurs as they learn to relate to God, other persons, and their own inwardness in ways that help to satisfy *four basic spiritual needs* which all men have, whether or not they are aware of them:

(1) The need for a meaningful philosophy of life and a challenging object of self-investment.

(2) The need for a sense of the numinous and transcendent.

(3) The need for a deep experience of trustful relatedness to God, other people, and nature.

(4) The need to fulfill the "image of God" within oneself by developing one's truest humanity through creativity, awareness, and inward freedom. These needs are not "spiritual" in some special "churchy" sense. Rather they are fundamental *human needs* which can be satisfied only as one interacts with the vertical dimension—the dimension of meaning and of God. As Dietrich Bonhoeffer put it so well: "To be a Christian does not mean to be religious in a particular way, to cultivate some particular form of asceticism . . . but *to be a man*." [27]

A minister's theological training should equip him to be a facilitator of spiritual growth. This is his unique and indispensable contribution in counseling. His knowledge of man's fundamental religious needs and the ability to help persons learn how to satisfy them are his crucial assets in counseling with reference to this dimension of human problems.

Erich Fromm holds that everyone has a deep, inescapable need for a "system of thought and action shared by a group that gives the individual a frame of reference and an object of devotion." [28] Counseling experience confirms the existence of a universal craving for a sense of meaning and some "ultimate concern" to which to commit one's life. Jesus taught that it is by such self-investment that one finds life.

Viennese psychiatrist Viktor Frankl's system of "logotherapy" is based on the conviction that the "will to meaning" is the dominant drive in human life, that a man lives in his meanings, and that the central task of therapy is to help a person find a sense of meaning. His basic thesis is that "life is transformed when a mission worth carrying out is uncovered." [29] Frankl points his patients to three kinds of values

[27] *Letters and Papers from Prison*, p. 166.

[28] *Psychoanalysis and Religion* (New Haven: Yale University Press, 1950), p. 21. A pioneer in child psychology writes: "Values permeate our development and personality to such a degree that they can never be left out of the picture" (Charlotte Buhler, *Values in Psychotherapy* [New York: The Free Press of Glencoe, 1962], p. x[illegible].

[29] Robert C. Leslie, *Jesus and Logotherapy*, p. 75.

—*creative* values, doing something worthwhile; *experiential* values, derived from experiencing a sunset, a good marriage, the fragrance of a flower, a precious memory; and *attitudinal* values, taking a constructive attitude toward even the worst situation. Frankl stresses the "defiant power of the human spirit," its ability to rise above past and present limitations. The religious man, in his view, is the "one who says 'yes' to life; the man who, in spite of everything that life brings, still faces his existence with a basic conviction in the worthwhileness of life."[30]

The emphasis of Frankl and other existentialist psychotherapists on meanings and values is directly relevant to pastoral counseling. The same is true of the emphasis on decision and commitment. The existential therapist seeks to help the person experience his existence more fully, and to discover what has prevented him from finding something to which he could commit himself unconditionally. Rollo May declares in a kind of counseling-for-decision passage: "The patient cannot permit himself to get insight or knowledge until he is ready to decide, takes a decisive orientation to life, and has made the preliminary decisions along the way."[31]

In counseling on value problems it is important to be aware of the ways in which the contemporary crisis in values makes it difficult for many people to find a viable philosophy of life—"so alive it bleeds when cut." Millions are uprooted from those relationships of mutual trust within which sound values flourish and existential anxiety can be handled constructively.[32] Rollo May articulates the challenge of life in our time of kaleidoscopic change:

> When a culture is caught in the profound convulsions of a transition period, the individuals in the society understandably suffer spiritual and emotional upheaval; and finding that the accepted mores and ways of thought no longer yield security, they tend either to sink into dogmatism and conformism, giving up awareness, or are forced to strive for heightened self-consciousness by which to become aware of their existence with new conviction and on new bases.[33]

[30] *Ibid.*, p. 14.

[31] *Existence*, p. 87.

[32] Tillich summarized the impact of our times: "The anxiety which, in its different forms, is potentially present in every individual becomes general if the accustomed structures of meaning, power, belief, and order disintegrate. These structures . . . keep anxiety bound. . . . In periods of great changes these methods no longer work" (*The Courage To Be*, p. 62).

[33] *Existence*, p. 17.

This insight has important implications for the "ministry of meanings" in pastoral counseling.

The clergyman should help his counselees discover ways of fulfilling their need for a sense of the numinous and the transcendent—the "ecstatic moment" (Tillich), something wonderful transcending the mundaneness of daily life. This is linked with the need for a sense of relatedness to nature, unity with life, a trustful relationship with other persons and with God. In his discussion of the self-actualizing person Abraham Maslow used the phrase "oceanic feeling" to describe the experience of feeling a part of the whole universe. Existentialist therapist J. F. T. Bugental says it this way: "Man is a part of The All. . . . Man is more than a creature, and in his sensing of The All, however dim, man is in a different relation to The All." [34]

The need of persons for a dynamic vertical relationship, summarized by Tolstoy's phrase "a thirst for God," [35] is not easily satisfied in our time. Much contemporary religion has lost its sense of wonder and become pale and anemic, lacking in the ecstatic and the transcendent. For modern man the prayer of St. Augustine, "Oh! that Thou wouldst enter into my heart and inebriate it," [36] has wistful overtones. When religion loses its lift, its sense of the numinous, many people turn to pseudo religions. Some attempt to make a chemical religion out of alcohol or drugs. All forms of idolatry eventually betray their worshipers.

Pastoral counseling on existential problems aims at helping people learn to live in harmony with the principles of the psychological-spiritual world, to enjoy loving interaction with nature and an open, maturing relationship with God. It seeks to help persons become aware of the fact that they are made to be active partners[37] of the living God who *is active in every relationship!* It seeks to help them renew their sense of "basic trust" by being aware of him, and to help them find healing for those dimensions of their brokenness which can only be healed in this vertical relationship. It seeks to help each person find his

[34] *The Search for Authenticity*, p. 412.

[35] Tolstoy credits this craving for God with keeping him alive during a long period of suicidal depression. See William James, *Varieties of Religious Experience* (New York: Modern Library [1902]), p. 153.

[36] *Confessions*, Bk. I.

[37] This is the theme of Theodor Bovet's book on pastoral care, *Road to Salvation, A Handbook on the Christian Care of Persons* (Garden City, N.Y.: Doubleday & Co. 1964).

mission, his cause—that which he can pour his God-given life into with abandon.

With the existential therapists, the pastoral counselor should aim at helping persons to become more fully human, to release that creativity, awareness, and inner freedom which constitute the *imago dei.* To the degree that a man actualizes his essential being as a man, he finds his place in the universe and is able to transform existential anxiety into a life-enhancing force in his experience. Fear of death loses its power to paralyze as one becomes more alive and authentic. The person who treats himself like a machine, who feels he has never lived, whose awareness, inner freedom, and creativity are trammeled by neurosis, is most terrified by death. Conversely, the person who has learned to relate, to create, to be aware and inwardly free, and thus moves toward fulfilling his most human potentialities, is able to transform his feelings about death into a stimulus for living more fully. He dies living rather than lives dying. The more his unique human attributes are fulfilled, the more he participates in what Bugental calls the "celebration of being."

A person who has passed forty and suddenly realizes, "My life is more than half gone!" may experience a wave of existential anxiety. If his life is empty of creative expression, he may be well-nigh overwhelmed by this experience. If, on the other hand, he has participated in biological creativity (i.e., has children) or if he has poured some of his vital energies into the ongoingness of life, he has a source of strength in something that he has created that will survive him. In the creative moment one transcends the shackles of finitude, rising above creaturehood, to become co-creator with God. The implication of this for counseling with older people is clear—help them find a channel of creativity.

METHODS OF EXISTENTIAL COUNSELING

When a parishioner talks in counseling about aging and death, his relationship with God (or lack of it), the meanings by which he lives (or his vacuous meaninglessness), his when-the-chips-are-down theology, his "ultimate concerns," it is probable that he is asking for help with the existential dimension of his problems. Often the cry for existential help is less obvious—perhaps disguised as a dull purposelessness or empty longing.

It is the clergyman's responsibility to lead people toward an awareness of the existential dimension in their dilemmas. In a sense the pastor's counseling has two aspects—the immediate problem in living and the "ground" of all one's problems. If a minister only helps a person handle his immediate problems more adequately, he has done but half his job, even though an important half. The other half is to help him release his humanity and to stimulate his growth on the vertical plane of his life. Bugental describes the two aspects in existentialist terms: "In simplest terms, the main undertaking of psychotherapy is that of aiding the patient in his efforts (a) to discard the distortions of awareness which arose to forestall existential anxiety, and (b) to accept the responsibilities and opportunities of authentic being in the world. The central concern in both phases is with authenticity." [38]

The pastoral counselor can encourage the person to move into the existential dimension by raising questions such as these: "Does your personal religion seem to be related to this problem, as you see it?" or "How do you see this decision, in the light of what's important, in the long run, in your life?" Questions of this type should be asked only within a strong counseling relationship, after the person has struggled with other aspects of his problem. So timed, such a question may open counseling doors for the exploration of blocks to a more vital religious life and more creative awareness in relationships. It may expose guilt feelings and immature religious feelings which are barriers to inner freedom and creativity.

When a person lacks awareness of any significant meanings, the questions may have to be more confrontational. In applying Frankl's methods to pastoral counseling Robert C. Leslie states:

> When the counselor is dealing with a lack of purpose, he has to provide active help in discovering the purpose. His task at this point is twofold: on the one hand he has to help the counselee to sense that life is worth living, that it does have a meaning; on the other hand he has to help the counselee find the specific personal meaning that beckons, that awaits fulfillment. In both these tasks active participation is called for.[39]

Frankl uses provocative questions to help people discover the meaning

[38] *The Search for Authenticity*, p. 31. He calls these the "analytic phase" and "ontogogic phase" of therapeutic work.

[39] *Jesus and Logotherapy*, pp. 43-44.

which is in their lives but of which they have not been aware. In effect, he communicates, "There *is* meaning in your life; it is part of your responsibility to find it, and I will help you do so."

Wayne E. Oates writes: "Pastoral counseling is spiritual communication about the durably meaningful things of life as they are separated from the transient things." [40] Many people need to make this separation but are afraid to do so. Their fear of finitude has produced heavy defenses against awareness of the transiency of their lives. In our death-denying culture many people are able to avoid confronting the fact that their lives are running out like grains of sand in an hourglass. But unless they find courage to face their finitude and use this awareness as a stimulus to creativity, their full rich humanness will remain largely unfulfilled. A trustful counseling relationship can give them the courage which will permit meaningful confrontation.

The pastoral counselor should not be timid about raising questions of human destiny. This is his area of greatest concern. He should help people ask and seek meaningful answers to the "big questions"—"What does my life mean?" "Why am I here?" "What is my relation to the All?" As a hospital patient put it: "As long as nobody asks the big questions, you can ignore them and let them be. But once they're asked, you can't put them down again until you have the answer." [41] The big questions are always present in a person's mind, often out of conscious awareness. If a person can bring them into awareness and deal with them, he is provided with an opportunity to confront his existential anxiety and to incorporate it into his self-awareness. The counselor may, for example, use a Frankl approach, asking a person to look at his life in terms of how he would feel if he were at the end looking back at the way he is now living. Searching questions such as, "Are the urgent things crowding out the important things in your life?" [42] may be used to make one aware of his problem of inverted values.

As Rollo May indicates, the existentialist thrust in psychotherapy does not seek to diminish anxiety but to help the person face it and use it to discover deeper dimensions of his existence. He states:

[40] *Protestant Pastoral Counseling*, p. 165.

[41] Bowers, *et al.*, *Counseling the Dying*, p. 12.

[42] This is a paraphrase of a statement by Robert Hutchins, "The job of the administrator is to distinguish the urgent from the important."

Everyone constantly faces the threat of nonbeing if he lets himself recognize the fact. Central here is the symbol of death, but such threat of destruction of being is present in a thousand and one other guises as well. The therapist is doing the patient a disservice if he takes away from him the realization that it is entirely within the realm of possibility that he forfeit or lose his existence and that may well be precisely what he is doing at this very moment.[43]

Following confrontational life experiences, existential issues are usually near the surface. One physician regularly asks patients who are well along the road to recovery from heart attacks, "What have you learned from this experience?" Even when the issues of ultimate meaning are not near the surface, the careful use of confrontational questions sometimes makes them accessible in counseling.

Helping people surrender their pseudo religious "solutions" is another way of letting them face their real spiritual needs. This is particularly useful with middle-aged persons who have overinvested in "success," are appalled by its lack of inner satisfactions, but do not know how to let go of this obsession. Releasing idols which have brought a semblance of security is very difficult until they begin to collapse. The mechanism of surrender,[44] as described previously (Chapter 9), is relevant at this point. Holding on to our grandiose self-sufficiency blocks the channels through which more vital experiences of God, nature, and people could come. Only when narcissism collapses does one "hit bottom" and, like the alcoholic, become open to life and help.

It is easy for a busy pastor to be seduced by superficiality (his own and his parishioner's) so that he avoids raising ultimate issues or dodges them adroitly when they emerge in counseling. A young man with a drinking problem and an attachment to "positive thinking" literature came to talk about religious problems on which he felt "pretty mixed up." The minister missed his existential emptiness, his search for meaning. He asked him briefly about his worries, suggested he consider revising his budget, and then gave him some glib advice about his religious life.[45] No future appointment was made. The young man was starving for bread but he went away with only a stone.

[43] *Existence*, p. 89.

[44] It should be emphasized that "surrender," as used here, is a *positive* movement away from self-idolatry and toward accepting the reality of one's finitude.

[45] See Cryer and Vayhinger, *Casebook in Pastoral Counseling*, Case No. 38, pp. 213-16.

THE RELIGIOUS SEARCH GROUP IN EXISTENTIAL COUNSELING

Educative group counseling methods are very effective in dealing with existential-religious problems. Spiritual growth takes place most rapidly in a group committed to religious values. Every church should have several spiritual search groups in which people can simultaneously deepen their relationships and their faith. Among the variety of patterns of such groups, two widely used types are the "*koinonia*" and the "Yokefellow" groups.

The *koinonia*[46] group method was developed by Robert A. Raines, who writes:

> In the last several years a number of people in our church have been rediscovering who they are as Christians and what their mission is. This experience was nothing that any of us planned or even anticipated. It came as a gift, a surprising outcome of meeting together in small groups for Bible study, prayer, and the sharing of experience. We know that the study of the New Testament has been at the heart of it. We have watched our friends changing radically and permanently in the context of these groups. We are convinced that real change in ourselves is necessary for the recovery of our mission. We know for ourselves the validity of Paul's declaration: "If any one is in Christ he is a new creation." [47]

Raines holds that offering adults an opportunity to acquire a basic knowledge of the Bible and to work out a more mature faith is crucially important in itself and the best way to attract a sizable number of adults into small groups. The groups offer a way of reaching people deeply and quickly, and of training "a hard core of committed and growing disciples who will serve as leaven within the local church." [48]

Koinonia groups, composed of eight to twelve people, meet for two hours twice a month, often in members' homes. Meetings begin with a fifteen-minute devotional period, including a time of corporate silence for "centering down." This is followed by one and one-half hours of serious grappling with the assigned material from a two-year cycle of New Testament study, beginning with Mark. The meeting ends with a

[46] *Koinonia* is the New Testament Greek word for the redemptive fellowship of the first century church.

[47] *New Life in the Church*, p. 18.

[48] *Ibid.*, p. 78.

period of "shared prayer." Each person may say a sentence prayer; those who wish to pass simply say "Amen."

Koinonia groups are not counseling or therapy groups, but there is no doubt that they are therapeutic. Raines reports, "No matter how academically I would start the discussion, the people would invariably bring it down to their daily lives where they needed help." [49] Lives were changed and marriages were re-created, as husbands and wives learned to communicate and minister to each other's needs.

A depth Bible study approach, as illustrated by the *koinonia* groups, offers an ideal format for group existential counseling in a church. The focus on biblical material has these values in addition to those mentioned by Raines:

(1) It takes the group directly to wrestling with theological-existential issues on a level of personal needs, doubts, fears, and conflicts.

(2) It is less anxiety arousing, for the leader and group members, than contentless group counseling approaches which focus *directly* on the members' problems.

(3) The combining of an objective and subjective focus helps keep a group from bogging down in fruitless psychologizing, as sometimes happens in counseling groups without a trained therapist.

(4) The life insights of the Bible can be used as an entrée, stimulus, and guide to deeper exploration of the inner problems of members. As Hiltner points out, religion is a channel of access which the pastor has to personality.[50] Spiritual and emotional problems are always intertwined. Both will be encountered no matter with which one begins.

(5) Depth Bible study can be led safely by persons with no formal training in group counseling, including laymen who have learned how to lead by participating in previous groups. The more training in group methods a person has, the more opportunities he will discover for group counseling within this context.

A spiritual group method which is explicitly counseling oriented is the Yokefellow group approach. Elton Trueblood began the Yokefellow movement as a way of reviving the use of the spiritual growth prin-

[49] *Ibid.*, p. 84. Robert C. Leslie writes: "Most study groups conducted under church resources that fail are failures not because of a lack of vital material to deal with but because the material is so commonly unrelated to immediate personal life situations" (*Jesus and Logotherapy*, p. 53).

[50] *Pastoral Counseling*, p. 118.

ciples of the Moravian Band class meeting.[51] The West Coast pattern of the "Yokefellow Associates" has adopted a modified group therapy approach.

One California church began a Yokefellow group about five years ago on a thirteen-week experimental basis. Four additional groups were started within the year. A central purpose was to help people to learn to communicate—particularly husbands and wives. The groups range in size from ten to fourteen for couples, and eight to ten for singles. Each member agrees to spend a minimum of thirty minutes a day in devotions, study, and prayer for other group members. The meetings begin with devotions, followed by centering on the areas in which the different members need to grow. Some groups follow a schedule of recommended reading. The minister of this church reports: "I think the Yokefellow groups have been the most helpful thing to the people of this church which we have ever undertaken. . . . It would almost take a book to describe the results." [52] Another minister who has used Yokefellow groups reports: "I have discovered that the people who have participated have experienced some tremendous changes and spiritual growth in their lives." [53] There is ample evidence that the Yokefellow approach has helped many people. The spiritual orientation tends to make these groups less threatening than unmodified group therapy.

Joseph Knowles cites certain limitations of the "prayer therapy" method [54] (which is used by many Yokefellow groups). It is my opinion that the group therapy Yokefellow approach cannot be used as safely by ministers and laymen with no group therapy training as can the depth Bible study *koinonia* group approach. To avoid "getting in over his head" and unwittingly doing harm, a Yokefellow group leader should have training in counseling and in group therapy methods. If he lacks

[51] Knowles, *Group Counseling*, p. 61.

[52] Letter from Vickrey Dougherty, August 26, 1965.

[53] Letter from Eugene E. Golay, September 10, 1965.

[54] *Group Counseling*, pp. 62-63. Knowles points to these dangers—That the Yokefellow Associates material may be used as a form of "The power of positive thinking"; that unproductive intellectualizing about problems may be encouraged; that the prayer therapy materials do not provide leaders with an adequate philosophy and methodology of group leadership. I would add that the system of mailing the group members mimeographed "spiritual growth slips," based on psychological tests, reflects a highly questionable practice, both therapeutically and in terms of the legitimate use of tests. The greatest danger of the Yokefellow approach—inadequate leadership—can be reduced by the careful selection, training, and continuing guidance of the laymen who function as leaders, or the use of persons from the mental health professions as leaders.

this, he should work under the supervision of a skilled group counselor.

The redemptive impact of any religious search group depends on the openness of communication and the *religious quality of its relationships.* It is not the use of religious words, nor the discussion of problems labeled "religious," which stimulates growth in relationships with God. As Buber has declared, "religion" can mask the face of God.[55] It is the achievement to some degree of a *koinonia* quality, a living embodiment of the "good news" in the fabric of group relations that nourishes spirits and changes lives. When this occurs, the small group becomes an instrument for proclaiming the gospel on a very deep and personal level.

THE USE OF RELIGIOUS INSTRUMENTS IN COUNSELING

Because spiritual growth is the ultimate aim of his counseling, a minister should use theological words, biblical allusions, and the religious resources of prayer, scripture, and sacraments with great care. Such symbols and practices mean many things to many people. For some they carry heavy emotional freight. Here are some ground rules for reducing the danger of blocking spiritual growth by the misuse of these instruments in counseling:[56]

(1) Use religious symbols and instruments sparingly and only after one is aware of the counselee's needs and "internal frame of reference," particularly with respect to religion. Otherwise one is likely to pray or read the Bible in an irrelevant or even harmful way.

(2) After praying or reading scripture, give the person an opportunity to discuss his feelings regarding the experience. The pastor may say: "What was going through your mind as I was reading?"

(3) Use these instruments in ways that do not diminish a dependent person's sense of responsibility. Avoid praying in ways that create magical expectations or block the catharsis of negative feelings by arousing guilt about them.

(4) Catch up the person's feelings, including his angry, bitter, or resentful feelings, in the prayer, indicating that God accepts these human feelings.

(5) Use religious instruments more extensively in supportive, crisis, confrontational, and existential counseling, and less in depth and in-

[55] "Buber on Good and Evil," *Saturday Review,* April 7, 1962, p. 18.

[56] For a discussion of the constructive use of the Bible in counseling, see Wayne E. Oates, *The Bible in Pastoral Care* (Philadelphia: Westminster Press, 1953).

sight counseling. Be aware that religious practices usually strengthen the authority image of the minister by activating the counselee's Child (Berne).

(6) Never use prayer as a "tool." Unless the minister honestly feels prayerful, he will confuse the counselee by his "act."

(7) Use religious practices to deepen a relationship, never as a substitute for relating.

(8) Never feel that one *has* to pray. God is continually active in all therapeutic relationships, whether or not formal "religious" practices are used.

The appropriate use of religious instrumentalities can stimulate and facilitate creative struggle with existential problems in counseling. It can help open a person to the power of the spiritual universe which is available to him. At the close of a counseling relationship a prayer of thanksgiving may be a fitting way to express gratitude for the new life that has come into one's inner world.

For some people it is helpful to see that the issues at the heart of counseling—alienation, guilt, anxiety, the search for wholeness, reconciliation, and rebirth—are essentially theological issues. In some cases it may be useful to formulate the ultimate goal of counseling in theological language—rebirth through reconciliation with oneself, others, and God. Skillfully employed theological language sometimes can catch the "feel" of the ineffable experiences which occur again and again in counseling.

THE PASTOR'S INNER RESOURCES

When a minister counsels in existential problems, his living theology—the way he handles *his own* existential anxiety—will influence the outcome more than his head-level theology. His degree of basic trust, his ways of coping with the "ego chill," [57] his courage to look into the abyss of nonbeing—these will be tested in relating to a man dying of cancer or an alcoholic teetering on the brink of meaninglessness and suicide. His real feelings about his own life and death will influence all his counseling, especially that with existential problems at the center.

Fortunately, the minister's effectiveness is not entirely dependent on

[57] Erik Erikson's term for existential anxiety.

his degree of spiritual maturation. As a representative Christian person he can draw on the resources of a rich tradition—wisdom about life tested by use in several thousand years of human struggle. Even at best he is an imperfect channel. But in spite of this, if he will be an "existential partner" [58] with the counselee, he often can transmit the transforming symbols and depth experiences of his heritage. Though his own faith is far from perfect, "the spiritually secure pastor knows that the life of his counselee is actually in the hands of God, and not his. The Holy Spirit and not he himself is the Counselor." [59]

It is important that the minister be in an attitude of prayer—i.e., openness to the universe—in counseling. As he enters a counseling session a silent prayer may help him keep out of the center. It may make him aware of the presence of the "Great Counselor," the Holy Spirit, working in the relationship. It may help open *him* to the energies of the spiritual universe which are always available, and make him *spiritually ready* to function as an enabler in the God-man encounter by helping to remove the blocks to vital relating—fear, guilt, hatred, self-rejection, and defensive pride. The work of the effective counselor in existential problems "springs from, and is sustained by, a deep and continuous interior transaction with God.[60] It is the vitality of a minister's relationship with God which undergirds his effectiveness in the vertical dimension of relationship-centered counseling.

THE EXISTENTIALISTS' PERSPECTIVE

The clergyman-counselor's effectiveness will be increased if he immerses himself in the *existentialist perspective* in psychotherapy.[61] Its emphases on values, awareness, creativity, freedom (choice and responsibility), authenticity, existential anxiety (and also existential guilt and joy), being, actualization, encounter, confirmation, dialogue, and meaning are all consistent with a religious view of human beings. Its nonreductionistic conception of man, in contrast to both behaviorism

[58] This term, from the existentialists in psychotherapy, describes the sense of common humanity and lack of professionalism on the therapist's part.

[59] Oates, *Protestant Pastoral Counseling*, p. 59.

[60] H. Richard Niebuhr, *et al.*, *The Purpose of the Church and Its Ministry*, p. 11.

[61] J. F. T. Bugental's outstanding book represents the ideal means for the clergyman to encounter this perspective.

and psychoanalysis, lifts up the *uniquely human in man.* J. F. T. Bugental states it well:

> Perhaps I can best summarize what existential psychology means to me by using this phrase: "It restores our divinity." I am not content to see man as mechanism or robot or even as organism. Man must partake in whatever he means by the concept of God. . . . Existentialism restores man to his central place in man's own experience and grants us the possibility of realizing our fondest and most extreme imagining about the human condition, if only we have the courage and perseverance to see them through.[62]

The "revised model" of pastoral counseling may increase, to some extent, the ever-present danger that the minister will see his counseling task in terms of techniques rather than relationships. I can think of no more salutary influence than the existentialists' perspective to protect him from this danger and to release his potentialities as a facilitator of authentic relationships.

RECOMMENDED READING

Margaretta K. Bowers, *et al., Counseling the Dying* (New York: Thomas Nelson and Sons, 1964).

J. F. T. Bugental, *The Search for Authenticity, An Existentialist-Analytic Approach to Psychotherapy.*

John L. Casteel, ed. *Spiritual Renewal Through Personal Groups.*

Howard J. Clinebell, Jr., "Philosophical-Religious Factors in the Etiology and Treatment of Alcoholism," *Quarterly Journal of Studies on Alcohol,* September, 1963.

Viktor E. Frankl, *The Doctor and the Soul, An Introduction to Logotherapy* (New York: Alfred A. Knopf, 1955).

Robert C. Leslie, *Jesus and Logotherapy* (Nashville: Abingdon Press, 1965).

Rollo May, ed., *Existence, A New Dimension in Psychiatry and Psychology.*

Robert A. Raines, *New Life in the Church* (New York: Harper & Row, 1961).

Edward E. Thornton, *Theology and Pastoral Counseling* (Englewood Cliffs, N.J.: Prentice-Hall, 1964).

[62] *The Search for Authenticity,* p. 20.

REALITY-PRACTICE SESSIONS

PARISHIONER'S ROLES: 1. You are Jim, a high school freshman who feels strong doubts about the existence of God and the effectiveness of prayer. You have been invited by the director of Christian education to discuss joining the youth membership training class, a step which you are unwilling to take because of your doubts.[63]

2. You are Mrs. T., age forty-five, married, with two teen-age daughters. Repeated surgery has shaken your faith. You feel that God has let you down. Your husband seems to have lost his faith. He resents the heavy medical expenses. Things look very dark. (You are in a hospital bed. Lie down during the reality-practice session.)[64]

PASTOR'S ROLE: Counsel with the above persons using the approaches described in this chapter. Be particularly aware of connections between interpersonal conflict and existential problems.

OBSERVER-EVALUATOR: Be aware of the interaction in these sessions, with particular reference to the pastor's success in encouraging the expression of feelings and avoiding a defense of God or an intellectualized discussion of theology.

[63] For a verbatim report of a D. C. E.'s counseling in this case, see Cryer and Vayhinger, *Casebook in Pastoral Counseling*, Case No. 26, pp. 147-52.

[64] *Ibid.*, Case No. 30, pp. 167-71. Other cases which involve existential counseling include Case No. 33, fear of death, pp. 182-87; Case No. 6, husband dying, pp. 51-54; Case No. 8, dying woman, pp. 59-63.

15

Depth Pastoral Counseling

The purpose in a man's mind is like
deep water,
but a man of understanding will
draw it out.—Prov. 20:5

Ful wys is he that can him-selven knowe.
—Geoffery Chaucer[1]

Depth pastoral counseling is a long-term helping process aimed at effecting depth changes in the counselee's personality by uncovering and dealing with hidden feelings, intrapsychic conflicts, and repressed, early life memories. The terms "insight counseling," "pastoral psychotherapy," and "depth pastoral counseling" are roughly synonymous. As noted in Chapter 8 depth methods seek to enhance self-awareness, thus producing basic intrapsychic as well as relationship changes. It should be emphasized that the depth of the counseling process is a matter of degree. Significant insight can occur on various levels of counseling interaction. In some cases helpful self-understanding may be achieved during short-term counseling. But generally speaking, "the longer the period, the deeper the material that tends to emerge." [2]

The "revised model," as has been evident, emphasizes short-term, non-uncovering, relationship-modifying counseling approaches which are best adapted to parish counseling. These approaches provide the

[1] *Canterbury Tales*, "The Monkes Tale," l. 3329.
[2] Hiltner, *Pastoral Counseling*, p. 88.

"treatment of choice" for the majority of those seeking pastoral help. With many people the use of non-uncovering counseling methods is more helpful than are depth approaches. Short-term, relationship-modifying methods may, in such cases, produce long-term and highly significant results.

Some people, however, *require* depth counseling if they are to be helped. Intense inner conflicts sabotage their efforts to improve their relationships through short-term counseling. Depth counseling is essential in order to reduce the intensity of these conflicts and enhance self-esteem. With them, relationship-centered counseling is not adequate.

What should the minister do to be of help to such persons? Seward Hiltner states:

> There is no inherent reason why extended counseling could not be a part of a pastor's work—if he were trained, had the time, and did not in the process step out of his role as pastor. That is, extended counseling is not inherently foreign to pastorship, but in a practical sense it is rarely wise or appropriate for most pastors to engage in it.[3]

Depth counseling is a complex, time-consuming process. The pastor with limited training in counseling should refer persons needing such help to a competent psychotherapist. Even if a minister is well trained as a depth counselor, he is wise to invest most of his counseling time in the short-term opportunities which occur frequently in pastoring. Over the years he can give significant help to many times the number of persons he could aid by majoring in long-term, depth counseling.

The levels at which a minister counsels should be determined by the points at which his skills intersect the needs of those who seek his help. In many areas qualified therapists are unavailable or in short supply. In most nonmetropolitan settings clergymen with even minimal counseling training have more training than anyone else in their communities. In such therapy-poor areas a minister's skills in depth pastoral counseling may be the only resource for helping those who desperately need psychotherapy. Even if psychotherapists are available in a particular area, their crowded schedules and high fees often make referrals impossible.[4] Thus, in most situations, the well-trained pastor has many

[3] *Ibid.*, pp. 89-90.

[4] It is a part of a minister's prophetic role to work with others to create community resources where psychotherapy is available on an ability-to-pay basis.

opportunities to use his depth-counseling skills, to whatever extent his time permits.[5]

In addition to providing a valuable service to the troubled, a limited amount of depth pastoral counseling tends to strengthen a man's total ministry. To relate to even one person at a time in the complexities of the deep roots of his problems helps to provide a depth dimension to one's ministry, diminishing the occupational hazard of shallowness in relationships. Depth counseling is demanding, both in time and emotional energy, but it is also highly rewarding when done effectively. Overinvestment in depth counseling weakens a man's total ministry by causing him to neglect the many for the few.

DEPTH UNDERSTANDING

A distinction should be made between depth *understanding* and the practice of depth *counseling*. Every pastor needs sufficient knowledge of the goals and methods of psychotherapy to make appropriate, skillful referrals. Furthermore, whether or not he has the training and time to do depth counseling, his total work with persons will be deepened and enriched as he increases his understanding of the unconscious forces which influence all behavior profoundly. He needs this understanding of psychodynamics to maximize his effectiveness in preaching, teaching, administration, and general pastoral care. The insights of depth psychology[6] are indispensable for ministering to persons in our age of anxiety.

The psychoanalytic views of psychosexual (Sigmund Freud) and psychosocial (Erik Erikson) development are invaluable pastoral resources for understanding behavior, beliefs, and relationships—of oneself and one's parishioners. The insights of Freud and his successors illuminate vast areas of human life which otherwise are shadowed enigmas. The contributions of Jung, the interpersonal schools of depth psychology (Adler, Sullivan, Fromm, and Horney in particular), and the existentialists in psychotherapy supplement and/or correct the view

[5] Hiltner suggests that there are four situations which call for extended counseling: When no better trained psychotherapist is available, when the minister is qualified by special training, when he can work in collaboration with professional therapists, and when the problem focuses in the spiritual area (*Pastoral Counseling*, pp. 90-93).

[6] "Depth psychology" refers to those approaches to understanding man's psyche which take cognizance of the importance of its unconscious aspects.

of Freud at crucial points.[7] By immersing himself in studying these sources a pastor can enhance his understanding of the amazing depths and heights in man. For the average parish pastor the psychoanalytic schools are of limited value in supplying useful *methods* of counseling, but they are valuable sources of new *understanding* of the persons to whom he ministers.

THE GOALS OF DEPTH COUNSELING OR PSYCHOTHERAPY

In terms of the counseling goals described in Chapter 1, depth counseling, or psychotherapy, seeks to remove the subsurface personality blocks which prevent some people from maintaining mutually satisfying relationships. The ultimate goal (which is never completely achieved) is the "fully functioning person." [8] Here are the directions of change in psychotherapy: the person moves toward—

(1) Self-awareness—listening to his own feelings and experiences.

(2) Insight—depth understanding of his feelings and relationships.

(3) Permitting the therapist to care about him and thereby beginning to perceive himself as a person of worth.

(4) Going deeper within himself, discovering that there is "no beast in man; only man in man."

(5) Dissatisfaction with his facade composed of his responses to the "shoulds" and "oughts" of others.

(6) Autonomy, self-directedness, choosing his own goals, trusting his own awareness of genuine values.

(7) Self-acceptance, which leads to acceptance of others.

(8) "The quiet joy of being oneself"—a primitive joy in life analogous to a lamb frisking about a meadow.

(9) Desiring to be all of oneself at a given moment—"to be the self one truly is." The most common despair is not choosing to be oneself. The deepest despair is to choose to be another than oneself.[9]

This view of the directions of change, reflecting Rogers' *intrapersonal* orientation, needs to be supplemented by an *interpersonal* perspective

[7] Ruth L. Munroe's book *Schools of Psychoanalytic Thought* is a comprehensive exposition and critique of the various psychoanalytic schools.

[8] See Carl R. Rogers, *On Becoming a Person*, pp. 183-96.

[9] From Kierkegaard's *The Sickness unto Death* (Princeton: Princeton University Press, 1941), p. 29. Quoted by Rogers in " 'To Be That Self Which One Truly Is': A Therapist's View of Personal Goals," *On Becoming a Person*, pp. 163-82. The directions of change are paraphrased from this and other papers by Rogers.

such as Erich Fromm's: "Analytic therapy is essentially an attempt to help the patient gain or regain his capacity for love." [10]

> Love is . . . a power which breaks through the walls which separate man from his fellow man, which unites him with others; love makes him overcome the sense of isolation and separateness, yet it permits him to be himself, to retain his integrity.[11]

Effective psychotherapy *enhances inner freedom*. After extensive depth pastoral counseling a woman could report: "I feel something is complete. For the first time in my life, I have access to the full range of my feelings. Having access, it is up to me what I do with them. Before, I had no choice." The stranglehold of past relationships on her present life had been broken. Genuine alternatives had been opened in her inner world. Spontaneity had become a prominent characteristic of her feelings and relationships.

Effective psychotherapy also increases one's sense of *personhood* (identity) and *aliveness*. Psychologist Abraham Maslow declares:

> Self-actualizing people have a wonderful capacity to appreciate again and again, freshly and naïvely, the basic goods of life, with awe, pleasure, wonder and even ecstasy, however stale these experiences may have become to others.[12]

> Their ease of penetrating to reality, their closer approach to animal-like or child-like acceptance and spontaneity, imply a superior awareness of their own impulses, their own desires, opinions, and subjective reactions in general.[13]

A person is alive to the extent that he is aware of, and in relationship with, the many facets of himself, other people, the universe, and God. Self-awareness is the path to greater aliveness. By it one moves beyond *knowing* to *being* oneself.

In the vocabulary of existentialist psychotherapy, the goal of psychotherapy is authenticity—realizing one's true being.

The distinctive and ultimate goal of *depth pastoral counseling* is a loving, growing relationship with God. Augustine's prayer expresses this well: "O God . . . may I know myself, may I know thee." [14] Pastoral

[10] *Psychoanalysis and Religion*, p. 87.
[11] *The Art of Loving* (New York: Harper & Row, 1956), pp. 20-21.
[12] *Motivation and Personality* (New York: Harper & Row, 1954), pp. 214, 215.
[13] *Ibid.*, p. 210.
[14] *Soliloquia* Book II, Chap. 1.

psychotherapy can be an effective instrument for the healing of deeply fractured relationships and the stimulation of growth toward that personhood represented so clearly in Jesus. His aliveness, self-affirmation, and inner freedom were wonderfully contagious, helping those with whom he related to become more vital, self-accepting, and free within.

THE METHODS OF DEPTH COUNSELING

In his survey of psychotherapeutic schools of thought, Robert A. Harper describes *thirty-six different approaches.*[15] Most practicing therapists are eclectic in their methodology, utilizing techniques from a variety of schools. It is beyond the scope of this book to describe depth counseling methods in detail. (Readers who wish to know more about particular approaches may consult the books by Harper, Stein, Munroe, or Ford and Urban listed under Recommended Reading.) The discussion here will be limited to an overview of the general process of psychotherapy, followed by a brief consideration of two methods of depth pastoral counseling—client-centered and psychoanalytic.

In general, depth counseling employs methods which allow one to gradually become aware of those out-of-awareness (repressed) feelings, images, impulses, desires, memories, and conflicts which are limiting one's effectiveness in living. Insight emerges within the context of a trustful, empathic relationship in which the person counseled feels safe enough to explore painful feelings. By "working through" deeper and deeper levels of feelings the person gradually penetrates inner blocks to self-understanding, developing expanding awareness of himself and his relationships. With the therapist's support and help he can deal with archaic, inappropriate feelings and resolve creativity-crippling conflicts from the past. Long-sealed doors to hidden rooms in the recesses of one's early experience are gradually opened. The ghosts of the past, grown powerful *because* they were shut off from the adult, reality-oriented part of the self, are shorn of their demonic power by being exposed to the light of present reality. A choice passage from Lewis Carroll's *Alice's Adventures in Wonderland* illustrates the tyranny of the past: "Alice knew it was the Rabbit coming to look for her, and she trembled till she shook the house, quite forgetting that she was now about a

[15] *Psychoanalysis and Psychotherapy: 36 Systems.*

thousand times as large as the Rabbit and had no reason to be afraid of it." [16]

The psychotherapeutic relationship and process allow the person to become aware of his hidden "rabbits." Healing comes by re-experiencing the past traumatic or need-depriving experiences within the strength of the therapeutic relationship. Pastor Oskar Pfister wrote to Freud: "You yourself have always taught that what matters is not remembering but *reliving*. . . . You have always insisted that memory is not sufficient, but that it must be charged with affect." [17] The point of this is that the *feelings* surrounding a damaging early life relationship or trauma must be reexperienced and worked through if healing is to occur. The therapeutic relationship permits the repair, to some degree, of the personality crippling caused by inadequacies in the parent-child relationship. The therapist goes down into the person's little private hell with him,[18] allowing him to face his inner "devils" and find release from them. Near the conclusion of long-term pastoral psychotherapy a woman reported that she was no longer engulfed by negative feelings toward her mother: "For the first time in my life I can feel real compassion for her because I am free enough from her not to feel crippled by her crippledness. Poor thing! She has lived with those feelings all her life." She commented on the meaningfulness of her relationship with the counselor: "Before I felt so cheated by not feeling close to my parents. Now one good relationship carries you through all the others. Before I was trying to gulp in from others what I couldn't feel myself." Experiencing the counselor's acceptance had enabled her to find and accept herself as separate from her mother. Self-acceptance allowed her to accept her mother. This illustrates the way in which depth counseling provides an experience of emotional reeducation and personal growth at a deep level.

Effective therapy reduces inner conflicts with their pain and wasted energy. It makes one more sensitive to the dynamics of one's relationships and to the pain of others. It helps one to find the courage to face the abyss of loneliness and existential anxiety. Clark Moustakas observes: "When man is removed from a fundamental truth of life, when he successfully evades and denies the terrible loneliness of individual exis-

[16] Quoted by Jerome D. Frank in *Persuasion and Healing*, p. 18.
[17] *Psychoanalysis and Faith*, p. 92.
[18] This is Louis J. Sherrill's apt description of the therapist's role.

tence, he shuts himself off from one significant avenue of his own self growth."[19] Therapy helps make one aware of his inescapable need for meaningful relationships with his own depths, with others, and with God. Equally important it helps him develop the *ability* to relate. It opens one to himself, to others, and to life.

Most depth therapies operate on the assumption that significant improvement in one's self-perception and self-acceptance will produce spontaneous positive changes in one's behavior and relationships. As therapy progresses the person experiments with new ways of relating and communicating, derived from his inner growth. Feedback of feelings from these experiments in relating often produces additional positive movement in therapy. Gradually the person learns to live more fully, relate more satisfyingly, and handle the continuing problems of reality more constructively.

CLIENT-CENTERED COUNSELING

As indicated in Chapter 2 the Rogerian or client-centered method of psychotherapy is useful with young or middle-aged persons who are reasonably intelligent, introspective, verbal, and motivated to do more than solve their immediate problems. As with any introspective, uncovering therapy, this method tends to be effective with persons possessing reasonably strong egos and whose problems in living can be characterized as *psychoneurotic* rather than *psychotic* or *character disorders* (see Chapter 8).

The client-centered approach is relatively safe for use by any minister who has a good foundation of clinical and academic training in counseling. Many clergymen with natural counseling aptitudes, but with limited formal training, can learn to do effective client-centered counseling by having their counseling supervised regularly by an experienced psychotherapist. A minister who is teachable can, by obtaining regular supervision, counsel safely and effectively at a considerably deeper level than would otherwise be possible.

The definitive books on client-centered therapy are readily available to clergymen (see the volumes by Rogers under Recommended Read-

[19] *Loneliness* (Englewood Cliffs, N.J.: Prentice-Hall, 1961), p. ix.

ing). Carroll A. Wise has applied the Rogerian approach to pastoral counseling in *Pastoral Counseling, Its Theory and Practice.*[20] Seward Hiltner's *Pastoral Counseling* also draws extensively on client-centered theory. Inasmuch as these sources are easily accessible, no attempt will be made to do more than merely summarize the Rogerian method.

In general, client-centered therapy has these phases: (a) Initial establishing of rapport and structuring of the therapeutic relationship; (b) the "expressive stage"—catharsis of negative followed by positive feelings; (c) the emergence of insight which gradually produces changes in self-perception and behavior; (d) the closing phase during which the relationship is terminated. In an unmodified Rogerian approach "the main function of the therapist is to provide the atmosphere in which the client feels free to explore himself, to acquire deeper understanding of himself, and gradually to reorganize his perceptions of himself and the world about him."[21] The content, speed, and direction of the counseling are determined by the counselee. The desired changes are seen by Rogers as occurring gradually and spontaneously by a kind of "natural childbirth" (of the psyche), as the counselor engages in the following activities:

> (1) Strong, consistent effort to understand the client's content of speech and feelings, conveyed by words, gestures, expressions, etc.; (2) an effort to communicate this understanding to the client by word or (more often) his general attitude of acceptance; (3) occasional presentation of a condensation or synthesis of expressed feelings; (4) occasional statement of the nature and limits of the therapeutic relationship, the expectancies of the situation. . . . (5) When question-asking and information-giving seem relevant to the client's working through of his problems, they are engaged in, but denied when they seem likely to increase the client's dependency; (6) while the therapist may interrupt the client to make sure he understands what the client is saying or feeling, he offers no interpretations other than those which seem to summarize what the client (not the therapist) is feeling; (7) likewise the client-centered therapist does not try to promote insight directly, or give advice, praise, blame or to teach, or suggest programs of activities, or to ask questions or suggest areas of exploration.[22]

[20] This volume contains helpful chapters on "The Counseling Relationship," "Insight as the Goal of Counseling," and "Counseling and the Christian Faith."

[21] Harper, *Psychoanalysis and Psychotherapy: 36 Systems*, p. 82.

[22] *Ibid.*, pp. 88-89.

The minister's effectiveness in extended as in short-term counseling is enhanced by the appropriate introduction of educative, action-oriented, confrontational, role-relational, and other methods described in this book. In most cases it is wise to begin with a Rogerian approach and then to modify it with flexibility, as indicated by the particular needs of the parishioner.

Let me reemphasize that doing extended counseling, using a Rogerian base, is within the potential competencies of many parish ministers. The mastery of this art provides a means of meeting human needs which cannot be met by short-term counseling. What is more, it is a valuable discipline which cannot but stimulate the growth of the minister in his own ability to relate deeply.

PSYCHOANALYTIC PASTORAL PSYCHOTHERAPY

In 1913, when the negative reactions to Freud's discoveries were at their peak, Henri Bergson wrote:

> To explore the more sacred depths of the unconscious . . . that will be the principal task of psychology in the century which is opening. I do not doubt that wonderful discoveries await it there, as important perhaps as have been in the preceding centuries the discoveries of the physical and natural sciences.[23]

It is fortunate for the church, for suffering persons, and for the advancement of the psychotherapeutic art that some clergymen are obtaining training which allows them to do psychoanalytically oriented psychotherapy skillfully. This is a form of depth pastoral counseling which deals with unconscious distortions by means of psychoanalytic methods such as free association, active imagination, and the analysis of dreams, fantasies, and transference feelings. This approach tends to go deeper than client-centered therapy and to elicit more powerful "transference" feelings which are projected into the relationship. It therefore requires a great deal of skill, to be used constructively, and *should not be attempted by anyone who has not had specialized training in this method,* including a personal analysis and extensive supervision of one's functioning as a depth therapist.

Some thirty years ago Anton T. Boisen, father of the clinical training movement, expressed this hope:

[23] From *The Independent,* October 30, 1913. Quoted by Lancelot L. Whyte in *The Unconscious Before Freud* (New York: Basic Books, 1960), p. 181.

> Instead of allowing the psychiatrist to remain the exclusive keeper of the lower regions, I am hoping and laboring for the day when the specialist in religion will be able with his help to go down to the depths of the grim abyss after those who are capable of responding, those in whom some better self is seeking to come to birth.[24]

The growing emphasis on depth pastoral counseling is gradually making Boisen's hope a reality.

If clergy-counselors should ignore psychoanalytic approaches, creative experimentation in this important form of depth therapy would become, by default, the exclusive concern of the nontheologically trained. While acknowledging our major debt to the other counseling professions, and recognizing our continuing need for collaboration with them, we cannot escape the fact that pastoral counseling should be adding its unique contributions from the theological perspective to the theory and practice of psychotherapy, including that which is psychoanalytically oriented. As Bergson predicted, vital discoveries concerning the depths of man's psyche are occurring; often these emerge in the psychoanalytic relationship. The church, with its concern for the *whole person,* has a huge stake in these new insights. It can ill afford to allow the depth therapeutic encounter to become the exclusive concern of the nontheologically trained.

If the full helping potentialities of the depth psychology revolution (in human self-understanding) are to be released within the life of the churches, then persons with both theological and psychoanalytic training must be engaged in depth counseling. With their particular background and perspective pastoral depth therapists may eventually develop methods and discover insights about man which will enrich the entire psychotherapeutic effort to free the captives of inner conflict. Writing to his friend Pastor Pfister, Freud declared:

> In itself, psycho-analysis is neither religious nor non-religious, but an impartial tool which both priest and layman can use in the service of the sufferer. I am very much struck by the fact that it never occurred to me how extraordinarily helpful the psychoanalytic method might be in pastoral work.[25]

[24] *The Exploration of the Inner World,* pp. 266-67.
[25] *Psychoanalysis and Faith,* p. 17.

Pfister is a superb example of the way in which what he called "the analytic cure of souls" (psychoanalytically oriented pastoral counseling) can be a valuable method for a clergyman. Around the turn of the century this warm-hearted Swiss pastor wrote a paper protesting "the sin of omission toward psychology of present-day theology." In 1909 he encountered the writings of Freud and, shortly afterward, the man himself. Thus began a lifelong, mutually enriching friendship. Pfister was a frequent and welcome visitor at the Freud household. In writing to thank him for a gift Freud commented that it would remind him of "a remarkable man who came to see me one day, a true servant of God, a man the very idea of whom I should have had difficulty in believing, in that he feels the need to do spiritual good to everyone he meets. You did good in this way even to me." [26]

Pfister was a pastoral psychotherapist who was unafraid to encounter his parishioners in depth. He remained a dedicated pastor on the Zurich circuit until his retirement in 1939, much loved by his congregation. He used psychoanalytic methods in his pastoral counseling and was one of the major pioneers in the "analytic cure of souls." He also made significant contributions to the development of psychoanalytic theory and practice in its application to children, adolescents, and education. His lifelong appreciation for Freud's genius did not cause him to adopt Freud's metaphysical views. Following the publication of *The Future of an Illusion* he wrote Freud candidly:

> Thus there remains between us the great difference that I practice analysis within a plan of life which you indulgently regard as servitude to my calling, while I regard this philosophy of life, not only as a powerful aid to treatment (in the case of most people) but also the logical consequence of a philosophy that goes beyond naturalism and positivism, is well based on moral and social hygiene, and is in accordance with the nature of mankind and the world.[27]

The minister who is trained in psychoanalytic therapy can do in our day what Pfister did so well, under more difficult circumstances, in his—bring together two mighty streams of healing—the time-tested resources of the religious heritage and the newer instruments and insights of the depth psychotherapeutic disciplines. He may help develop a

[26] *Ibid.*, p. 24.
[27] *Ibid.*, p. 116. Letter dated November 24, 1927.

creative synthesis of these streams out of which may eventually be born a uniquely pastoral form of depth therapy. Because of the richness of his transference image as a clergyman, and the depth symbols of religion, he has unique assets as a depth therapist.[28]

A form of depth therapy which is particularly well fitted for use by the pastoral psychotherapist is the "existential-analytic approach" developed by J. F. T. Bugental. This represents a wedding of psychoanalytic and existentialist concepts and methods. Its philosophy and objectives are much more in harmony with the pastoral orientation than are those of the unmodified psychoanalytic approach. (See Chapter 14.) Especially relevant to depth *pastoral* counseling is Bugental's two-phase conception of therapy—an approach which makes a place for dealing with existential value considerations, following the analytic phase:

> When psychotherapy goes effectively through the analytic phase and thus aids the person in resolving his resistances and reclaiming his life, there is often need for a constructive phase to supplement the therapeutic work. . . . Just as the resistances on the negative side prevented the realization of human potential, so on the positive side confrontation with the ontogogic givens of living can facilitate the actualization of that potential.[29]

In addition to client-centered, psychoanalytic, and analytic-existential approaches, a number of other methods offer promise as useful instruments in pastoral psychotherapy. For example, several specialists in pastoral counseling are convinced that *image therapy* offers the ideal way of integrating theological insights into psychotherapy.[30] Image therapy draws on the concepts of Wilfried Daim, Melanie Klein, W. Ronald D. Fairbairn, and W. Earl Biddle.[31] Persons are seen as blocked from wholeness by captivity to their internalized "bad parent" images. Therapy aims at freeing them from these and helping them learn to relate to

[28] Since psychoanalytic therapy requires advanced specialized training and is not an approach which can be used safely and productively by most parish ministers, its methodology will not be discussed here. Readers who wish to know more about its methods are directed to Karl Menninger, *Theory of Psychoanalytic Technique* (New York: Basic Books, 1958) and to the books by Stein, pp. 338-71, and by Ford and Urban, pp. 109-78, in Recommended Reading.

[29] *The Search for Authenticity*, p. 15.

[30] Included are Carroll J. Wright, Paul Fairweather, and Merle Jordan. The latter has applied image therapy to pastoral counseling in a Th.D. dissertation, "The Idolatry of a 'Bad' Parental Image as a Frustration to Becoming a Whole Person," School of Theology at Claremont, 1965.

[31] See W. Earl Biddle, *Integration of Religion and Psychiatry* (New York: The Macmillan Company, 1955).

their good parental images within. Wilfried Daim holds that the central image around which an emotionally disturbed person organizes his life becomes absolutized and therefore an idol. This idolatry stultifies the soul's "natural freedom to unfold itself." [32]

Another method which holds promise for pastoral psychotherapy is based on the observation (by Jung and others) that many of the images and symbols of the Bible are directly related to universal human experiences and to the unconscious.[33] In some counseling a direct route to the person's central problem is the simple question, "What is your favorite (or least liked) Bible story?" Jane, a bright adolescent who was failing in school, responded: "It's the Adam and Eve story."

COUNSELOR: Tell me about it.

JANE: Adam and Eve were in the garden and ate the fruit of the tree of knowledge. That was the beginning of their trouble. They got kicked out and had to take care of themselves after that!

COUNSELOR: Are you saying, Jane, that when we gain knowledge, pain often follows?

JANE: Uh huh.

In the next session, Jane began to see that succeeding in school was equated in her mind with growing up and leaving the dependency relationships of childhood, her personal "Garden of Eden." As she faced and worked through her fears of adulthood, her school work improved.

Projective painting, drawing, and clay modeling are productive methods in depth pastoral counseling. The person is asked simply to express his feelings, with no planning in advance and no attempt to produce a work of art. When the painting, drawing, or model is brought to the counseling session, it is used in much the same way as dreams. The person is asked to free-associate on the entire work and on each part. Profound feelings often can be expressed in a visual medium long before they can be recovered through verbalizing alone. Religious symbols appear frequently in projective pictures, even those created by persons who do not think of themselves as "religious."

Well-trained pastoral counselors should experiment with a variety of

[32] *Depth Psychology and Salvation* (New York: Frederick Ungar Publishing Co., 1963), pp. 40-41.

[33] See Edgar Draper, *et al.*, "On the Diagnostic Value of Religious Ideation," *Archives of General Psychiatry*, September, 1965, pp. 202-7.

psychotherapeutic methods, including both the uncovering types (Rogerian, psychoanalytic, image therapy) and the non-uncovering approaches such as "reality therapy" and the learning-theory therapy.[34] The latter types aim at changing destructive or maladaptive behavior without attempting to find the hidden causes. Learning-theory approaches alter harmful behavior by rewarding more constructive responses and by punishing or withholding rewards from the negative behavior. Thus the person is reconditioned to a more constructive way of functioning without the necessity of uncovering the stimulus which originally triggered the negative response. Learning-theory therapy has been used with considerable success with autistic children, as well as with chronic delinquents and others with character disorders.

If depth pastoral counseling is to realize its rich potentialities, its practitioners must be open to varied therapeutic thrusts. The unique pastoral forms of psychotherapy which may eventually be developed will probably utilize approaches from various therapeutic schools, perhaps adding certain distinctive methods (such as the therapeutic use of religious symbols). Their integrating principle should be that view of the meaning of existence which sees the God-man relationship as the center and axis of all other relationships.

CHURCH-RELATED COUNSELING PROGRAMS

The emergence of pastoral counseling as a specialty within the ministry and the mushrooming of church-related counseling services are highly significant twin developments in the contemporary religious scene. The well-trained clergyman who is engaged in a full-time ministry of counseling, on the staff of a local church or a pastoral counseling center, represents a major new resource for accomplishing three things: (a) providing pastoral counseling services, *including pastoral psychotherapy*, at a level of competence which specialization makes possible; (b) carrying on creative experimentation with new methods of individual and group pastoral counseling which eventually will strengthen the entire field of pastoral counseling; (c) developing new, grass-roots training programs in many communities for helping parish ministers increase their counseling skills by means of pastoral case

[34] For an overview of learning-theory therapies, see Perry London, *The Modes and Morals of Psychotherapy* (New York: Holt, Rinehart & Winston, 1964), pp. 70-125.

conferences, consultation, and supervision sessions. The presence within the life of the churches of a growing group of clergymen who, through clinical and academic training and personal therapy, have developed special awareness of the importance of depth relationships, cannot but have a leavening influence on the churches and the ministry.

Clergymen and theological students who wish to prepare for specialized ministries of counseling should consult the training requirements of the American Association of Pastoral Counselors,[35] the professional organization which has established minimum standards in this field. Churches or councils of churches which are contemplating the employment of a "minister of counseling" or a pastoral counseling service staff member should make certain that the person has had training which would make him eligible for clinical membership in AAPC. Standards for the operation of accredited church-related counseling services and training centers are also available from AAPC. These can serve as guidelines for churches in the process of setting up counseling centers.

In summary, pastoral psychotherapy has an important place in the church's total ministry of creative caring. When practiced by well-trained minister-counselors, it strengthens the dimension of depth understanding and service which should be present in all pastoral care.

RECOMMENDED READING

J. F. T. Bugental, *The Search for Authenticity.*

Donald H. Ford and Hugh B. Urban, *Systems of Psychotherapy, A Comparative Study* (New York: John Wiley & Sons, 1963).

Robert A. Harper, *Psychoanalysis and Psychotherapy: 36 Systems* (Englewood Cliffs, N.J.: Prentice-Hall, 1959).

Ruth L. Munroe, *Schools of Psychoanalytic Thought* (New York: Holt, Rinehart and Winston, 1955).

Carl R. Rogers, *Client-Centered Therapy*, pp. 3-231.

———, *Counseling and Psychotherapy.*

———, *On Becoming a Person.*

Morris I. Stein, ed., *Contemporary Psychotherapies* (New York: The Free Press of Glencoe, 1961).

Carroll A. Wise, *Pastoral Counseling, Its Theory and Practice.*

Lewis R. Wolberg, *The Technique of Psychotherapy.*

[35] For information about membership requirements and standards, write The American Association of Pastoral Counselors, 201 E. 19th Street, New York, New York 10003.

16

The Layman's Ministry of Pastoral Care and Counseling

Bear one another's burdens, and so fulfil the law of Christ.—Gal. 6:2

Any emphasis on the ministry of the laity means not only training but a special kind of pastoral care. Laymen and women should be encouraged to use the pastoral gifts that many of them possess. Mutual care of members by each other as well as by the clergy is needed in the Church. Christians have many natural opportunities for the pastoral care of neighbours, workmates and others.
—Report of the Second Assembly of the World Council of Churches [1]

Since World War II there has been a dramatic rediscovery of a striking fact—*every Christian has a ministry because he is a Christian,* whether or not he is ordained. This awareness gives the layman a new self-image. He is no longer a second-class Christian who leaves "spiritual" work to the clergyman. Because he is a layman he has a vital, unique ministry to the world beyond his church—to his neighbor, his business associates, his union, his friends, his enemies, and to the disadvantaged, rejected, and exploited in his community. The vitality of the ministry of the laity has already reached a level which has not existed since the early decades of the Christian movement.[2] The poten-

[1] *The Evanston Report* (New York: Harper and Brothers, 1955), p. 170.
[2] See Howard Grimes, *The Rebirth of the Laity.* This movement has been called the "lay renaissance" by Hendrik Kraemer.

tialities of this development are almost unlimited. It is like a fresh wind blowing across the church, awakening a growing group of lay men, women, and youth to an exciting ministry to persons.

This lay renaissance is based on the rediscovery of the New Testament understanding of the church as (a) the *people of God*—a fellowship bound together by a covenant with God; (b) the *body of Christ*—an organic unity in which every member is an instrument of his healing spirit in the world; (c) the *community of the Holy Spirit*—a caring, reconciling community in and through which the living Spirit can work. The New Testament word *laos,* from which "laity" and "layman" are derived, refers to all Christians! The "ministry of reconciliation" (described in II Cor. 5:17) was entrusted to the whole church, not to a set-apart professional ministry.

What, then, is the clergyman's function? He is, by his training and ordination, equipped and designated to function as a leader and a specialist in that which is the work of every Christian. Instead of being a one-man band who plays each Sunday for a passive congregation, he should be the conductor of an orchestra, who helps each person make his unique contribution to the symphony of the good news. His key role is described in Ephesians—"to equip God's people for work in his service." (4:11-12, NEB.) His job is to train, inspire, guide, coach, and work alongside the lay ministers as a "teacher of teachers," "pastor of pastors," and "counselor of counselors." [8]

IMPLICATIONS FOR PASTORAL CARE AND COUNSELING

The implications of the lay renaissance for pastoral care and counseling are profound and challenging: A local church should strive to become a healing, growth-stimulating, redemptive organism. Pastoral care, rightly understood, is a function of the entire fellowship. The aim of the church's program should be the development of a dynamic climate of mutual concern which gradually seeps into and saturates the whole fellowship. Church administration and the small group program should be oriented toward this objective. To the extent that *koinonia* exists in a congregation, mutual pastoring occurs spontaneously as individual members seek to give themselves, in Luther's words, "as a Christ to my

[8] H. Richard Niebuhr *et al., The Purpose of the Church and Its Ministry,* pp. 83 ff.

neighbor."[4] Every member has a pastoral care opportunity that is uniquely his. Only as increasing numbers of us accept this challenge can our churches become centers of healing, help, and growth.

The ministry of the laity is essentially *a ministry to persons in need*—in the congregation and in the community. The challenge of Jesus' parable of the man who was robbed and beaten beside the Jericho Road was directed to all his followers. The criteria in his description of the last judgment were all matters of loving service:

> For I was hungry and you gave me food, I was thirsty and you gave me drink, I was a stranger and you welcomed me, I was naked and you clothed me, I was sick and you visited me, I was in prison and you came to me. (Matt. 25:35-36.)

As the "*pastorhood of all believers*" (Hiltner) becomes a reality in a congregation, laymen escape from their "spectatoritis" and begin to fulfill their personal ministries. Their own spiritual growth is stimulated as they put their faith to work in direct service. The unmet human needs in every church and community are so numerous and varied that a clergyman working alone can only scratch the surface. A church's caring ministry to the community's lonely, sick, aging, bereaved, shut-ins, strangers, institutionalized, and a host of other suffering human beings, can be tripled or more by involving trained laymen in pastoral work. When dedicated laymen become informal pastors to their neighbors, associates, and fellow church members, *they become the church*—the body of Christ serving those in need.

TYPES OF LAY PASTORAL MINISTRIES

A heartening variety of lay pastoral ministries has emerged in many places. A dozen Church of the Brethren congregations have sponsored homeless alcoholics as they are released from institutions. The plan is similar to that of sponsoring refugees. Housing, a job, and most important, acceptance by the congregation, are provided. A group within the congregation is trained to function as lay pastors in this project.

The social welfare department of the Denver Council of Churches conducted a workshop to train laymen in visiting the elderly. This led

[4] John Dillenberger, ed., *Martin Luther, Selections from His Writings* (Garden City, N.Y.: Doubleday & Co., 1961), p. 75.

a number of churches to "adopt" nursing homes. Residents are visited regularly and offered the kinds of services which volunteers in hospitals give.

Laymen are used to minister to persons in the institutions of the Honolulu area. This program is under the direction of the chaplaincy coordinator of the local council of churches. For a number of years several hundred laymen, divided into thirteen groups, have provided a volunteer ministry in the police court, jail, general and mental hospitals, juvenile court, women's prison, and children's homes of the Louisville area.[5]

A Methodist church in San Francisco sponsors a halfway house for young adults in outpatient psychiatric treatment and those recently released from mental hospitals. Twenty-three laymen completed a sixteen-week training course in preparation for their roles in this project.[6] Laymen in a suburban Southern California church have set up an inner city project to help disadvantaged minority group members find jobs. In Pasadena, California, a group of laywomen, sponsored by the council of churches, calls regularly and carries on a helping ministry to the wives and children of men who are in prison.[7]

The women of a Presbyterian church in Berkeley, California, have organized a "Christian Service Center," a personalized telephone service "open to all comers and equipped to give out information about the community and sources of help for needs of all sorts." [8] The project grew out of a retreat at which the women faced the searching question of their personal roles in meeting the needs of a transient population in a rapidly changing metropolitan area. The center is staffed from 9:00 A.M. until 5:00 P.M., Monday through Friday. Twenty-two women give four hours every other week at the center. They participate in eight two-hour training sessions to prepare them for this work. The church's minister of outreach reports:

> In effect the Center is a clearinghouse for information, and a kind of matchmaking service that brings persons with needs and existing resources . . .

[5] See George Stoll, *Laymen at Work* (Nashville: Abingdon Press, 1956).

[6] For a fuller description see Clinebell, *Mental Health Through Christian Community*, pp. 252-53.

[7] *Ibid.*, pp. 278-79.

[8] Letter from Donald P. Buteyn, minister of outreach, First Presbyterian Church, Berkeley, California, August 18, 1965.

> together. We stress to the women the danger of trying to counsel . . . where problems are sticky. Their function is to direct persons to qualified sources of help and then to follow up and make certain that the needed encounter has taken place. Above all, the program has required a cooperative approach to the entire community. This in itself has produced refreshing new points of entrance for the church into the world.[9]

The problems encountered include marital difficulties, housing problems, runaway children, senior citizen needs, unwed mothers, employment, and home nursing needs. Warm personal interest, follow-up calls, and continuing contacts in some cases have helped to implement the project's philosophy—that only "person to person relationships in our fragmented culture can really build the bridges so desperately needed." [10]

A telephone counseling service is carried on by the Life Line Centres, church-sponsored programs in Australia. A year before the Sydney Center opened, Alan Walker and his staff began training carefully selected laymen as accredited "telephone counselors." That centre now receives some ten thousand calls for help a year. About half are from impoverished people in physical distress. The others are from what Walker calls the "new poor"—those impoverished in terms of their psychological and spiritual needs. Nearly one tenth of all the calls are for help with marital problems. Some 150 volunteers answer the phones twenty-four hours a day with these words: "This is the Life Line Centre. Can I help you?" Professional persons—ministers, physicians, social workers, and psychiatrists—are always available to back up the lay counselors when complex problems are encountered. Approximately one hundred professionals have linked themselves as volunteers to the Sydney program, agreeing to take up to three cases at a time. In emergencies such as threatened suicides, "trouble teams" in radio cars are dispatched to give direct help. (See Recommended Reading.)

The American Baptist City Mission Society in Los Angeles sponsors a similar program called the "Help Line Telephone Clinic." It provides information, guidance, and referrals, without charge, for "anyone with a problem." Volunteers—both laymen and ministers—man the phones from 9:00 A.M. until 10:00 P.M. During one three-month period a total

[9] *Ibid.*
[10] *Ibid.*

of 1,475 calls came to the clinic. An experienced pastoral counselor conducts call-back sessions, counseling at a somewhat deeper level with the more serious cases. Another minister makes home calls where this is indicated. During one month, one or more persons with these problems called the clinic for help: alcohol, desertion, drugs, employment, emotional, family, finances, health, juvenile, loneliness, mental, morals, sexual, legal, unwed parent. The volunteer staff members received an initial series of training sessions including lectures, demonstrations, dialogues, and field trips. Special emphasis was put on developing sensitivity to the feelings of the persons calling for help.

A Minneapolis church has formed a lay committee on grief therapy "to surround the bereaved persons with Christian concern."[11] Since it is a downtown church many of its members are victims of "urban isolation." When a loss occurs, the supportive circle of friends and family which often surrounds the grieving person in a smaller community is lacking. This void is precisely what the lay ministry of the church seeks to fill. The Woman's Society prepares dinner for those attending the funeral, if this is desired. One or two persons from the grief therapy committee are assigned to each family. In the training sessions provided by the church, the forty-two persons who volunteered to be a part of this ministry were trained in the principles of helping the bereaved. They begin calling about ten days after the funeral. By that time the bereaved person is usually alone and in need of an opportunity to talk through his feelings. Callers usually ask two key questions during the initial visit: "When did it happen?" and "How did it happen?" Contacts continue for a period of several months.

So successful has the "healing fellowship of Christian friends" been in its forays against grief that it has taken on another larger assignment for itself: to surround shut-ins and nursing home residents with the same atmosphere of concern.[12]

HOW TO IMPLEMENT A LAY MINISTRY

Here are some guidelines for developing a lay pastoral ministry:

(1) *Organizing:* Although pastoral care is the function of the whole

[11] Irene E. Clepper, "'Grief Therapy'—New Role for Laymen," *Together*, September, 1965, pp. 45-46.

[12] *Ibid.*, p. 46.

congregation, some group should be carefully selected and trained to spearhead this ministry. Every church member should be challenged to become a part of the network of supportive, growth-nurturing relationships which is the church at its best, and to engage spontaneously in compassionate service to persons as opportunities arise. But within the church there should be one or more task forces composed of those committed to pastoral care as their primary focus of lay ministry.

In some situations it may be best to see if an existing organization or committee will accept the challenge of sponsoring such a service. Some denominational structures charge certain regular committees, along with the pastor, with care of the ill and others in special need.[13] In such cases it is the minister's role to help these groups understand and fulfill their responsibility effectively. Many churches have calling committees or committees on social problems which can provide leadership in pastoral care projects. In other situations the pastoral action of the laity may be furthered with more alacrity by recruiting a special *pastoral care team*. This may focus on one problem area (e.g., bereavement) or be available to augment the general pastoral work of the minister, at his discretion and under his guidance.

Lay pastoring arose spontaneously in Robert A. Raines's church as a result of the spiritual deepening of *koinonia* group experiences. A depressed, convalescing woman was helped so much by a visit from a friend in her group that, quite informally, she took up a lay ministry to the sick and hospitalized. Raines reports:

> One morning in a sermon I mentioned what this woman was doing and asked any persons who were interested in this kind of ministry to speak to me. The response was amazing. I discovered that a veritable well of compassion existed which had only been waiting to be tapped. Approximately twenty-five persons said they wanted to take up this ministry. I am now working with them, informing them when people are hospitalized, sending them to visit the sick, shut-ins, those in hospitals, new mothers, and in some instances bereaved families.[14]

(2) *Selection:* One of the advantages of recruiting a special pastoral care group is that persons with natural pastoral aptitudes can be invited.

[13] For example, in The Methodist Church the Commission on Christian Social Concerns is charged with concern for the alcoholic, the mentally ill, the aged, prisoners, and others in special need.

[14] *New Life in the Church*, pp. 126-27.

Those with natural therapeutic personalities—in Paul's words, who have "gifts of healing" [15]—should be urged to participate. In every congregation there are persons with a high degree of the personal qualities which are associated with therapeutic change in counseling—unconditional positive regard, empathic understanding, congruence, and identity.[16] They possess personal warmth, a love of people, sturdy self-esteem, and a substantial degree of emotional and spiritual maturity. They make other people feel "tall" and worthwhile in their presence. In contrast the so-called "do-gooder," who is strongly motivated by self-aggrandizing needs in his desire to be of service, should be avoided like the plague. Equally essential to avoid is the person who cannot keep confidences inviolate. The team must be bound by the seal of professional confidentiality.

If possible a pastoral care team should include a physician, a lawyer, an experienced businessman, a staff member of a community agency, a teacher, a member of one or more of the counseling professions, a stable AA member, and an Al-Anon member. Other warm, growing Christians of various ages and backgrounds round out the team.

(3) *Training:* The effectiveness of lay pastoring projects is directly correlated with the strength of their training programs. To release the helping potential of his lay pastors, a minister must apply the insights and skills which he has acquired in the area of pastoral care to training, inspiring, and coaching them. Even persons with natural therapeutic abilities need to develop these by the continuing discipline of in-service training.

Various formats have been used in training. In most cases a series of intensive training sessions is held before a lay pastoring project begins. Participants then have biweekly or monthly sessions with the minister for continued training, based on feedback from the experiences of the group. The lines of communication with the minister and other professional persons on the team should always be open for consultation and referral. Once or twice a year the team should have a weekend retreat to deepen their fellowship and sense of vocation in lay pastoring.[17]

[15] "Within our community God has appointed . . . those who have gifts of healing, or ability to help others or power to guide them." (I Cor. 12:28, NEB.)

[16] See Chapter 17 for a full discussion of these characteristics.

[17] The Life Line workers attend weekly "College for Christians" classes, have three all-day conferences and one "live-in" conference per year.

The small, spiritual growth group (by whatever name) should occupy a central place in lay pastoral training. In his book on group counseling Joseph W. Knowles states:

> The ministry of the church is the ministry of the entire people of God. Group counseling can become one means by which the pastor fulfills his essential function "to equip God's people for work in his service" . . . and through which laymen perform their priesthood as members of the Body of Christ.[18]

Hopefully, the pastoral care team itself will become a nurture group, as interpersonal ties deepen through working together. The atmosphere should be that of an educative therapy group where honest discussion of feelings and relationships stimulates growth in interpersonal skills and sensitivities. The use of role-playing and an observer of group process enhances self-awareness. The attempts of members to help—successful and unsuccessful—should be reviewed regularly (and confidentially) to permit the group to learn from its experiences. The pastoral care group can become a kind of modern equivalent of the Methodist class meeting, in which pastoral care was a function of laymen. It should become a place of inspiration, renewal, and depth relationships.

The content of training experiences should be of two kinds—*theological* and *clinical*. In the Life Line movement workers take courses to deepen their Christian understanding as well as enhance their counseling skills. It is important to keep lay pastoral projects theologically oriented. The participants should see their work as *a ministry*. Their function is to help overcome the *spiritual* as well as *interpersonal* loneliness of the persons to whom they minister.

The content of the clinical sessions should include such matters as are covered in Chapters 4 (common elements), 5 (informal), 8 (supportive), 9 (crisis), and 10 (referral). The particular needs of those with such prevalent problems as bereavement, alcoholism, marital conflict, and aging, should be discussed with anonymous case illustrations. Team members with special competence can brief the others on particular problems—e.g., the AA member can help his team colleagues understand alcoholism and AA. Mental health professionals from the congregation and community should be invited to meet with the team occasionally as resource persons.

[18] *Group Counseling*, p. 8.

(4) *Functioning:* It is usually wise to use newly trained lay pastors in a ministry to newcomers, shut-ins, the lonely, and the aged. This gives them experience in types of pastoral care work which require sophisticated counseling skills relatively infrequently. Those who demonstrate particular aptitudes can gradually be moved into those crisis situations where the need for counseling skills occurs more frequently—e.g., the sick, the bereaved, families of the mentally ill, and the alcoholic. In addition to accepting specific assignments by the minister, lay pastors should seek to leaven their entire church with a shepherding concern[19] by being sensitive and responsive to the needs of persons in the congregation and community.

SELF-HELP GROUPS

Some experienced lay pastors should be encouraged to draw together a small group of their fellow church members in self-help groups using the Yokefellow or *koinonia* group models. Another approach which offers great promise is the AA type group. Alcoholics Anonymous has demonstrated convincingly (some 350,000 times) that an unsuspected gold mine of helping resources is present in certain laymen. It has also demonstrated the healing power of a spiritually centered and growth-oriented group.

A church should be bold and imaginative in experimenting with a variety of self-help groups, including a group in which the twelve-step recovery program of AA [20] is applied to the problems of living of a small group of church members. The AA steps represent a systematizing of some of the basic thrusts of our religious tradition—awareness of need, repentance (surrender of self-sufficiency), dependence on God, self-examination, honest confession, restitution and renewal, deepening one's contact with God, and sharing the new life one has found with others in need. It may well be that these steps provide a path by which a distinctively religiously oriented approach to group counseling eventually will be evolved.

As groups like Al-Anon, Gamblers Anonymous, Overeaters Anony-

[19] While this chapter was being written I witnessed a vivid example of an entire congregation rallying around a couple whose child was critically ill. The minister said of his people, "They care for each other even if they don't talk about it. They rally around when trouble strikes."

[20] See *Alcoholics Anonymous* (New York: AA Publishing Co., 1955) and *Twelve Steps and Twelve Traditions*, by a co-founder of AA (New York: Harper & Row, 1952).

mous, and Narcotics Anonymous have discovered, the AA steps are readily adaptable to nonalcoholic problems. The problem in developing such a group for "normal" people with better-hidden problems is that many are unaware of how much their freedom and creativity are crippled by problems. To be effective a group should be composed of persons who are *hurting* in some area of their lives and *aware of their* suffering. The leadership of such a group should probably rotate. The leader should have a "lay" perspective. That is, he should make his own needs clear and be a participant in the group's search for wholeness and help. He cannot stand apart as a "leader" or "therapist" without damaging the basic therapeutic dynamic of a self-help group. A person who has experienced and found workable solutions to problems similar to those shared by most of the group makes an ideal leader, provided he has genuine humility and is aware of his need for continued growth. Without these qualities he will alienate others by his unrealistic "I've-got-it-made" attitude. He should serve as a "model" (as in integrity therapy)[21] of openness in discussing his own difficulties in living and in sharing what has worked for him. Such openness is contagious. Preparation for leading an AA-patterned self-help group should include study of the AA principles and attendance at a number of open meetings of that fellowship.

The report of the Second Assembly of the World Council of Churches declared: "The Church is sent into the world as a ministering community, not only in the sense that the parts serve each other, but that all serve the world."[22] As the "pastorhood of all believers" is taken seriously and implemented in church after church, a new healing force is being released into the life of our communities.

RECOMMENDED READING

Arnold B. Come, *Agents of Reconciliation* (Philadelphia: Westminster Press, 1960).

John W. Drakeford, *Counseling for Church Leaders* (Nashville: Broadman Press, 1961).

Mark Gibbs and T. R. Morton, *God's Frozen People* (Philadelphia: Westminster Press, 1965).

[21] Drakeford reports that laymen can be used as leaders of "integrity therapy" groups. Such groups apparently utilize only one aspect of the AA approach—i.e., the moral inventory and group confession aspect. See Drakeford's book *Integrity Therapy*, Chapter 13.

[22] *The Evanston Report*, p. 70.

Howard Grimes, *The Rebirth of the Laity* (Nashville: Abingdon Press, 1962).

Louis J. Cantoni and Lucile Cantoni, *Counseling Your Friends* (New York: William-Frederick Press, 1961).

Handbook for Volunteer Group Counselors, Michigan Department of Corrections.

Hendrik Kraemer, *A Theology of the Laity* (Philadelphia: Westminster Press, 1959).

Esther Pike, ed., *Who Is My Neighbor?* (New York: Seabury Press, 1960).

Charlie W. Shedd, *The Pastoral Ministry of Church Officers* (Richmond: John Knox Press, 1965).

Alan Walker, *A Ringing Call to Mission* (Nashville: Abingdon Press, 1966), pp. 75-96.

December 1964 issue of *Pastoral Psychology* on the "Pastorhood of the Layman."

17

How to Increase Skill as a Pastoral Counselor

Counseling is not merely the use of certain techniques. It is first of all the counselor's use of himself in a manner that helps the counseled to do something constructive about his trouble. The key is not so much the techniques employed, important as they are, as it is the total attitude of the counselor, how he feels about people, what he believes about them and about himself.

—Dean Johnson[1]

Teachers of pastoral counseling are occasionally queried by pastors and theological students who ask, in effect: "Where should I go from here? I'm aware of my need for greater competence in counseling. Having grasped some of the basic concepts, what should I do to move ahead? What skills and sensitivities are essential and what training experiences are most helpful in acquiring them?" These are good questions. This chapter is my attempt to give meaningful answers.

THE KEY—THE PASTOR'S PERSONALITY

Empirical studies, reported by Rogers, have identified three crucial counselor characteristics.[2] When they are present in a counselor *and* are perceived by the counselee, the counseling process tends to produce positive change and growth in the person. They are—*congruence, unconditional positive regard,* and *empathic understanding.*

[1] *Marriage Counseling, Theory and Practice,* p. vii.

[2] *On Becoming a Person,* pp. 47-49. Rogers relates these characteristics to personal maturity when he writes: "The optimal helping relationship is the kind of relationship created by a person who is psychologically mature" (*Ibid.,* p. 56).

Congruence, in this context, means inner genuineness, integration, and openness. Rogers observes: "The most basic learning for anyone who hopes to establish any kind of helping relationship is that it is safe to be transparently real." [3] The opposite of congruence is "being a phony" or "putting on an act." In such a person there is an incongruence between his words and his real feelings.

Persons who have had to hide their real feelings from others for extended periods in order to feel accepted may eventually become unaware of their own feelings. Such repressed feelings produce emotional blind spots, frequently in the areas of hostility, aggressiveness, sexuality, and tenderness. A counselor's emotional blind spots prevent him from being inwardly congruent in those areas—from being the self he truly is. This will keep him from relating therapeutically to others in these blocked-off areas. "Each person is an island unto himself. . . . He can only build bridges to other islands if he is first of all willing to be himself." [4]

To experience **unconditional positive regard** is to experience grace in a relationship. Rogers declares:

> Actually it is only the experience of a relationship in which he is loved (something very close, I believe, to the theologians' *agape*) that the individual can begin to feel a dawning respect for, acceptance of, and finally, even a fondness for himself. It is as he can thus begin to sense himself as lovable and worthwhile, in spite of his mistakes, that he can begin to feel love and tenderness for others.[5]

Unconditional positive regard is a blend of warmth, liking, caring, acceptance, interest, and respect for the person. A significant study by Julius Seeman "found that success in psychotherapy is closely associated with a strong and growing mutual liking and respect between client and therapist." [6] The counselor becomes a companion-guide in a warm, human relationship which helps the person find courage to face his situation, bear his load, or go on the often frightening journey into the unexplored areas of his personhood. Unconditional positive regard, in

[3] *Ibid.*, p. 51. The counselor may choose not to verbalize certain of his own feelings, but he should be *aware of them.* Otherwise they will interfere with the relationship in hidden ways.

[4] *Ibid.*, p. 21.

[5] Review of Reinhold Niebuhr's *The Self and the Dramas of History* in *The Chicago Theological Seminary Review*, January, 1956, p. 14.

[6] Carl R. Rogers, *On Becoming a Person*, p. 44.

Buber's familiar terms, is the counselor's ability to establish I-Thou relationships.

Empathic understanding means entering into the person's inner world of meanings and deep feelings through listening with awareness. The counseling pastor's continuing prayer might well be the hymn line, "Take the dimness of my soul away." Fortunately for most of us, even "a bumbling and faulty attempt to catch the confused complexities of the client's meanings" [7] is helpful to him.

One of the barriers to empathic understanding is self-centeredness. Those who are overly invested in themselves find it extremely difficult to enter into another's inner world. Self-centeredness and depth self-awareness are opposite psychological conditions. The self-centered person is aware mainly of his own painful insecurity and demanding need for attention. The consuming question, "Will I get *my* needs for approval satisfied?" blocks awareness of his own deeper feelings and strangles his capacity for empathy.

Herschel McLandress[8] has devised a means of measuring an individual's degree of self-absorption. The method (which attaches considerable importance to the appearance of "I," "me," and "my" in written and spoken material) measures the longest span of time during which a subject's thoughts remain centered on something other than himself. A "McLandress Coefficient" of two minutes means that the person can remain diverted from himself for a maximum of two minutes. Eleanor Roosevelt was found to have a McLandress Coefficient of two hours, John F. Kennedy twenty-nine minutes, and Elizabeth Taylor three minutes.[9] To be an effective, empathic counselor, a minister needs a reasonably high McLandress Coefficient—the ability to focus outside himself.

In addition to the three counselor qualities described above, I would add a fourth—a **sturdy sense of one's identity** as a person. A theological student, reflecting on a reality-practice session in which he was the "parishioner," said of the counselor: "I felt his compassion but not the hope that his strength and know-how would help me 'pull myself to-

[7] Rogers, *On Becoming a Person*, p. 53.

[8] Former professor of psychiatric measurement at Harvard Medical School.

[9] Mark Epernay, "The McLandress Dimension," *Esquire*, October, 1962, pp. 79 ff. The McLandress methodology was discussed in the *Journal of Psychiatric Measurement*, Autumn, 1962.

gether' and set me up for a working-together relationship. I felt I had pulled him down in the hole with me." To avoid this, a pastor needs that firm sense of his identity, personal worth, and competence which are at the nucleus of ego strength. A counselor is able to be "sensitive and responsive to the needs of others" to the degree that he possesses this strong inner awareness of his own value and personhood.

A fifth essential counselor quality is a therapeutic attitude. This results from a vivid awareness of one's affinity with the sickness and sin, loneliness, alienation, and despair of the disturbed person. The therapeutic attitude begins to dawn as the minister senses, in the presence of the person with psychosis, alcoholism, or suicidal impulses, that "there but for the grace of God (and a good mother) go I!" It emerges more fully as he moves beyond this to the deflating awareness—"*There go I!*" This fellow feeling somehow lowers the walls which block the flow of healing forces in relationships. Retaining this fellow feeling is very difficult for most of us. To identify with the essential humanness of the despairing threatens our fragile defenses against our own despair. To recognize that the regressed catatonic on the back ward of the mental hospital is more like than different from oneself [10] shakes the very foundations of our defensive self-image. To accept this truth at a deep level is possible for most of us only to a limited degree. It requires an inward surrender of subtle feelings of self-idolatry and spiritual superiority. One student referred to this as "getting off the omnipotence kick." Even a partial surrender of one's defensive superiority feelings helps to open the door to mutually redemptive relationships. Somehow it melts a hole in the icy barrier of pride which freezes real self-esteem and keeps people—especially disturbed people—at a distance.

DEPTH TRAINING FOR CREATIVE COUNSELING

What kinds of "learning" enable a minister-counselor to use the many facets of his complex personality creatively? Experiences that will enhance his inner congruence, unconditional positive regard, empathic understanding, sense of identity and worth, and reduce his defensive

[10] The late Frieda Fromm-Reichmann once declared that effectiveness in dealing with psychotics is contingent on the therapist's awareness of this fact (lecture at the William A. White Institute of Psychiatry, 1948). Ernest E. Bruder's book *Ministering to Deeply Troubled People* communicates the importance of the minister's attitudes toward himself and others. He writes, "What a minister is in himself matters far more than what he does" (p. 70).

pride. Carroll A. Wise puts his finger on the key: "The pastor needs to *know himself* as well as to understand the dynamic processes of personality as they find expression in the counselee." [11] Being able to form a helping relationship with another is dependent on forming a "helping relationship to myself." [12] The pastor's self-awareness catalyzes the process of self-awareness in others. His inner freedom awakens the freedom of the spirit in others. Rogers summarizes: "The degree to which I can create relationships which facilitate the growth of others as separate persons is a measure of the growth I have achieved in myself." [13] Grace-communicators must have experienced grace. Growth-facilitators must be growing persons. Renewal agents must know firsthand the discipline and lift of continuing personal renewal.

What experiences available to clergymen stimulate growth in self-awareness and self-acceptance most effectively? Most academic courses, seminars, and books on pastoral counseling, *per se*, have relatively limited effect on this level, although they may be valuable on a cognitive level. There are five types of experiences which provide, in varying degrees, the deeper *self-encounter* which accelerates the counselor's growth: personal psychotherapy, clinical pastoral training, supervision of one's counseling, sensitivity training groups, and reality-practice. The learning which accrues from these experiences, to quote a choice Shakespearean line, "adds a precious seeing to the eye." [14] It increases the capacity for "thouness" in relationships.

Optimally, *personal psychotherapy* should be an integral part of the training of every clergyman. The ministry of even the healthiest individual invariably is deepened and enriched by it. It sharpens his interpersonal awareness and makes previously unused facets of his personality available for person-maximizing relationships. A minister's personality is his only instrument for communicating the Good News through relationships. Psychotherapy is a means of removing the inner blocks which diminish its ability to be the fine, effective instrument it could be. Of course psychotherapy cannot eradicate all inner conflicts, but it can make one enough aware of those which remain to drastically reduce their interference with creative relationships. Thus the minister becomes

[11] *Pastoral Counseling, Its Theory and Practice*, p. 11. Italics mine.

[12] Rogers, *On Becoming a Person*, p. 51.

[13] *Ibid.*, p. 56.

[14] *Love's Labour's Lost*, Act IV, Sc. 3, l. 333.

freer not to distort his counseling by blindly projecting his inner conflicts into his relationships.

Group psychotherapy, with a therapist well trained in this technique, can function on any therapeutic level from depth analysis to interpersonal adjustment, depending on the methods employed. For many clergymen group therapy is more effective than individual psychotherapy because it offers wider opportunities to become aware of interpersonal distortions, to be confronted with one's subtle dishonesties, and to experiment with more creative relating. Individual therapy is indicated where distortions in relating stem mainly from need deprivation in the preschool years. Group therapy is ideal for rectifying distortions derived mainly from later inadequacies in peer relationships.

The growing prevalence of therapy groups for ministers, theological students, and their wives, is a fresh source of creativity in the church. It is imperative that psychotherapy, individual or group, be done by a highly trained professional person—a psychiatrist, social worker, clinical psychologist, or specialist in pastoral counseling.[15] Because of the extensive training required, and the relative scarcity of qualified therapists, the cost is usually high. Ordinarily, group therapy is less expensive than individual. But, whatever the cost, personal psychotherapy is a valuable investment in one's total ability to relate more redemptively. Ministers often have to make financial sacrifices to obtain therapy. With few exceptions they report that the benefits were more than worth the costs. In fact, clergymen who have had depth therapy usually describe it as the most valuable aspect of their education, paying rich dividends through the years in their personal as well as their professional lives. To the minister contemplating therapy, I would pass along the words which Fritz Kunkel inscribed on the fly leaf of my copy of one of his books: "Good luck on the journey down and up!"

Clinical pastoral training (CPT) also provides a depth encounter with oneself. In some two hundred accredited centers, located mainly in general and psychiatric hospitals and in correctional institutions, theo-

[15] To be most effective in helping a minister to depth self-discovery, a therapist should have psychoanalytic training, including a personal analysis. He need not be a psychoanalyst (a subspecialty within psychiatry in the United States), but he should be skilled in dealing with unconscious material—dreams, fantasies, free associations, transference feelings. Other forms of intensive psychotherapy can be valuable as training experiences, but not on the same depth level.

logical students and ministers spend twelve to forty-eight weeks working under a chaplain supervisor with people in crisis. Some seminaries require one quarter (twelve weeks) of CPT for graduation. If all seminaries required this or something comparable, the ministry would experience remarkable revitalization in one generation.

Clinical training has many values. It forces the person to ask searching and disturbing questions concerning the dynamic meaning of religion in troubled people's lives. It raises the confronting question of relevancy: "How is my understanding of religion relevant to the real needs of this mental patient (or delinquent, drug addict, cancer patient)?" CPT, like therapy, reveals the strengths and weaknesses of one's pattern of relating. It provides opportunities to learn to work with the other helping professions, and to define one's professional function and identity in relation to them and in the light of one's tradition. CPT involves participation in a personal growth group, a therapy or self-awareness group composed of fellow students and the chaplain supervisor.

Parish ministers who take a three-month "sabbatical" from their churches for clinical training usually find it to be one of the richest experiences of their lives. Some accredited centers offer "supervised clinical experience" on a one or two days-per-week basis, for those who cannot arrange to take full-time CPT. Clinical training, both full- and part-time, offers unique opportunities to strengthen one's total ministry to persons.[16]

One of the best resources for enhancing interpersonal skills is available at the fingertips of most clergymen, often without their being aware of it. I refer to opportunities to obtain *supervision of one's counseling.* Competent supervision is a direct, efficient way of upgrading counseling skills. Any minister who lives within reasonable driving distance of a well-trained counselor or psychotherapist can obtain this valuable training by a modest investment of time and money. The procedure is simply to arrange with that person to have weekly or biweekly sessions at which one receives guidance in the handling of counseling cases. Most mental health professionals are glad to multiply their therapeutic

[16] Information concerning CPT can be obtained from the Council for Clinical Training, 475 Riverside Drive, New York, New York, or the Institute of Pastoral Care, P.O. Box 57, Worcester, Massachusetts.

influence by helping clergymen do their counseling more effectively. I know of a number of small groups of ministers (three to eight in size) who have made arrangements with psychiatrists for group supervision, dividing the cost among them.[17]

Significant new resources for helping parish ministers increase their counseling skills have emerged in recent years in the training programs developed by a growing number of church-related counseling centers. These training programs complement the clinical training and seminary counseling courses. Broadly distributed geographically, they offer hope for an eventual breakthrough in closing the gap between the counseling training of most parish clergymen and the actual counseling demands placed upon them. It is my conviction that every church-related counseling program should devote at least one third of its staff time to providing training experiences.

A West Coast pastoral counseling center sponsors "pastoral case conferences" following this pattern: The group, limited to ten parish ministers, meets once a week for two hours. The leader is the center's director, a clergyman with advanced training in counseling. At each session one minister is responsible for making a detailed presentation of one of his counseling cases. Other counseling problems are discussed as they are raised by group members. Occasionally the leader discusses some new development in pastoral counseling. Tapes of actual counseling sessions are used regularly, as are reality-practice techniques. Each minister pays a modest sum per session to the center's treasury for this service.

Supervision is more widely and readily available than any other form of counselor training. In many situations all that is required is for the minister to take the initiative in arranging for such an experience, with a small group of his colleagues or by himself, with a therapist. In long-term[18] supervisory groups the interaction often approaches the group therapy level. Depth understanding of any counseling relationship throws as much light on the counselor as on the counselee. Like clinical

[17] Staff psychiatrists with public mental health facilities sometimes provide consultation for clergymen as a public service. As the federal legislation to provide community mental health centers is implemented, psychiatric consultation for ministers may become available in more and more places.

[18] To be of substantial value supervision should continue for at least a year, preferably longer, under a highly competent therapist.

training, supervision can sharpen a minister's self-awareness as it strengthens his ability to help the troubled.

Sensitivity training groups offer valuable learning experiences for pastors, though they should not be regarded as a substitute for personal therapy, clinical training, and long-term supervision. Such groups are widely used in workshops and human relations labs to enhance the participants' skill in relating by increasing their awareness of themselves and others. Often called "T Groups" (T for training), the approach was pioneered by the National Training Laboratory in Group Relations located in Bethel, Maine. A small aggregation of persons is given the simple (and anxiety-arousing) instructions, "Become a group." A trained observer helps them become aware of themselves and their interaction. Such labs usually last for a week or two. Several denominations are using sensitivity training groups in their leadership training conferences. One theological seminary provides semester-long "group interaction" for all first-year students, to help them become more aware in their relationships. These groups tend to move beyond sensitivity training to modified group therapy. A recent three-seminary research project demonstrated the value of two-semester therapy groups in preparing seminarians for a person-centered ministry. This project gives convincing evidence that sensitivity training and therapy groups should be an integral part of every seminary's program.[19]

UNDERSTANDING OF BASIC CONCEPTS

I have discussed clinical experiences first to emphasize their indispensability in any sound approach to counselor training. The deepening of self-other awareness is essential if conceptual tools are to be genuinely useful. Otherwise the mastery of concepts makes one a clever technician—a functioneer but not a growth-stimulator. But as a minister grows as a person his conceptual grasp of psychodynamics and counseling theory becomes increasingly valuable in ministering to the troubled. Through disciplined reading and academic courses a minister or theological student should acquire a workable understanding of the following:

(1) *Normal personality development,* including child, adolescent,

[19] The Lilly Foundation financed this project during the school year 1964-65.

and adult psychology. Erik Erickson's "eight stages" are a useful conceptual framework for understanding the life cycle.

(2) *Marriage and family dynamics.*

(3) *Group dynamics.*

(4) *Psychopathology* (abnormal psychology).

(5) *Methods of individual counseling.*

(6) *Methods of group counseling.*

(7) *Community referral resources.*

(8) *Personality and culture* (socio-economic forces as they influence personality, health, and growth).

(9) *History and theory of pastoral care.*

(10) *Theology and counseling,* including the theology *of* counseling.[20]

This list may arouse the response expressed by Chaucer's line: "The lyf so short, the craft so long to lerne." [21] But these are fundamental subject areas which should be mastered at some point during a minister's education—college, seminary, or post-seminary—if he is to be equipped for effective work with people in all the dimensions of his profession.

Many seminaries have made significant progress in the psychological aspects of their curricula since World War II. As a major study of theological education states:

> *When one considers the revitalization of much in the theological curriculum today through new emphases in psychology and pastoral counseling, it must be concluded that a significant new turn in the education of the ministry has been taken. Powerful new resources are available throughout the curriculum because of work in this field.*[22]

However, as many of us in theological education are aware, much more needs to be done, particularly in clinical education, before seminary graduates in general will enter parishes with even minimal competence in pastoral care and counseling. A number of seminaries are providing refresher courses for parish ministers in the area of counseling. Many

[20] This list is adapted from the membership standards of AAPC.

[21] "The Parlement of Soules," l. 1.

[22] H. Richard Niebuhr, Daniel Day Williams, and James M. Gustafson, *The Advancement of Theological Education* (New York: Harper & Row, 1957), p. 128.

more are needed. New seminary programs leading to graduate degrees in pastoral counseling should be developed and existing ones strengthened, to equip highly competent specialists to staff church-related counseling centers which can provide top-quality training experiences for parish ministers.

The January issue of *Pastoral Psychology* renders a valuable yearly service by listing both clinical and academic training opportunities throughout the United States. Each year the list lengthens encouragingly. Communication with churchmen who are developing counseling training resources in other countries is gradually developing.[23] Hopefully this will have a broadening and mutually stimulating effect in the growth of this pastoral art.

Counseling, of course, is only one aspect of the clergyman's work. If he perceives the importance of this skill in the lives of burdened people, however, his motivation to grow in this area will be strong. Many ministers are realizing that to be "too busy" to participate in such experiences as personal therapy, supervision, refresher courses, and workshops on counseling, is to be something like the carpenter who is too busy to sharpen his tools. Those who choose their advanced training programs with care almost always find that the benefits more than justify the investment.

PRESENT EFFECTIVENESS AND HOPE FOR THE FUTURE

In spite of the inadequate counseling training of many clergymen, the majority apparently do remarkably effective counseling. In the previously cited national survey of where people take their troubles, it was found that 65 percent of those who had gone to ministers reported that they had been "helped" or "helped a lot." Another 13 percent reported that they had been helped, but in a more limited way. Only 18 percent indicated that such contacts did not help.[24] The percentage of those who felt they had been helped by ministers was higher than was true of any other professional group (though only slightly higher than nonpsychiatric physicians). A counselee's perception of how much he was helped is, of course, a subjective criterion. However, these figures do

[23] This is one of the activities of AAPC.
[24] *Americans View Their Mental Health*, p. 319.

show that clergymen in general are giving *significant help* to the majority of their counselees.

These statistics should not blind us to the drastic need for upgrading the counseling skills of many ministers. The survey showed that most of the counselees were helped by "advice" (34 percent), "comfort" and "ability to endure" (23 percent). Ten percent were helped by a change effected in another and 9 percent by breaking a negative relationship. *Only 7 percent described a positive change in himself or in a troubled relationship as the mode of help!*[25] Undoubtedly some of those who were helped by supportive and advising approaches could have been helped in deeper, more lasting ways had the counselors been better prepared. Certainly the study shows the need for *broadening the range* of ministers' counseling skills.

The helping potential of the ministry of counseling has barely begun to be released. Only as more and more of us strengthen our competence as counselors will this potential wellspring of healing and growth become more available to the millions who desperately need what it can give. The challenge which confronts each of us is to help release this potential by becoming *incarnational counselors*—persons whose relationships allow the liberating Word to become flesh and dwell among us in healing power, causing those who enter these relationships to discover their real humanity.

SOME FINAL PERSPECTIVES

In the practice of the counseling art it is helpful to remember these perspective-giving facts:

(1) The pastor's focus on the acute needs of individuals who seek counseling should always be balanced by a broad, sustaining ministry of pastoral care to the congregation as a whole. Many people need their minister's concern and inspiration who do not need counseling.

(2) One can help many troubled people without being an "expert" in counseling. Every pastor—lay or professional—should maximize his helping abilities. But at every level of mastery there are opportunities to be of genuine help.

(3) Every counselor, however skilled, fails to help some people. It

[25] *Ibid.*, p. 323.

is well to remember the inevitable limitations of all counselors and all helping relationships. Jesus' lack of success with Judas, in spite of his close association, is a striking case in point. As in Jesus' parable of the sower, the counselor's seeds do not always fall on receptive soil. His job is to keep sowing, trusting the growth forces, and remembering that, at best, he is an instrument of healing resources beyond himself.

(4) Increasing one's counseling skills and sensitivities is a continuing, lifelong challenge. One never "arrives." The heart of the counseling art can be learned only by experience. This learning is accelerated immensely if one's experience is exposed to systematic reflection and evaluation. This is why supervision, consultation, and reality-practice are so fruitful.

(5) Whatever else a troubled person needs, his first and most pressing need is to be understood.[26] Becoming an understanding listener is an attainable goal for most ministers who have a fervent desire to help others grow.

(6) Finally, having examined a variety of theories and methods of counseling, it is important to reemphasize the heart of the matter—*the person-to-person relationship*. Jung's advice to psychotherapists is relevant to pastoral counselors: "Learn your theories as well as you can, but put them aside when you touch the miracle of the living soul. Not theories but your own creative individuality alone must decide."[27] Engraved in every pastor's mind should be these words: *Relationship—the Instrument of Help!*

Without a warm, accepting relationship, the methods of counseling described in these pages become mere techniques—sterile, manipulative, and ineffective. But when skillfully employed *within an accepting therapeutic relationship*, they become means by which the relationship's healing power is released.

Paul Tillich once declared:

> The power which makes acceptance possible is the resource in all pastoral care. It must be effective in him who helps, and it must become effective in him who is helped. . . . This means that both the pastor and the counselee . . . are under the power of something which transcends both of them. One can call this

[26] Dean Johnson, *Marriage Counseling, Theory and Practice*, pp. vi-vii.

[27] *Psychological Reflections* (New York: Pantheon Books, 1953), p. 73.

power the new creature or the New Being. The pastoral counselor can be of help only if he himself is grasped by this power.[28]

The minister who thus has been grasped becomes a channel by which this power brings release of the prisoners, the recovery of sight to the blind, and lets the broken victims go free!

[28] "The Theology of Pastoral Care," p. 4.

INDEX